TechBook

Index of Articles | 2020

Published by Bullseye Glass Co.
3722 SE 21st Avenue
Portland, Oregon 97202
www.bullseyeglass.com
503.232.8887

Cover: Quick Tip, *A Riot of Effects*
Reactions between French Vanilla Sheet,
Silver Foil and Aquamarine Frit.

⊚ Table of Contents

TechNotes

TECHNOTES ❶

A Technical Supplement from Bullseye Glass Co.

Knowing Your Kiln

To achieve control in firing glass, it is necessary to understand how heat is distributed within the kiln you are using. Kiln heat is rarely even. Top-fired kilns tend to be hotter in the center. Side-fired kilns are frequently hotter around the perimeter. The pyrometer reads only one point within the kiln chamber and may not give you an accurate indication of the heat treatment the glass is receiving. In working with a new kiln, making a few preliminary tests will help you to understand the kiln's heating patterns and gain better control over your results.

TESTING THE "LOW END"

At the low end of the temperature range—generally below 1200°F (649°C)—you will be slumping, bending and/or annealing the glass. Understanding heat distribution in this temperature range will be important for two reasons:

For bending and slumping: The heat pattern in the kiln will determine how and where to set up the project.

For annealing: The heat pattern will determine whether the kiln can properly anneal projects that cover a large area within the kiln chamber. If heat distribution in the kiln is uneven, large projects may break, due to annealing strain.

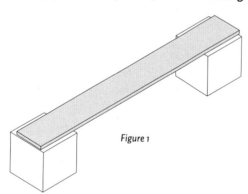

Figure 1

Figure 1 shows a 6" x 3/4" x 1/8" (152mm x 19mm x 3mm) strip of glass suspended over two 1" (25mm) tall mullite blocks. On a 20" (508mm) square kiln shelf, 13 such set-ups should be spaced evenly over the surface of the shelf. Use the same style of glass, preferably all from the same sheet or production date, for all 13 set-ups. (See Figure 2 for arrangement.)

Fire the kiln, using this schedule:

	RATE	TEMPERATURE	HOLD
1	500°F (278°C)	1000°F (538°C)	:05
2	300°F (167°C)	1150°F (621°C)	:05

Allow kiln to cool below 700°F (371°C) with the door closed. No annealing necessary.

READING THE RESULTS

If the glass strips around the perimeter are more deeply slumped than those in the center of the kiln, the perimeter is heating more than the center. (Figure 2)

If, instead, the center strips show a greater curve, the center is the area of greater heat work.

If all strips are equally slumped, the kiln is firing evenly.

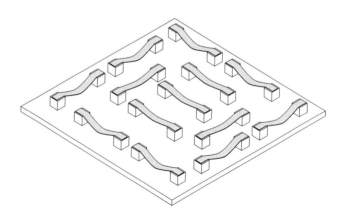

Figure 2

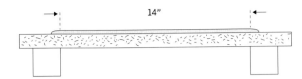

14"

Figure 3

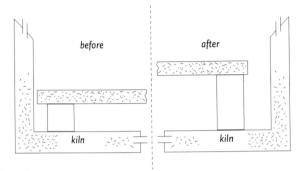

before   after

kiln   kiln

Figure 4

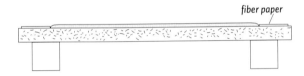

fiber paper

Figure 5

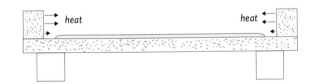

heat   heat

Figure 6

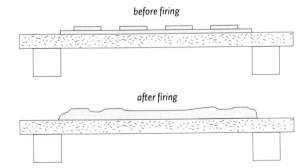

before firing

after firing

Figure 7

CORRECTING FOR UNEVEN HEATING

If the test results indicate that your kiln is firing unevenly, you can choose from the following actions to correct the problem:

1. Use a slower firing cycle.

2. Reduce the size of the glass project relative to the size of the kiln shelf. For example, rather than covering the full 20" (508mm) width of a shelf with a piece, limit the dimensions of the piece to 14" (356mm). (Figure 3)

3. Reduce the size of the kiln shelf and raise it further off the kiln floor to allow greater heat circulation around the shelf and the piece. (Figure 4)

If the test results indicate that the outer edges of the kiln are cooler than the center, try the following:

1. Insulate the edges of the glass piece with ceramic fiber paper, blanket, or board. This will slow down heat release from the edges. (Figure 5)

2. Create a perimeter wall of hard brick around the outer edges of the piece. Upon heating, the hard brick will absorb heat. Upon cooling, this absorbed heat will radiate back toward the glass and prevent its edges from cooling too rapidly. (Figure 6)

If the test results show an asymmetrical heating pattern (i.e., some areas along the perimeter of the kiln are hotter relative to the center, while others are colder), the elements within the kiln may not be firing properly. Turn the kiln to full fire and observe the elements. Are they glowing equally? If not, they will need either to be replaced or repositioned.

Note: Coiled-wire heating elements, if not properly secured to the kiln walls or ceiling, have a tendency to move, bunching up in corners or at the ends of the elements. The elements also tend to become brittle with prolonged use and may break or weaken if manipulated while cold.

Caution: Adjusting kiln elements is best done when the elements are hot (the power having just been disconnected). Such adjustments should be made only by qualified kiln technicians. In some cases, it may be most sensible to replace the elements. Make certain that replacement elements are secured in such a fashion that they are unlikely to move within the element grooves or along the element hangers.

4

UNDERSTANDING THE "HIGH END"

At the high end of the temperature range, where fusing occurs, you may get different results within different areas of the kiln, due to:

· The type of kiln (top- or side-fired)
· The type of kiln insulation (brick or refractory fiber)
· Kiln power and rate of heating
· Soak time
· The size of the shelf relative to the size of the kiln.

In a top-fired kiln, the corners or perimeter of the shelf are frequently colder than the center. Since the center of the kiln fires hotter than the edges or corners, the finished piece may have an uneven surface. (Figure 7)

With a side-fired kiln, the opposite is likely to occur. The temperature will be higher around the perimeter of the shelf than in the center. This faster firing at the edges can cause bubbles by trapping air between layers of glass and/or cause thin, ragged edges ("needle-pointing"). (Figures 8, 9)

FINDING OUT HOW YOUR KILN FIRES AT ITS HIGH END

By using an external, hand-held pyrometer and taking thermocouple readings at the middle and edges of your kiln, you can get a general idea of the heating differential within your kiln. (Figure 10)

You can get a more thorough understanding of your heating differential by performing the following test:

Assemble 5 stacks of test tiles, using Bullseye Clear (001101-0030F), Black (000100-0030F) and White (000113-0030F) glass. The bottom 2 layers should be 3" (76mm) square Clear tiles; the center layer, a 1" x 3" (25mm x 76mm) strip of Black; the next layer, a 1" x 3" (25mm x 76mm) strip of White; and the top layer, a 1/2" (13mm) square Black tile. (Figure 11)

Optional: By placing frits, stringers, or chips of other glass on the corners, you can learn more about the behavior of these materials at full fusing temperatures.

Place the tiles directly on the primed kiln shelf as shown in Figure 12. Do not place the tiles on fiber paper, as they will stick to the fiber and that will influence the test result. (Figure 12)

Fire the kiln at 1490°F (810°C) for 10 minutes, using this cycle:

	RATE	TEMPERATURE	HOLD
1	500°F(278°C)	1000°F (538°C)	:05
2	600°F (333°C)	1490°F (810°C)	:10
3	AFAP*	900°F (482°C)	:30
4	200°F (93°C)	700°F (371°C)	:30
5	AFAP*	70°F (21°C)	:00

*As fast as possible.

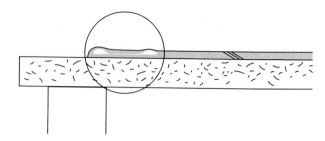

Figure 8: Cutaway showing Bubbles caused by faster fusing of the edges and consequent air entrapment between layers.

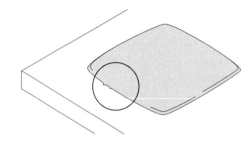

Figure 9: A thin, ragged edge ("needle-pointing") caused by increased pulling inward at the hotter, outer edges.

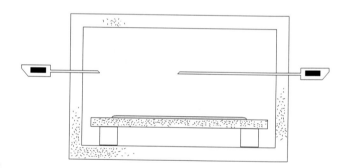

Figure 10

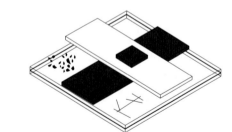

Figure 11

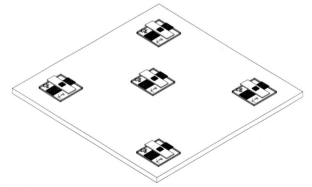

Figure 12

If the fired test tiles all have the same surface—congratulations! You have a kiln that fires evenly.

If, instead, the surfaces of the tiles are not all the same, there are ways to compensate for the variation.

ADJUSTING FOR UNEVEN FIRING AT THE HIGH END

1. Soaking your project with a longer hold at process temperature will help to even out the temperature differential. To avoid overfiring, you may need to reduce your maximum temperature by 10°F (5°C).

2. To prevent trapping air between layers when firing in a side-fired kiln, insulate or baffle the perimeter of the glass with ceramic fiber paper or brick, and/or consider adding a programmed hold somewhere in the range 1150–1250°F (621–677°C) to "squeeze" out any air from between the layers of glass.

3. Use a dense ceramic shelf. This will conduct heat well, allowing it to penetrate and escape from the bottom of the glass with ease.

4. Use a smaller kiln shelf. This will result in better heat circulation and, consequently, help to even out the temperature.

5. Make sure that your kiln shelf is not sitting on large bricks or strips. Try to minimize the amount of contact between the kiln shelf and its supports. Hollow supports are ideal.

6. Finally, if you are firing a number of different projects on one shelf, arrange them to take advantage of the heating pattern in your kiln. For example, if your kiln fires colder around the perimeter, you may want to put softer glasses to the outside and stiffer glasses to the middle of the shelf.

Remember: Understanding your kiln and the way it transfers heat to the glass is a major factor in ensuring the success of your kilnformed projects. If you find discrepancies in how uniformly your kiln heats (and therefore cools), you can make some corrections. Ultimately, however, corrections can only go so far. If your kiln is not firing uniformly, you may want to consider repairing or replacing it. The kiln is the most valuable tool (outside of yourself) that you have in your studio. A kiln that fires unevenly can result in lost time and lost work.

TEMPERATURE CONVERSION CHART

Use this table to look up a known temperature and find the corresponding temperature in °C or °F. Examples: To convert 100°F to °C, look up 100 in the center column and read the box directly to the left (38°C). To convert 100°C to °F, look up 100 in the center column and read the box directly to the right (212°F).

°C	TEMP	°F	°C	TEMP	°F	°C	TEMP	°F
-12	10	50	210	410	770	432	810	1490
-7	20	68	216	420	788	438	820	1508
-1	30	86	221	430	806	443	830	1526
4	40	104	227	440	824	449	840	1544
10	50	122	232	450	842	454	850	1562
16	60	140	238	460	860	460	860	1580
21	70	158	243	470	878	466	870	1598
27	80	176	249	480	896	471	880	1616
32	90	194	254	490	914	477	890	1634
38	100	212	260	500	932	482	900	1652
43	110	230	266	510	950	488	910	1670
49	120	248	271	520	968	493	920	1688
54	130	266	277	530	986	499	930	1706
60	140	284	282	540	1004	504	940	1724
66	150	302	288	550	1022	510	950	1742
71	160	320	293	560	1040	516	960	1760
77	170	338	299	570	1058	521	970	1778
82	180	356	304	580	1076	527	980	1796
88	190	374	310	590	1094	532	990	1814
93	200	392	316	600	1112	538	1000	1832
99	210	410	321	610	1130	543	1010	1850
104	220	428	327	620	1148	549	1020	1868
110	230	446	332	630	1166	554	1030	1886
116	240	464	338	640	1184	560	1040	1904
121	250	482	343	650	1202	566	1050	1922
127	260	500	349	660	1220	571	1060	1940
132	270	518	354	670	1238	577	1070	1958
138	280	536	360	680	1256	582	1080	1976
143	290	554	366	690	1274	588	1090	1994
149	300	572	371	700	1292	593	1100	2012
154	310	590	377	710	1310	599	1110	2030
160	320	608	382	720	1328	604	1120	2048
166	330	626	388	730	1346	610	1130	2066
171	340	644	393	740	1364	616	1140	2084
177	350	662	399	750	1382	621	1150	2102
182	360	680	404	760	1400	627	1160	2120
188	370	698	410	770	1418	632	1170	2138
193	380	716	416	780	1436	638	1180	2156
199	390	734	421	790	1454	643	1190	2174
204	400	752	427	800	1472	649	1200	2192

WATCH OUT!

Use the table above only to convert specific temperatures. **Do not use it to convert heating and cooling rates.** If you apply the temperatures listed on a conversion chart to a heating or cooling rate, you will always be 32° off.

For example, if you fire at a rate of 600°F per hour (DFPH) to 1270°, you will arrive at 1270° in 2 hours (2:00). If you use this chart to convert 600°F to 316°C per hour (DCPH) and fire to 688°C, you will arrive at 688°C in 2 hours and 10 minutes (2:10), or 10 minutes slower.

To convert a Fahrenheit rate to centigrade, simply divide the Fahrenheit number by 1.8. Conversely, to change a centigrade rate to Fahrenheit, multiply by 1.8.

A Technical Supplement from Bullseye Glass Co.

The Vitrigraph Kiln
Creating a New Vocabulary in Fused Glass

Fused glass is frequently characterized by a cut-and-fit approach to design. Various shapes of colored glass are cut and fired to a base blank, often a tile or plate. While this is a valid method of working the material, it comes more from a collage or mosaic than a painterly tradition.

Originally trained as a painter, Narcissus Quagliata has worked in stained glass since the early 1970s. Probably more than any other modern flat glass artist, Quagliata has succeeded in imparting the fluidity of a painter's sensibility to leaded glass through both painstaking selection of unique glasses and a highly expressive use of the lead line. Invited to take part in the Connections program of artist exchanges at the Bullseye factory in 1993, Quagliata quickly enlisted the assistance of Rudi Gritsch, equipment-builder extraordinaire (and at that time Bullseye's kilnworking director) to devise a way of generating lines in hot glass that could approximate the spontaneity of the pen or brush stroke. These glass lines and the techniques of shading and modeling with frits became the core of a methodology of fusing that Quagliata came to call "light paintings" — a revolutionary approach to working glass in the kiln that combines the expressiveness of paint with the vibrancy of light.

The key tool in creating these lines is an ingenious small kiln, designed by Rudi Gritsch, called the "vitrigraph."* Since then Bullseye has built and tested numbers of them, and sent replicas off to studios around the world. This article describes the equipment and processes developed by Quagliata and Gritsch, in the process creating a whole new vocabulary for fused glass.

Narcissus Quagliata during the creation of *Summer Buddha*, fused panels employing hot drawn glass lines.

* From the Latin "vitri–" (glass) and the Greek "–graph" (writing). Not to be confused with "vitreography," the process of making prints from glass plates.

CALDERA BULLSEYE EDITION KILN SPECS
· Interior: 8 x 8 x 6 3/4 in (20 x 20 x 17 cm)
· Exterior: 11 3/4 x 14 x 19 1/2 in (30 x 36 x 50 cm)
· Electrical Requirements: 120 V / 15 A
· Power Consumption: 1.68 kW
· Plug: Standard (NEMA5-15p)
· Shipping Weight: 46 lb (21 kg)
· Product Number: 8823

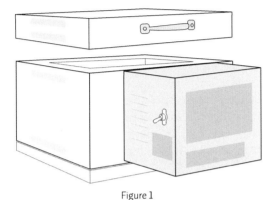

Figure 1

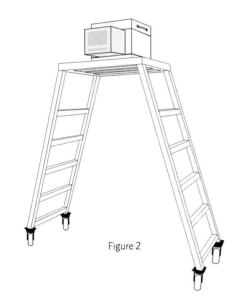

Figure 2

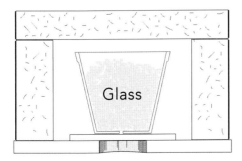

Figure 3

Construction of a Linemaking Mini-Kiln

The original vitrigraph kiln was composed of a stack of three component kiln rings. We now use the Paragon Caldera because it has a programmable controller (the original did not), requires less power, and is more versatile. (Figure 1)

To be used as a vitrigraph, the Caldera is set on top of a panel of 1" (2.5 cm) thick rigidized fiber or vermiculite board that replaces the bottom of the kiln. This 12" (30.5 cm) square panel has a 2.5" (6 cm) diameter circle cut out of its center. The entire unit is mounted overhead either to a wall or on a sturdy ladder-like structure. Our vitrigraph is mounted with the bottom about 5'9" (1.75 meters) off the floor. It is, in essence, a miniature bottomdraw glass furnace. (Figure 2)

Within the heating chamber, a pair of mullite strips (the same material kiln shelves are made of) bridge the center opening to support a clay Vitrigraph Pot (8822) 4.5" tall by 5.5" diameter (114 x 140 mm). If purchasing your own, avoid pots with hairline (or larger) cracks, as these will widen as they reach molten glass temperatures. In our experience, unglazed Italian terra cotta pots are more durable. Even so, these are generally a single use item. A Sentry Xpress digital temperature controller mounted on the outside of the kiln controls heating to the kiln chamber. Instructions for programming this controller are included with the kiln.

Glass Feedstock

Any scrap pieces of Bullseye compatible sheet glass or coarse (-0003) frit can be melted down to make lines or "stringers." Avoid glass granules smaller than coarse frit, as they produce a seedier stringer due to the greater amount of air trapped between the smaller particles.

Loading The Glass

We typically load the glass into the pot outside the kiln, while it is at room temperature, and then place the loaded pot into the kiln so that it is supported by the mullite strips. (Figure 3) When working with frit or extremely small pieces of scrap sheet glass, place a small square of Bullseye compatible sheet glass the same color as the feedstock over the hole to prevent the glass from falling out. Then fill the pot with the feedstock.

Firing The Kiln

Before firing the vitrigraph, read the safety notes on page 4. Make sure that all electrical cords are secured and the kiln platform you've selected is stable. If your platform doesn't include a ladder system, you'll need a sturdy metal ladder next to the kiln to access the top lid for charging.

CHARGING: We advise loading the amount of glass needed for a run of stringer while the pot is cold, and then cooling between runs. If time forces you to do continuous melts, or if it becomes necessary to add more glass to the pot during the melt, here are a few things you need to keep in mind:

- Turn the power off during charging.
- Use extreme care in filling the pot. Glass scraps or frit which miss the pot and land on the electrical elements can damage the elements.
- Glass scraps or frit that melt against the refractory brick will corrode it.

FIRING CYCLES AND PROCESS TEMPERATURES FOR VARIOUS GLASSES: Different types of glasses behave differently in the melting and forming process. Those with lower melting temperatures, like Black (000100), will need to be heated more slowly and to a lower process temperature to avoid their running too freely. Certain glasses, like White (000113), will cool more quickly than others and have a narrower "working range." Transparent cadmium/selenium glasses such as Yellow (001120), Red (001122), and Orange (001125) have a tendency to opalize in the remelting process. Only by working with the various glasses will you come to understand their idiosyncrasies.

Firing the vitrigraph too rapidly may result in a very seedy melt, with many air bubbles trapped in the resulting stringers. It may also cause the feedstock to thermal shock, sending chips and shards into the elements and refractory bricks. Firing too quickly can also result in an uneven melt, with the glass in the top of the pot extremely hot and the glass in the bottom still relatively cold. As a result, the glass initially flows very slowly before suddenly flowing at an uncontrollable rate. The following cycle works well to achieve a very controlled line for most glasses:

RATE (DEGREES/HOUR)	TEMPERATURE	HOLD
450°F (250°C)	1680-1725°F* (916-941°C)	2:00

*Most transparent glasses and Black (000100) will work well at process temperatures of 1680°F (916°C). Most opalescent glasses will work well at process temperatures of 1700°F (927°C). Stiff glasses such as White (000113) and French Vanilla (000137) work well at 1725°F (941°C). Depending on your experiences and the types of stringers that you are trying to create, you will find process temperatures that suit your specific needs.

FORMING: During the forming stage the temperature will determine the quality of line produced. Setting the kiln at 1680°F (916°C) while melting Black (000100) should produce a thick, fairly slow-moving stream. At this temperature it is very easy to manipulate the glass by handpulling and using the simple tools described below. Fine-tune the quality of the stream by starting at a low melting temperature and then slowly increasing it. If the glass stream is moving so fast that it becomes impossible to control, turn the kiln off and lift the kiln lid to allow heat to escape. When the glass is back under control, close the lid and restart the kiln.

Some Tools and the Line Qualities They Produce

HAND PULLING: Many types of lines require only handwork (while wearing Zetex or Kevlar gloves). If the glass is viscous enough you can pull it at intervals to create stringers of fluctuating thickness. At these low temperatures the glass can also be pulled into curves. At very high temperatures when the stream is extremely thin and fast moving you can make delicate bird's-nest shapes by allowing the stream to freefall.

TONGS: If you don't feel comfortable hand-pulling the stream of glass, there are a variety of long-handled metal tong-like tools available, such as the 9" (23 cm) long hemostat shown here.

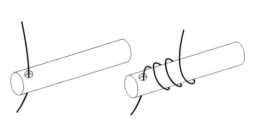

PIPES: You can make stringers in the shape of spring-like coils using a 1" (2.5 cm) diameter steel pipe. These coils can then be carefully cut into sections that will form perfect circles when kilnformed. The pipe illustrated here is 15" (38 cm) long with 0.5" (1 cm) holes drilled through the wall about 1" (2.5 cm) from the pipe's end. Pull the glass stream through the drilled holes. As the glass flows, twirl it around the pipe and then cut or break it at the end of the pipe.

TRAY: A 2-foot (61 cm) square stainless steel tray held at a 45° angle about 16" (41 cm) below the bottom of the kiln makes a good working surface for creating flat curlicue S-curves, and other curves.

Melting Cycle and Pot Life

Because of its long working range, Black (000100) is a good stock for your initial experiments in linemaking. To work in other colors using the same pot, cycle through the spectrum so you gradually transition from lighter to darker colors. Any time you transition from one color to another, the beginning of the run will produce stringers that have a thin, often streaky layer of the previous glass on the outer surface. As the run progresses, this will disappear.

A gray or metallic appearance to the pot after firing is iron in the clay that has migrated to the surface. This indicates that the pot (and the glass inside it) became much hotter than it needed to be.

Note that rapid cooling will also shorten pot life.

Avoid refiring a used pot. The risk of cracking is far greater than the minimal expense of a new pot. As mentioned above, watch out for cracks. They widen and eventually break on firing.

Safety Considerations

- Keep the kiln away from flammable surfaces and materials.
- Whichever mounting support system you choose, make sure it's sturdy and non-flammable. Any wall brackets should be firmly connected to structural wall studs.
- A freestanding system needs to be properly counter-balanced so it won't tip over during normal operation.
- Use heavy (12 gauge) electrical extension cords. A standard light-duty cord will overheat and could start a fire.
- Make sure that all primary electrical and extension cords are out of the way and taped down. Taping cords also protects them from the heat of the kiln and the pulled stringer, both of which can melt through the insulation and create a shock and fire danger. If cords are on the floor, tape them down.
- As noted by the manufacturer, the temperature inside the kiln should never exceed 2350°F (1288°C).
- Never leave the kiln unattended, especially above 1500°F when the glass is starting to soften and flow.
- If you charge the kiln using a metal scoop or tool, be certain to turn off power to the kiln first and avoid contact with the elements. There is a significant risk of electrical shock when working with metal tools this close to the kiln elements.
- A piece of sheet metal on the floor directly beneath the kiln will help prevent a structure fire.

Protective Gear

SAFETY GLASSES: A must at all times. Glass will sometimes thermal shock while being loaded into a preheated pot, and bits of glass will tend to fly when stringer is broken from the glass stream.

GLOVES: Zetex or Kevlar gloves are necessary for charging the kiln and for any direct contact with the hot glass. However, the bulkiness of these gloves makes it difficult to manipulate the forming tools. A thinner leather glove on the working hand allows you to handle the tool and provides some protection from the heat, while a Kevlar glove on the other hand allows you to break the hot stringer from the glass stream.

CLOTHES: Wear cotton pants with long legs and long-sleeved cotton shirts, and be sure to wear closed-toe shoes. Avoid wearing synthetic materials/fabrics as these are more likely to catch fire.

Additional Resources
Vitrigraph Kiln: Basic Use (video lesson)
Drawing with Glass (video lesson)

Featured Products
Paragon Caldera Kiln (8823)
Vitrigraph Base Board (8827)
Vitrigraph Pot (8828)
Vitrigraph Pot, 4 Pack (8816)
Vitrigraph Pot Supports, Set of 4 (8829)

A Technical Supplement from Bullseye Glass Co.

Compatibility of Glasses
COE Does Not Equal Compatibility

By Daniel W. Schwoerer, Bullseye Glass Co.

A misunderstanding that the compatibility or "fit" of two glasses is solely a function of their expansion properties has led to an overemphasis on "expansion" and the numerical value of the coefficient of expansion (COE) of glass. Studio artists continually ask us for the COE of a glass, hoping to predict whether it will "fit" other fusing glasses or their own furnace glass. We say the same thing each time: Matching COEs is simply not an accurate measure of compatibility.

The viscosity characteristics of a glass are equally important as its expansion characteristics. Together, these two properties determine whether one glass will fit another. But it will be useful to first discuss each individually as it pertains to this subject.

Expansion affects compatibility throughout the full temperature range (from the annealing point to room temperature). This is because by nature most materials—whether solid or liquid—expand upon heating and contract upon cooling. It is commonly assumed that if they expand and contract similarly they will "fit" or be compatible once fused together. But this is not necessarily true. In fact we have tested some glasses with the same COE and found them to be incompatible.

Measured and Calculated COEs

The expansion of a glass may be determined by calculation or by measurement. A common laboratory test (using a dilatometer) measures the expansion properties of a glass over a given temperature range, for instance 20°–300°C. (A COE number must always be accompanied by the temperature range over which it was measured or it is meaningless.) Unfortunately, the equally important range in this measurement—from 300°C to the annealing point—is ignored. It is a well-known fact that the

expansion properties of a glass change significantly through the transition range.[1] Therefore it is obvious that this measured COE number is not intended to describe the expansion characteristics of a glass for compatibility purposes. In actuality there is no one number that can describe the expansion properties of a glass through the full temperature range since it is not constant (linear). Furthermore, it is highly unlikely that an entire line of "compatible glasses" would all have the same COE.

To further confuse the issue, many manufacturers publish a so-called "calculated COE." This calculated COE is a meaningless number when comparing the COE of different glasses in the context of studio usage. The calculated number[2] should only be used to compare projected relative changes in expansion of a given glass with changes in composition of the same glass, or in comparing very similar glasses to each other—such as one soft soda lime glass to another soft soda lime glass. It should never be assumed to represent a real COE. It is a tool that a glass formulator can use to predict changes in expansion when making raw material changes such as substituting magnesium for calcium or sodium for potassium. However, we encourage glass and batch suppliers—and educators—not to publish this number. Unless they provide considerable explanation as to its use, it is very misleading to users in the studio glass community, implying a meaningful COE for furnace-melted glass, which it clearly is not.

---

1 F.V. Tooley, The Handbook of Glass Manufacture, Vol. 2, 1974, pp 906–907.

2 There are many methods for making this calculation, among them English and Turner, OI, Winkelman and Schott. They all utilize an expansion factor for each raw material, assume an additive mathematical result, and do not take into account the melting cycle of the glass.

Why a Measured COE Alone Does Not Insure Compatibility

As stated above, the fitting of two different glasses is a function of both viscosity (resistance to flow) and expansion. Whereas expansion affects the compatibility predominantly in the lower temperature range—below the strain point—the viscosity properties affect compatibility predominantly in the annealing range, from the annealing point to the strain point . Differences in viscosity between two glasses will cause compatibility problems. If one glass is stiffer than the other, they will strain each other as they cool through the annealing range.

Compatibility Via Compensating Differences

For glasses of different viscosities to be compatible (which is frequently the case) their expansions must be different. In actuality, what happens is a process of compensating differences. Two different glasses will be compatible if the strain set up by the mismatch in viscosity is cancelled out by the strain introduced by the mismatch in expansion (once cooled to room temperature and assuming, of course, that proper annealing has occurred). For instance, if the viscosity differences result in tension between the two glasses and the expansion differences result in an equal amount of compression between the two glasses, the two stresses cancel each other out. This is the critical phenomenon that results in compatibility of two glasses with different expansion/viscosity properties. This explains why glasses of very different viscosity/expansion characteristics actually fit such as a stiff opalescent with a soft transparent. If you were to have samples of these two types of glasses measured for expansion you would find that they could have COEs[3] differing by as much as five or more points.

This, furthermore, is why the only practical test for compatibility is one that takes both phenomena into account. One example is the chip test for fusing. Looking at the COE alone is very misleading and cannot accurately predict compatibility. The chip test can.

Bullseye developed the chip test in the late 1970s, based on the input of Robert Barber. It has been used since that time and is an industry standard for determining compatibility. Our records allow us to track the compatibility characteristics of every sheet of glass that we have made since that time.

The test is done by placing 12.5-mm-square chips atop a 63.5-mm-wide base sheet of a known clear test glass. The chips are positioned with at least 25 mm between each test chip and 25 mm between the chips and the edge of the base of clear test glass. (See Figure 1.)

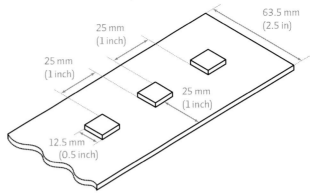

Figure 1: The chip test layup.

The arrangement is then fired to 1500°F (816°C) and held at that temperature for 15 minutes before cooling and annealing. Once cooled, the test is viewed for stress through cross-polarized light and graded accordingly using very strict criteria for acceptable strain. Glasses that are known to be fairly stable are tested in a single firing. Glasses known to be less stable are chip-tested in three consecutive firings to ensure good performance under typical fusing and slumping conditions (such as those used to make a simple plate).

This test works exceptionally well in predicting the compatibility of the glasses tested. Unlike calculated COEs or even measured COEs, the test takes into account both the expansion and viscosity characteristics of the glass. It also tests the glass in a manner in which it will actually be used, and results in meaningful data.

No test can take into account every process to which someone might subject a particular glass. If you intend to use a process that requires significantly more heatwork than described above, we recommend that you perform your own chip tests using the same cycles that you intend to use.

Some processes that may not immediately appear to exceed the parameters of the test for compatibility actually do. Firing some glasses very slowly or holding them for long times in the devitrification range starting at about 1375°F (746°C) can cause those glasses to change dramatically.

Conclusion

It would be better if we in the glass community had never focused so much attention on the coefficient of expansion. The only accurate measure of compatibility is testing a sample in a manner appropriate for the intended type of forming—whether fusing, kilncasting, blowing, or combining processes such as blowing and fusing—and viewing the results for strain. Unfortunately, there are those who continue to promote misguided and confusing concepts. In many cases, this can lead to failure for people using the material. Bullseye would rather have users feel confident about using the material and empowered to test their limits.

---

3   Assuming that all measured COEs were measured from 20°–300°C.

Heat & Glass

Understanding the Effects of Temperature Variations on Bullseye Glass

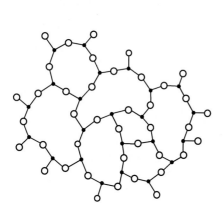

Amorphous structure

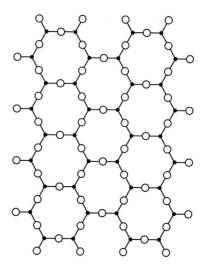

Crystalline structure

The Unique Nature of Glass, the Supercooled Liquid

Glass is an *amorphous* material. Its molecules are not arranged in a regular, specific pattern, like those of a crystalline material, but are random in their configuration.

Because of its amorphous molecular configuration, glass reacts to heat differently than do other materials. Whereas metals change from a solid to a liquid and a specific temperature (a *melting point*), glass goes through a very gradual transformation—from a material that behaves like a solid to a material that behaves like a liquid. It is this unique characteristic of glass that allows it to be blown or to be worked in the myriad ways we call *kilnforming*.

Even in its solid form, glass exhibits the molecular structure of a stiff liquid. For this reason, glass at room temperature is sometimes referred to as a *supercooled liquid*. As it is heated, glass gradually begins to behave more and more like a liquid until, at temperatures above 2000°F (1093°C), it will flow easily, with a consistency similar to honey. The temperatures at which glass is worked in a kiln are usually between 1000–1700°F (538–927°C). Within this range, a wide variety of effects may be achieved by using a variety of processes.

Behavior of Glass When Heated

The following chart gives a broad overview of how Bullseye glasses act in different temperature ranges. Not all Bullseye glasses behave identically. Some slight variations can occur, depending on the viscosity of the individual glass. Furthermore, the specific kiln, setup, and firing cycle used will have a direct impact on the results achieved at any given temperature.

Below 1000°F (538°C)	What You See	What is Happening Physically	Kilnforming Process
 1 Layer 3 mm (1/8") 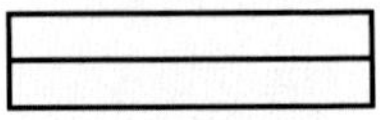 / 2 Layers 6 mm (1/4") 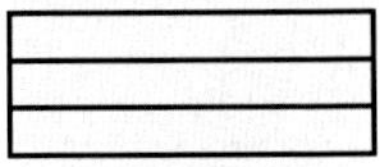 / 3 Layers 9 mm (3/8")	1 Layer: Rigid, no visible changes, edges sharp. 2 & 3 Layers: Same as above.	Glass expanding or contracting at a rate determined by its *coefficient of expansion*. Subject to *thermal shock* below approximately 850°F (454°C).	Upper end of this range is where *annealing* occurs, at the *anneal soak temperature* of 900°F (482°C).

Cold starting width

1000°–1250°F (538°–677°C)	What You See	What is Happening Physically	Kilnforming Process
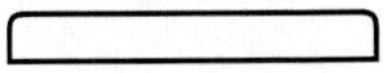 1 Layer 3 mm (1/8") 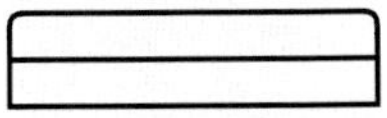 / 2 Layers 6 mm (1/4") 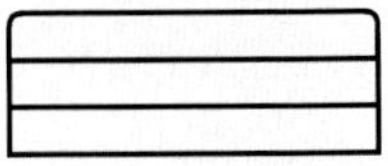 / 3 Layers 9 mm (3/8")	At upper end of range: 1 Layer: Edges just begin to soften and round. 2 & 3 Layers: (Same as above.) Layers appear to be sticking together.	Glass is beginning to soften and act like a stiff liquid, but still maintains its original shape. Glass is transitioning from behaving like a solid to behaving like a liquid; also known as the *transformation range*.	Most *painting* or *enameling* is done at these temperatures. Bullseye glass will bend or *slump* if held at the upper end of range. A soak in the 1150°–1250°F (621°–677°C) range is often employed to remove air from between layers, which reduces the number and size of bubbles in the finished piece.

Cold starting width

1250°–1350°F (677°–732°C)	What You See	What is Happening Physically	Kilnforming Process
1 Layer 3 mm (1/8")	1 Layer: Edges of glass slightly rounded, surface begins to look glossy.	If held at the top end of this range too long, crystals may grow: *devitrification*.	*Fire polishing*, the removal of fine abrasions on the glass surface, can be accomplished.
2 Layers 6 mm (1/4")	2 & 3 Layers: (Same as above.) Layers appear to be sticking together.		Glass begins to sag fully at upper end of range. Glass surfaces will stick together, called *sintering* or *tack fusing*.
3 Layers 9 mm (3/8")			

← Cold starting width →

1350°–1400°F (732°–760°C)	What You See	What is Happening Physically	Kilnforming Process
1 Layer 3 mm (1/8")	1 Layer: Starts to contract and bead up at edges.	Surface tension is overcoming gravity. Devitrification may occur.	Glasses stick together with edges rounded, called *tack fusing*.
2 Layers 6 mm (1/4")	2 & 3 Layers: Layers are stuck together, upper edges rounded; footprint of glass remains constant.		
3 Layers 9 mm (3/8")			

← Cold starting width →

1400°–1500°F (760°–816°C)	What You See	What is Happening Physically	Kilnforming Process
1 Layer 3 mm (1/8") 2 Layers 6 mm (1/4") DAM 3 Layers 9 mm (3/8") ← Cold starting width →	**1 Layer:** Center of piece may become extremely thin as perimeter thickens and *needlepoints*. **2 & 3 Layers:** Layers fully fused at upper end of range. Glass begins to move beyond original footprint unless constrained by dams or molds.	At upper end of range, gravity begins to overtake surface tension. Any air trapped between glass and shelf or between layers will expand.	At the lower end of the range, *tack-fusing*. At the upper end of the range, *full fusing* or *kilncarving* with fiber paper.

1500°–1600°F (816°–871°C)	What You See	What is Happening Physically	Kilnforming Process
1 Layer 3 mm (1/8") 2 Layers 6 mm (1/4") DAM 3 Layers 9 mm (3/8") ← Cold starting width →	**1 Layer:** Air trapped between the thin center of the glass and the top surface of the shelf may rise up and form a bubble. **2 & 3 Layers:** Surface smooth and watery, bubbles within glass or trapped between layers may rise to surface. Unless contained, glass will flow freely until it reaches 6 mm (1/4") thickness.	Viscosity continues to decrease, allowing glass to flow under the force of gravity. Glass also becomes more reactive with materials with which it is in contact. At the upper end of the range, glass sticks more readily to shelf separators and mold materials, and compatibility characteristics may begin to change.	*Full fusing* or *kilncasting*. At upper end of range, glass is flowing sufficiently to fill small cracks in molds.

1600°–1700°F (871°–927°C)	What You See	What is Happening Physically	Kilnforming Process
1 Layer 3 mm (1/8")	**1 Layer:** Bubble will burst, leaving crater.	Viscosity continues to decrease, and flow is increased.	Glass is fluid enough to perform *combing* with wet metal rod, and *kilncasting*.
2 Layers 6 mm (1/4")	**2 & 3 Layers:** Glass is flowing like molasses. Glass may flow off edge of shelf. Must be constrained by molds or dams. Bubbles rising from lower layers will pull lower glass up to surface.		
DAM **3 Layers** 9 mm (3/8")			

Cold starting width

Above 1700°F (927°C)	What You See	What is Happening Physically	Kilnforming Process
1 Layer 3 mm (1/8")	**1 Layer:** Crater fully opened.	Viscosity continues to decrease.	*Kilncasting* with a plugged crucible/reservoir that is unplugged to allow the glass to flow, once it is fully molten.
2 Layers 6 mm (1/4")	**2 & 3 Layers:** *Boiling* type of activity continues.		
DAM **3 Layers** 9 mm (3/8")			

Cold starting width

Goals of a Firing Schedule

Understanding the behavior of glass within different temperature ranges allows you to create a *firing schedule* or series of steps that will properly heat and cool glass in a kiln. Using a firing schedule, you can accomplish the two basic objectives of kilnforming, which are:

- To bring the glass body to a temperature where it can be formed in the manner or process selected.
- To return the glass to room temperature in a stable condition (i.e., free of unwanted internal stress).

A firing schedule (sometimes called a *firing cycle* or *firing profile*) may be subdivided in various ways.
At Bullseye, we generally break the firing schedule down into the following eight stages:

I. INITIAL HEAT: ROOM TEMP TO 1000°F (538°C)
Until glass reaches a temperature of about 850°F (454°C), it can shatter (undergo *thermal shock*), if heated too quickly or unevenly. Because the glass is always cooler than the thermocouple during initial heat, we extend the initial heating range to 1000°F (538°C) to make sure the glass is at least at 850°F (454°C) before moving to rapid heat. There are no negative consequences to heating too slowly in this range, other than lost production efficiencies. Therefore, at Bullseye, we are generally very conservative in our heating rate for first firings: ~400°F/hr (222°C/hr).

The smaller the individual pieces making up the project, the faster the initial heating can be.

2. PRE-RAPID HEAT SOAK: 1000°–1250°F (538°–677°C)
This optional-but-useful stage in the cycle, in which the glass is held at a specific temperature, is designed to even out the temperature within the glass body before the rapid ascent to process temperature, to allow for a faster ascent, and, in some cases, to *squeeze* air from between layers or within any gaps in the interior lay-up. A pre-rapid heat soak at ~1225°F (663°C) is required for a gold-bearing striking glass to achieve its target color.

3. RAPID HEAT: 1000°F (538°C) TO FORMING / PROCESS TEMP
The primary objective in this temperature range is to move as quickly as possible to the process temperature so as to avoid *devitrification* (growth of crystals on the glass surface), but not to fire so rapidly as to cause bubbles to be trapped between layers.

4. PROCESS SOAK: 1000°–1700°F (538°–927°C)
This is the temperature range at which glass can be formed by using various processes, such as slumping, tack fusing, full fusing, or kilncasting. The same effects or processes can be accomplished whether firing to a lower temperature for a longer time or to a higher temperature for a shorter time. This interplay between firing temperature and firing duration is the basis of *heat work*. In general, one has greater control with a longer process soak at a lower temperature, as long as this temperature is not within the devitrification range. At Bullseye, we soak for an average of 10 minutes at process temperature for most basic firings.

5. RAPID COOL: PROCESS TEMP TO 900°F (482°C)
Glass should be brought down to the anneal-soak temperature as quickly as possible, once it has been formed, to avoid devitrification and save unnecessary cooling time.

However, Bullseye does not recommend opening the kiln widely to vent at these temperatures. Opening to vent can set up a temperature differential within the glass body that will necessitate increased time at a lower temperature to bring back temperature equilibrium.

Rather than opening the kiln to vent, we recommend allowing the kiln to cool at its own rate (which will vary based on the kiln-wall insulation and mass of material in the kiln), to about 900°F (482°C).

6. ANNEAL SOAK: 900°F (482°C)
As glass heats, it expands; as it cools, it contracts. These processes set up stresses within glass, especially between the interior and the surface of a glass body. To relieve these stresses, which can lead to strain or breakage at room temperatures, it is necessary to cool glass in a very controlled manner, through a predetermined temperature gradient. This controlled process for cooling glass is called *annealing*.

The first phase of the annealing process is the anneal soak, which should help to equalize the temperature throughout the glass and relieve any stress that is present.

We soak Bullseye glasses at 900°F (482°C). The duration of the soak at this temperature depends upon both the thickness of the glass and how it is set up in the kiln. The goal is to achieve uniform temperature throughout the body of the glass.

7. ANNEAL COOL: 900°–700°F (482°–371°C)
Once the temperature within the glass body has become uniform during the anneal soak, it is gradually cooled through the rest of the annealing range. The rate of cooling required depends upon both the thickness (and variations in the thickness) of the glass and how it is set up in the kiln. The goal is to keep the temperature difference throughout the body of glass to within 10°F (5°C) from 900°–800°F (482°–427°C), and within 20°F (11°C) from 800°–700°F (427°–371°C).

8. FINAL COOL TO ROOM TEMPERATURE:
700°–80°F (371°–27°C)
Cooling to room temperature can be accomplished as quickly as possible, as long as the rate is not so rapid as to cause thermal shock.

In the Bullseye studio, for most firings of moderately-sized pieces of even 1/4" (6 mm) thickness, we allow the kiln to cool at its own rate, with the door closed, until the interior reaches about 200°F (93°C) or lower. The kiln can then be vented slightly until it reaches room temperature, allowing the glass

IDEALIZED FIRING GRAPH

Shown on a time/temperature firing graph, the eight firing stages might look like this:

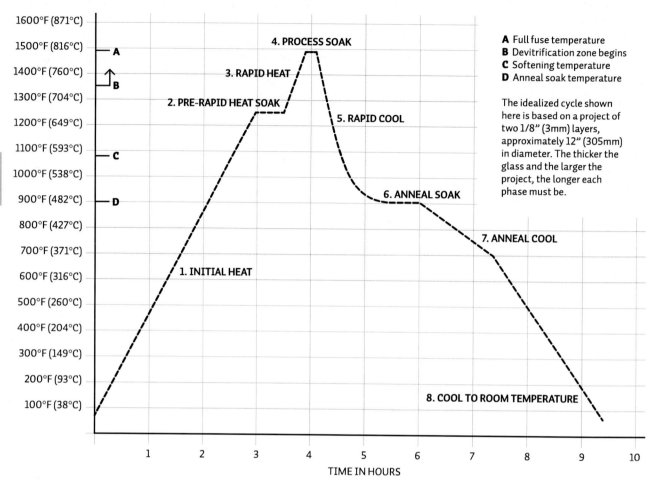

A Full fuse temperature
B Devitrification zone begins
C Softening temperature
D Anneal soak temperature

The idealized cycle shown here is based on a project of two 1/8" (3mm) layers, approximately 12" (305mm) in diameter. The thicker the glass and the larger the project, the longer each phase must be.

piece to cool down until it can be handled with bare hands. For thicker work and works with variation in thickness, we keep the kiln door closed until the interior has reached room temperature.

The Anti-Sucker Process

Sometimes, fully three-dimensional pieces, such as those made in the lost-wax casting process, will come out of the mold with depressions or wrinkles that were not present in the original model. Such areas, called *suckers*, will appear to have taken on detail from the mold and shrunken away from it or *sucked-in*. Suckers can form during the cooling process, while the glass is shrinking or contracting in general. Hot glass has a lower viscosity than cold glass and, therefore, may become the focal point of shrinkage for the entire piece. If the entire piece of glass cools and contracts uniformly while it is in its plastic state, no suckers will form. However, suckers may form if there are thicker areas in the piece or areas that are likely to stay hot longer than other areas during the cooling process.

At Bullseye, we have found that suckers can usually be prevented through a series of processes. 1) Soaking/holding the glass at around 1250°F (677°C) during the rapid cooling stage to unify the temperature throughout the glass. 2) Cooling the glass as uniformly as possible from this point

to the anneal soak temperature. 3) Incorporating a large reservoir into the casting that will remain full enough to be the thickest part of the casting and, therefore, the last area of the piece to cool off. It may be necessary to cover this reservoir with refractory fiber blanket to keep it from cooling too quickly. After firing, such a reservoir will have a concave meniscus that otherwise would have appeared as a sucker elsewhere on the body of the casting.

Kilnforming Process Temperatures

PROCESS	TEMPERATURE RANGE	
Combing/Boiling	1600–1700°F	871–927°C
Kilncasting	1500–1600°F	816–871°C
Full fuse	1480–1550°F	804–843°C
Kilncarving (bas relief)	1500–1550°F	816–843°C
Strip technique	1470–1550°F	799–843°C
Tack fuse (edges soften slightly)	1290–1435°F	699–779°C
Sagging (cross section changes)	1255–1350°F	679–732°C
Fuse-to-stick (sintering)	1255–1330°F	679–721°C
Slumping (no thickness change)	1100–1300°F	593–704°C
Painting	1000–1250°F	538–677°C

Practical Application

It is important to keep in mind that firing schedules are only one part of the total firing story. While it is fine to solicit or share firing schedules, they should be treated only as points of departure because they constitute just one of many conditions and variables that can affect the outcome of a glass project. For instance, every kiln fires a little differently, and this is true even for two kilns of the same model. Other factors include, but are not limited to: the type of glass, the type and placement of the shelf in the kiln, the type and location of the thermocouple, and whether the piece is being fired for the first, second, or third time.

In the Bullseye Research and Education studio we take a fairly conservative approach to most firings. The following schedules are typical for the cycles we use for many projects. In each case, it should be fairly clear how the firing theory from previous pages applies to these real schedules.

SCHEDULE 1

First full-fuse firing of a 12" (305 mm) diameter piece, composed of two layers of 3 mm (1/8") "-0030" glass in a Paragon GL24 with top, side, and door elements:

STEP	RATE (DPH)		TEMPERATURE		HOLD
1. Initial heat Pre-rapid heat soak	400°F	222°C	1250°F	677°C	:30
2. Rapid heat Process soak	600°F	333°C	1490°F	810°C	:10
3. Rapid cool Anneal soak	AFAP*		900°F	482°C	:30
4. Anneal cool	150°F	83°C	700°F	371°C	:00
5. Final cool	AFAP*		70°F	21°C	:00

SCHEDULE 2

Slumping schedule for the same piece. See notes.

STEP	RATE (DPH)		TEMPERATURE		HOLD
1. Initial heat Process soak	300°F	166°C	1180°F	638°C	:10
2. Rapid cool Anneal soak	AFAP*		900°F	482°C	1:00
3. Anneal cool	100°F	55°C	700°F	371°C	:00
4. Final cool	AFAP*		70°F	21°C	:00

SCHEDULE 3

First tack-fuse firing of a piece composed of one layer of 4 mm base glass and an application of frits and powders. See notes.

STEP	RATE (DPH)		TEMPERATURE		HOLD
1. Initial heat Process soak	600°F	333°C	1275–1450°F	691–788°C	:10
2. Rapid cool Anneal soak	AFAP*		900°F	482°C	1:00
3. Anneal cool	100°F	55°C	700°F	371°C	:00
4. Final cool	AFAP*		70°F	21°C	:00

* As Fast As Possible will be whatever cooling rate results from the kiln power being cut off by the controller. We do not advocate crash cooling. Rather, we advocate leaving the kiln closed, allowing it to cool naturally to the next temperature.

FIRING NOTES FOR SCHEDULE 2

· Notice that the initial heat for this schedule is more conservative than that recommended for schedule 1. This is because the piece being heated is now one solid, thicker piece of glass, which should be fired more slowly to ensure that it will heat evenly throughout.

· Notice that there is no pre-rapid heat soak in this schedule. This is because the piece in question has already been fused together, and there is no opportunity to remove air from between layers of glass, as there was in the initial firing.

· Slumping temperatures and hold times vary widely, depending upon the type and design of the mold, the glasses being slumped, and the desired effect. Slumping should always be confirmed visually.

· Because the slumped piece will be in contact with a mold that will have some thermal mass and may not be of a completely uniform thickness, and because a slumped piece will tend to cool unevenly, both the anneal soak and the anneal cool should be more conservative than they would be for pieces of comparable thickness that were merely flat fused.

FIRING NOTES FOR SCHEDULE 3

· The initial rate of heat for a single layer of glass with an application of frits and powders in a first firing is often faster than that used for two or more layers of glass. In practical application, such faster firing rarely presents a problem. In theory, however, such a piece could be more difficult to heat evenly if it is a less uniform arrangement of material than a piece made of even layers of sheet glass.

· Notice that there is no pre-rapid heat soak in this schedule. This is because the piece in question is composed of one layer of sheet glass with frits added on top. There are no top layers in this piece under which air could be trapped, as there were for the project described in Schedule 1.

· Process temperatures for tack-fused pieces depend upon the desired effect as well as the forms and colors of the glasses in question. Black powder (000100-0008), for example, will begin to fuse at a much lower temperature than White coarse frit (000113-0003).

· Notice that the anneal-cool stage for the tack-fused piece is more conservative than that proposed for the thicker, fully fused piece from Schedule 1. This is because tack-fused pieces tend to cool unevenly and should, therefore, be cooled more slowly to compensate.

A Technical Supplement from Bullseye Glass Co.

Volume & Bubble Control
Understanding Distortion and Trapped Air When Firing Bullseye Glass

Two common problems encountered when fusing glass are distortions of shape and unanticipated bubbles. To avoid these effects—or to engineer them into your work—you need to learn how to control volume and trapped air during firing.

Understanding Volume

When held at its full fusing temperature for an adequate amount of time, Bullseye glass will follow the Six Millimeter Rule and assume a thickness of 6 mm (0.25") unless contained by dams, molds, or other restraints. This equates to two standard layers of Bullseye 3 mm (0.125") sheet glass.

With less than two standard layers, the glass will pull in at a full fuse to assume a 6 mm thickness. As a result, the project "footprint" or surface area will be smaller after firing.

With more than two standard layers, the glass will flow out at process temperature to assume a thickness of 6 mm resulting in a larger project footprint.

These general principles may be modified slightly by the viscosity of the glass.

Viscosity

Viscosity is the resistance of a liquid to flow. For example, molasses is a highly viscous material, while water has very low viscosity.

Heated to sufficiently high temperatures, glass behaves like a liquid. But different glass styles have different viscosities, depending on their composition. A glass with low viscosity is sometimes said to be "soft." A glass with high viscosity is considered to be "hard" or "stiff."

While all Bullseye glasses will flow in accordance with the general principles discussed above, the viscosities of the individual glasses may modify flow slightly.

Black (000100) is a soft glass. The surface area it will cover when multiple layers are fired to full fuse temperature will be slightly larger than that covered by the same amount of a stiffer glass, such as French Vanilla (000137), fired under the same conditions.

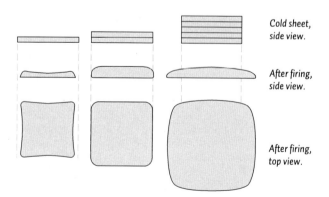

Cold sheet, side view.

After firing, side view.

After firing, top view.

1 1/2" (4 cm) squares of standard-thickness glass in 1, 2, and 5 layers.

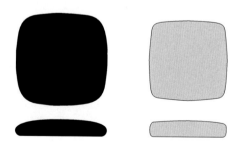

After firing, 5 layers of Black (left) vs. 5 layers of French Vanilla (right).

The Softening Temperature

Just as various types of glass differ in viscosity, they also differ in the rates at which they soften. Some glasses will begin to flow at lower temperatures than others. This fact can affect the design of a fused project.

For example, Black softens before White (000113). When Black is placed on top of the stiffer White, the Black softens and flows out over the surface of the White before sinking into the base.

By contrast, if the stiffer White is set on top of the Black, the White will sink into the base rather than softening and spreading over the surface.

Top views and cross sections of Black and White squares laid on each other.

Note that the footprint of the Black square will be slightly larger after firing than the White square. Note also that the corners of the Black square will be slightly more rounded.

Once you become aware of viscosity and its impact on the fusing process, you'll be able to take advantage of it in designing your work.

Effect of Volume on Design

As noted above, compositions thinner than 6 mm will contract, while those thicker than 6 mm will flow out. These effects will be most noticeable around the perimeter of a fused project. If unrestrained pieces of glass are stacked thickly at the edge of your work, they will flow out beyond the perimeter of the original footprint, creating an irregular edge. If areas close to the edge are less than 6 mm thick, they will tend to shrink in toward the mass of the work and result in an irregular perimeter.

If you are designing a project with areas of varying thickness, keep the variations away from the edge to minimize distortion of the shape or footprint.

Controlling Bubbles

Fusing art glass almost always results in the formation of some air bubbles. Controlling the size, shape, and number of bubbles is mostly a matter of paying attention to how air can become trapped between glass layers and between glass and the kiln shelf.

HOW AIR GETS TRAPPED BETWEEN LAYERS

Many air bubbles are generated as a direct result of the firing cycle. If glass is heated too rapidly, the edges of larger pieces can soften and fuse before their interiors do. This earlier fusing of edges may trap air between layers, resulting in bubbles. You can reduce unwanted air bubbles by adding a pre-rapid heat soak to the firing cycle. For a typical 6 mm project, hold the kiln at a temperature from 1150–1250°F (621–677°C) for 15–45 minutes. At this temperature, the glass will soften enough to begin moving, but not enough to fuse. Thus, the top layer can settle onto the bottom layer, squeezing out the air laterally from between the layers. Likewise, using a slower rate of heat in the rapid heat segment of your firing—for example, 400°F (222°C) per hour instead of AFAP (as fast as possible)—may reduce the number and size of bubbles.

If the edges of your project are too close to the kiln elements, or if the kiln has only side elements, the direct heat can cause your layers of glass to seal up at the edges before air can escape. Ceramic fiber paper or kiln dams can be placed on the edges of the shelf to baffle, or shield, the heat from the edges of your glass, thus allowing air to escape from between layers.

Another variable that can contribute to bubble formation is the flatness or waviness of the glass sheets being used in a project. For example, single-rolled (-0000) glasses are less flat than double-rolled (-0030) glasses and tend to trap more air between stacked layers.

Other bubbles may result from the design of a piece of work. For example, bubbles can form between layers from air pockets created when stacking component pieces of a design, or when cut pieces do not fit together well.

Also, consider the weight of the materials you add to the top layer of a piece. If you take two unfused layers of sheet glass and put a "frame" of sheet glass, frit, or powder around the top perimeter of those sheets, the extra weight along the edges of the piece can prevent air from escaping laterally from between the bottom two layers. Air will be trapped, causing bubbles. To prevent such bubbles, consider pre-firing the bottom two layers and then adding the frame element in the second firing, or else start the project using 6 mm glass.

Placing accessory glasses such as frit, powder, or stringers between layers is an almost certain recipe for bubbles. Instead, place accessory materials on the top layer of your project, or pre-fuse them in separate firings to the point where they are smooth and so less likely to trap air when stacked for a subsequent firing.

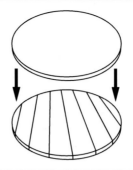

Tip: To fire two identical disks together, cut the lower disk into strips no more than 4 cm (1.5") wide, reassemble the pieces, and cap with the uncut disk. If the strips are tightly fitted together, they will be barely noticeable after fusing, and the piece will be relatively bubble free. This technique also allows air trapped between the glass and the kiln shelf to escape.

Two-layer disk with bottom layer strip-cut.

HOW AIR GETS TRAPPED BETWEEN GLASS AND THE KILN SHELF

Hot air rises. If it can't escape from underneath a piece laterally, it will force the softened glass upward. The resulting distortion, while not technically a bubble, will generally be undesirable. Fired to a high enough temperature, the trapped air will push completely through the softened glass, forming a crater or hole in the fused work.

Very large areas of glass, especially if constructed of layers with a total depth of less than 6 mm, will tend to trap air. Other conditions can aggravate this effect.

Moisture in a kiln shelf will turn to steam upon heating, and steam will create bubbles faster than hot air will. Make sure that your kiln shelf is thoroughly dry before firing by heating it to 500°F (260°C) and holding it at that temperature for 20 minutes. Using ceramic fiber paper instead of kiln wash will ensure that any moisture trapped below the glass can escape. The porosity of the ceramic fiber paper will also ensure an escape route for any trapped air.

A shelf that is not flat can also cause bubbles to form. A shelf containing a dip of 1.5 mm (0.0625") can create a significant bubble problem for typical fused projects that are 6 mm thick. To avoid the problem, check your shelves for flatness by using a straightedge. Shelves that are distorted enough to cause bubbles or other problems may still work if fiber paper is used between the glass and the shelf.

Otherwise, distorted shelves should be discarded, cut up for other uses, or used as "foundation" shelves for something like a sand bed.

Excessively rapid heating during the firing cycle can result in some areas of a glass project changing in thickness faster than others. This is especially likely to happen around the perimeter of pieces less than 6 mm thick, causing the "escape channels" for air between the glass and the shelf to be impeded. To avoid this, consider using a more conservative heating cycle or firing on a breathable shelf separator, such as ceramic fiber paper, to allow air that would otherwise be trapped to escape.

Bubbles can form between glass and a mold during slumping. This happens for a variety of reasons.

- If a mold is not porous and contains no holes through which air can escape as the glass slumps into the form.

- If holes become blocked before the glass has finished slumping.

- If the glass is in contact with the mold for too long or at temperatures that are too high.

- To prevent these problems, review your program and visually confirm the slump. Best results in slumping are usually obtained by holding the glass at lower temperatures for a longer period of time, rather than at higher temperatures for a shorter period of time.

TO PREVENT THE FORMATION OF BUBBLES BETWEEN LAYERS

1. Incorporate a pre-rapid heat hold in the firing cycle.
2. Increase the amount of time spent in the rapid-heating stage.
3. Baffle the edges of the piece with fiber paper, kiln dams, or pieces of sawn-up kiln shelf.
4. Eliminate air pockets from the design.
5. Pre-fire layers when necessary or work with 6 mm (0.25") glass.
6. Consider cutting the bottom layer of a piece to allow air to escape. (See tip above.)

TO PREVENT THE FORMATION OF BUBBLES OR DISTORTIONS BETWEEN YOUR GLASS AND KILN SHELF

1. Use layers of glass with a thickness of at least 6 mm (0.25")—for example, two layers of standard 3 mm (0.125") sheet glass.
2. Make sure that your shelf is thoroughly dry.
3. Use fiber paper between the shelf and the glass.
4. Increase the firing time up to full fuse in the rapid-heat stage.
5. Make sure that your shelf is flat.
6. Be certain that holes in slumping molds are properly positioned.
7. Confirm slumping visually.
8. Use smaller component pieces in laying up the work. (See tip above.)

Tip: Flip-Firing

This technique prevents bubbles from disfiguring a glass surface. The work is first fired with its face side down. During this "flipped" firing, the bubbles rise toward the top surface. When the piece is turned over for the second firing, the former top surface (toward which bubbles have risen) becomes the underside of the piece. The new top surface (the face) will be free of the bumpy texture resulting from bubbles. It can be fire polished on a second firing, though it may need to be sandblasted or overglazed.

Flip-firing was developed by Ray Ahlgren, owner of Fireart Glass in Portland, Oregon, during the fabrication of Silvia Levenson's *Un Mondo Migliore* at the Bullseye factory in 1996.

What If You Want Bubbles?

Just as you can prevent bubbles in your work by controlling your glass and firings, you can also purposely design bubbles into your work.

CREATING BUBBLES WITH TEXTURED GLASS

Textured glasses can be manipulated to create bubbles. Bullseye reeded glass (-0043 and -0053) has a tight linear pattern of ridges and grooves. Placing textured surfaces together with the ridges running at right angles to each other will create a grid-like pattern of air pockets, regularly spaced between layers. Fire to full fuse to create tiny, evenly spaced bubbles within the glass.

Bullseye accordion glass (-0045 and -0055) has a linear pattern of regularly increasing and decreasing spaces between its ridges. Use it with itself or combined with reeded glass to form another variety of bubble pattern.

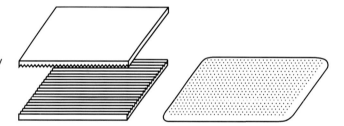

Reeded glass laid up at right angles and resulting bubble pattern.

CREATING BUBBLES WITH GLASS STRIPS

Crosshatching strips of glass and sandwiching them between two full layers of glass can yield bubbles that are large, defined, and dramatic.

STRINGER-PATTERNED BUBBLES

Crosshatching 1 mm or 2 mm glass stringers between layers of sheet glass will create an effect similar to that achieved by the glass-strip method, but with smaller bubbles.

There are other ways to trap air in a controlled fashion within a kilnformed piece, including combinations of the techniques listed above.

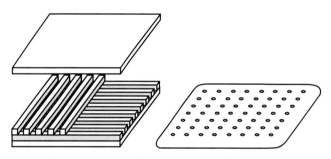

Glass strips laid up at right angles and resulting bubble pattern.

Conclusion

The basic concepts of volume and bubble control provided here are just starting points. Investigating these ideas through your own tests and experiments will strengthen your skills and craftsmanship in kilnformed glass. We encourage you to discuss these ideas and post questions and on the Bullseye Forum: bullseyeglass.com/forum

TECHNOTES ⬤6

A Technical Supplement from Bullseye Glass Co.

Preparing the Shelf System For a Large Kiln

25

Figure 1: Pearl-56 bullseye edition kiln with finished shelf system

Creating large, finished glasswork that is flat, uniform, and well annealed is highly dependent upon having a reliable shelf system. An ideal shelf system for a large kiln must have a continuous, seamless surface and be level, stable, smooth, durable, flat and able to transfer heat uniformly. With this TechNote, we recommend one such shelf system and the information needed to prepare it.

You will find that preparing this shelf system is not difficult, but it is process-intensive and will require several days. Taking your time, without rushing or cutting corners, will help you to establish a reliable firing surface that, with proper care, will last for many years.

The three major steps in preparing the shelf system are: leveling the kiln floor in its operating location, establishing a mullite subshelf system, and preparing a fiberboard shelf.

Step 1: Leveling the Kiln in its Operating Location

Ideally, you will be able to position the kiln in a level operating location.

Once the kiln is positioned, you will need to determine how level its floor is. Do this by placing a level on the kiln floor, taking readings from side to side, front to back, and corner to corner (Figure 2). If your level is short, set it on a long straightedge to evaluate a larger span.

If you find that your kiln floor is not level, you will need to make adjustments. Some slight leveling can be accomplished later, by positioning shims under sections of the mullite subshelf (Step 2). But if one side of the kiln floor is 0.125" (3 mm) lower than the other, the kiln itself should be leveled. In general, for the sake of stability, it is better to level the kiln than to rely on shims.

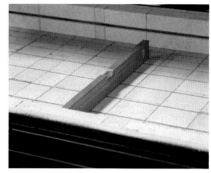

Figure 2: Checking the kiln floor with a level.

TWO OPTIONS FOR LEVELING THE KILN

If your kiln has adjustable leveling feet, use them.

OR

Add washers between the casters and mounting plates on the low side of the kiln.

Step 2: Establishing a Mullite Subshelf System

Once the kiln is level, the next step is to establish a mullite subshelf system that is stable, level, and flat. Such a subshelf system will provide strong support for glasswork and will help to ensure the uniform transfer of heat to glass.

Materials and tools you will need:
- Mullite subshelf units
- Kiln posts
- Stainless-steel shims
- A level, a square, and a measuring tape

PROCEDURE FOR ESTABLISHING THE MULLITE SUBSHELF SYSTEM

1. Calculate the total shelf size by subtracting 4" (10 cm) from both the length and the width of the interior kiln dimensions. This will leave a 2" (5 cm) air space between the shelf and sides of kiln, which will help to ensure uniform firing.

2. Using a tile saw, cut the mullite subshelf units. We recommend that the units be of an equal size to help provide uniform heat distribution, symmetrical post layout, and subshelf stability.

Figure 3: equidistant post placement.

3. Measure the kiln floor (Figure 3) and mark the intersections where support posts for the mullite units should be placed. (Subshelf corners will meet in the centers of the posts.)

4. Place one post at each intersection. If your posts are slightly different in height, you can saw or grind tall ones and add mullite shims to raise short ones. Cover posts with 3" x 3" x 0.5" (8 x 8 x 1.3 cm) mullite squares to increase subshelf stability. You can also place squares beneath posts. This will protect the brick flooring and the added height will also promote uniform firing.

5. Position the mullite subshelf units so that their corners meet in the centers of the posts (Figure 4). The units should fit together evenly but have narrow gaps between them—about 0.0625" (1.5 mm) in all directions. Gaps will allow the mullite subshelf system to expand during firing. If gaps are not present, the expanding system will shift during firing and may become uneven.

Figure 4: positioning the mullite subshelf units.

1. Once the subshelf units are laid in, you will need to level the entire subshelf. Measure how level it is by checking it with a level from front to back, side to side, and corner to corner. If you discover areas that are not level, try rotating or flipping the mullite subshelf units to correct the problems. Some units may be slightly bowed and some corners may be thicker than others. If a unit is bowed, always flip it so that the raised corners are facing downward and the bow is arching upward. Sharp, raised corners could dent or scratch the fiberboard shelf.

2. Finally, insert stainless steel shims between the posts and the shelving units to raise any areas that are still low. (Figure 5)

If many areas of the shelf need shimming, it may be useful to draw a map of the low areas so that you can plan the number, type, and location of shims you need and insert them in an orderly fashion.

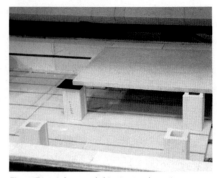

Figure 5: stainless steel shim inserted to raise a low corner.

Note: Do not use shims made of wood, tin, iron, aluminum or any material that will be compromised by firing. Use only shims made of stainless steel or refractory materials.

Step 3: Preparing a Fiberboard Shelf

The goal of this step is to prepare a fiberboard shelf that it is flat, smooth, and durable. To accomplish this, you will need to treat all of the shelf's surfaces with the same materials and processes so that they will have similar properties. Uniform surfaces will help the shelf to remain flat throughout its lifetime.

Note that fiberboard is somewhat fragile, especially when wet, and should be handled with care.

IN PREPARING THE FIBERBOARD SHELF, YOU WILL:
- Cut the shelf to size (if not pre-cut).
- Apply and dry colloidal silica, a fiber-rigidizing agent.
- Apply, dry, and sand multiple layers of Unifrax QF-180, a refractory-surface strengthener.
- Weight the shelf and burn out the product binders.

CUTTING THE SHELF TO SIZE
Wear a respirator and work in a well-ventilated area when following this procedure

3. Cut the fiberboard shelf to the same size as the mullite subshelf. (Or order the fiberboard shelf cut to size from the supplier.) For cutting, you can use an ordinary handsaw, recognizing that this will dull the blade significantly. You can also use a handheld tile-cutting saw.

4. Once the shelf is cut to size, sand the corners and edges until they are slightly rounded. Rounded corners and edges are less likely to be damaged during use than are sharp ones.

APPLYING AND DRYING COLLOIDAL SILICA
Colloidal silica is a liquid used to rigidize fibers in the manufacture of high-temperature kiln brick and ceramic-fiber refractories. When applied to your fiberboard, it will saturate and strengthen the material.

Materials and tools you will need:
- A handsaw or handheld tile-cutting saw with a circular blade
- A half-gallon or larger plastic container
- A painter's brush with fine bristles
- Sheet plastic
- A plastic watering can with showerhead spout
- A sanding block with carbide sandpaper, drywall screen, or diamond-cloth pad
- A respirator
- Liquid-proof gloves
- 1" thick, unfired fiberboard with a minimum heat rating of 2300°F (1260°C)
- Colloidal silica, a fiber-rigidizing agent
- Unifrax QF-180, a refractory-surface strengthener
- Dense kiln bricks
- A HEPA vacuum cleaner

Note: that as long as the colloidal silica in your shelf is wet, the shelf will be quite fragile. You could easily dent or break it with improper handling. A large, wet shelf can weigh more than 30 pounds—enough to cause the shelf to sag and break if it is moved without sufficient support. As a general rule, if your shelf is longer than 60″ (152 cm) or wider than 30″ (76 cm), you should prepare the shelf on a plywood support that will allow you to carry it to the kiln and slide it safely onto the mullite subshelf for drying. You could also prepare such a shelf on a worktable at the same height as the mullite subshelf, and then slide the fiberboard shelf onto the subshelf from the table. If your wet shelf is less than 60″ long or less than 30″ wide, two people should be able to carry and place it into the kiln safely. When in doubt, support the shelf well and slide it rather than picking it up.

FOLLOW THIS PROCEDURE FOR APPLYING COLLOIDAL SILICA TO THE FIBERBOARD SHELF:

1. Prepare your work surface with sheet plastic to contain the overflow of colloidal silica. Secure the plastic to the work surface with tape to prevent it from sliding.

2. Place your fiberboard shelf on the prepared work surface.

3. Wearing liquid-proof gloves, mix enough colloidal silica and water in a ratio of 1:1 to coat one side of the shelf (16 oz / sq ft or 0.5L / 929 sq cm of mixture). Pour the mixture into a plastic watering can with a showerhead spout.

4. Use the watering can to apply an even coating of rigidizer to the top and edges of the shelf. (Figure 6)

5. Next, with the help of an assistant, load the fiberboard shelf onto the mullite subshelf for drying.

6. With the kiln vented, fire the shelf at 275°F (135°C) until dry, usually 3 to 5 hours. You can check for dryness periodically by holding a mirror over the vent. If condensation appears, the shelf is still drying. If no condensation appears, the shelf is dry. (Figure 7)

7. When the fiberboard shelf is dry and cool enough to handle, remove it from the kiln and place it with the non-rigidized side up on your work surface, which should be covered with clean plastic.

8. Treat the non-rigidized side of the shelf using the method described above.

APPLYING, DRYING, AND SANDING MULTIPLE LAYERS OF UNIFRAX QF-180

Once the shelf has been rigidized, you will need to apply several layers of Unifrax QF-180, a high-temperature surface strengthener. In manufacturing, QF-180 is used as a coating cement to strengthen the outer surfaces of refractory materials. With several applications, it will provide a durable surface for your fiberboard shelf.

Note: If you will not be able to move the fiberboard safely after saturation, the colloidal silica mix can be applied with the shelf inside the kiln. In this case, be sure to protect the kiln's elements and interior surfaces with sheet plastic.

Figure 6: a watering can with a showerhead spout will control the flow of colloidal silica.

Note: The colloidal silica mixture can be applied with a large, disposable paintbrush rather a watering can. However, the result may not be as uniform and it will take longer to apply the mixture.

Figure 7: using a mirror to check for condensation.

FOLLOW THIS PROCEDURE TO APPLY, DRY, AND SAND QF-180:

1. Prepare your work surface (the floor or a table) with a clean, dry sheet of plastic. Secure the plastic to the work surface with tape to prevent it from sliding.

2. Place the fiberboard shelf on the plastic-covered work surface.

3. Wearing liquid-proof gloves, stir the QF-180. QF-180 separates easily and will need to be re-mixed frequently throughout this process.

4. After stirring the QF-180, pour about 2 cups (0.5 liter) into a disposable plastic container. If the surface of your shelf is smooth, mix the QF-180 with collodial silica in a 1:1 ratio. If the surface of your shelf is textured, use the QF-180 full-strength for the first coating only. (In subsequent coatings, mix it with collodial silica in a 1:1 ratio.)

Figure 8: Brushing qf-180 onto the fiberoard shelf.

5. Using a good painter's brush with long bristles, apply a single, even coating of the QF-180 mixture to the top surface of the shelf (Figure 8). Stir the liquid with your brush frequently to keep it well mixed. Coat the edges of the shelf, being careful not to layer excess material onto the top surface.

> **Note:** A good brush will ensure a smooth coat and therefore, less sanding.

6. Load the fiberboard shelf onto the mullite subshelf with the coated surface facing up.

7. With the kiln vented, fire the shelf at 275°F (136°C) until it is dry, about 30 to 60 minutes.

8. While the shelf is drying, cover the plastic bucket containing QF-180. Store your paintbrush in a container of water between coatings.

9. Prepare to sand the QF-180 by setting up a worktable outdoors, under a ventilation hood, or in an area where particulates can be safely contained or removed.

10. Prepare a large sanding block with diamond cloth, drywall sanding screen, or carbide sanding paper (60- to 120-grit). Using this block will help to ensure uniform pressure while sanding.

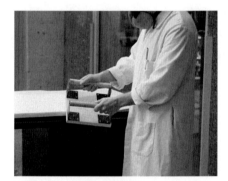
Figure 9: sanding the shelf using a large sanding block.

11. When the shelf is dry and cool enough to handle safely, move it to the sanding area. Wearing a respirator, sand the top and edges of the shelf to even out the surfaces. (Figure 9)

12. When you have finished sanding, vacuum the dust from the shelf and work area, using a HEPA vacuum (Figure 10). Alternatively, wipe up the dust with a damp sponge, rinsing as needed. (Do not use a regular shop vacuum, which will put more particulates into the air.)

13. Repeat the entire process described above until the top and edges of the shelf are as smooth as possible. Typically this requires 3 or 4 coatings of QF-180.

14. Once the top and edges of the shelf are finished, repeat the entire procedure for the untreated side of the shelf.

Figure 10: vacuuming dust from the shelf after sanding.

WEIGHTING THE SHELF AND BURNING OUT THE PRODUCT BINDERS

This final procedure will take several hours and will generate a fair amount of smoke. Be sure the kiln area is adequately ventilated for this firing.

Follow this procedure for weighting the shelf and burning out the product binders:

1. Place the fiberboard shelf in the kiln atop the mullite subshelf.

2. Place dense (heavy) kiln bricks at a minimum of 12-inch intervals all along the shelf surface. Stack double bricks at the corners (Figure 11). The weight of the bricks will flatten the shelf during firing.

3. Once the weights are in place, close the kiln lid and the vents and fire according to the following schedule:

RATE (DEGREES PER HOUR)		TEMPERATURE		HOLD (HR:MIN)
300°F	166°C	1550°F	843°C	2:00
300°F	166°C	70°F	21°C	:00

4. When the shelf has been fired and is cool enough to handle, turn it over and repeat the entire process described above.

5. Once both sides of the fiberboard shelf have been fired, the shelf should be ready to use.

If, however, the shelf shows a tendency to bend at the corners or to bow in the center (both of which can be caused by firing too hot or too fast), repeat the burnout firing. Stack bricks on top of a bowed surface to flatten it. Flip the board and stack double bricks on bent corners to flatten them (Figures 11, 12). Keep an eye on your shelf's flatness, especially during the first month of firing. If the corners bend up more than 0.125" (3 mm), consider weighting them with bricks during firing or repeat the weighting and firing procedure.

A NOTE ABOUT FIRING GLASS ON THIS SHELF

At Bullseye, we do not fire glass directly on this shelf. Rather, to prevent the possibility of damaging the shelf, we place fiber paper and ThinFire over it before firing.

Repairing a Dented Fiberboard Shelf

If your fiberboard shelf gets dented or gouged, you can repair it:

Fill the dent or hole with high-temperature caulk. (We recommend Pyroform E-Z Fill, available from Paragon.) Smooth the caulk and allow it to dry. You can speed the drying process by using a heat gun. Sand the caulk and then apply a coating of dilute QF-180 over the repaired surface. Dry that coating with the heat gun and sand. Apply and sand QF-180 on the damaged area until the shelf surface is uniform (usually 2 or 3 coatings).

OR

Saturate some ceramic fiber or ceramic wool with QF-180 and pack it tightly into the dent or hole so that it is level with the shelf surface. Allow the patch to dry or speed the process by using a heat gun. Sand the repaired area, then apply and sand QF-180 until the shelf surface is uniform (usually 2 or 3 coatings).

Figure 11: weighting the fiberboard shelf with bricks.

Warning: Never fire the kiln at full speed during the shelf-preparation process. Doing so could distort the fiberboard shelf.

Figure 12: example of a bowed fiberboard shelf corner.

Product Suppliers

- **Pearl-56 Shelf Kit (8839)**
  Available only with purchase of Pearl-56 Bullseye Edition kiln.
- **Unifrax LD Duraboard**
  Unifrax (www.unifrax.com)
- **Mullite Kiln Shelf (8840)**
- **Kiln Posts (8889)**
- **Colloidal Silica**
  Western Industrial (wicinc.com)
- **Fiberfrax Coating Cement**
  Western Industrial (wicinc.com)
- **Bullseye Bricks (8896)**
- **Pyroform E-Z Fill**
  Paragon (paragonweb.com)

Monitoring Kiln Temperatures for Successful Annealing
With a Multiple-Point Measuring System

When kilnforming glass, especially large-scale work, it is important to cool the glass uniformly throughout the annealing range. The temperature difference within the glass—from top to bottom, side to side, or end to end—should be no greater than 10°F (5°C). Such uniformity prevents a number of problems, including the creation of annealing strain, which can lead to glass failure.

At Bullseye, to ensure uniform cooling and proper annealing of large-scale work, we monitor temperatures at multiple points within the kiln during firing.

Our multiple-point temperature monitoring system involves the use of thermocouples and a pyrometer. The pyrometer displays temperatures that are sensed by the thermocouples, which are placed at two or more locations within the kiln. (Figure 1)

Information gathered and displayed by the pyrometer indicates how the glass and the kiln are heating and cooling and whether kiln temperatures need to be modified to prevent annealing strain—either by adjusting heat output from the top, bottom, or side elements (if they are controlled separately) or by slowing the cooling rate.

A multiple-point temperature monitoring system is well worth the small investment in equipment and energy required for installation. In this document, we discuss when to employ such a system, the equipment that is needed, where to find the equipment, how to install it, and how to use the information gathered to help ensure successful annealing.

WHEN TO USE A MULTIPLE-POINT TEMPERATURE MONITORING SYSTEM

There are two main reasons to use a multiple-point temperature monitoring system:

- To monitor a project's cooling rate throughout the annealing range
- To determine how well a kiln is firing

Even a kiln that you have used for many years should be monitored with a multiple-point system because heating and cooling in such a kiln may not actually be uniform.

While it is advisable to monitor temperatures any time you are firing large-scale work, it is especially important to do so when firing:

- Thick glass
- Projects that may be difficult to cool uniformly, such as complex forms
- New types of work—with unfamiliar shapes, sizes, or mold materials
- Kilns that are new or new to you
- Kilns that have not been fired for a long time.

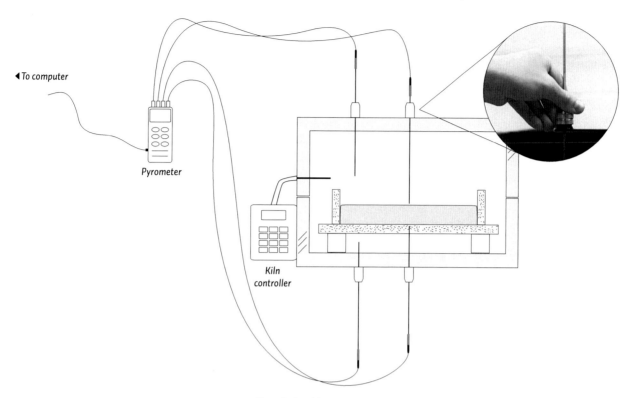

Figure 1: A multi-point monitoring system

**TO SET UP A MULTIPLE-POINT MONITORING SYS-
TEM, YOU WILL NEED**

- A 2 to 4 channel pyrometer
- 2 to 4 thermocouples
- 2 to 4 connectors
- 2 to 4 mounted collets (keyless chucks)
- Extension wire (in some setups, to connect thermocouples and pyrometer)

Models and vendors are recommended on page 3.

How to Install the Equipment

- A pyrometer requires little installation. It can be either handheld or mounted to a convenient, flat surface. Thermocouples, however, must be positioned with considerable care to ensure readings that are both consistent and useful for each project being monitored.

ENSURING THERMOCOUPLE CONSISTENCY

- It is critical that all thermocouples within any setup read temperatures to within 2°F (1°C) of each other. Most new thermocouples will read together as a group within this range. However, one malfunctioning thermocouple could render your entire monitoring system inaccurate; therefore, it is essential to test your thermocouples before installing them. Our simple testing procedure is described on page 5. Do not skip this necessary step.
- Once determined to be reading together as a group, your thermocouples should provide consistent readings for many years, provided they are installed and cared for properly.

BE SURE TO AVOID THE FOLLOWING SITUATIONS, WHICH CAN CAUSE INCONSISTENT READINGS:

- Loose connections (by far, the most frequent cause of problems)
- Damaged or kinked thermocouples
- Extension wire that is kinked, stretched, or spliced together
- Extension wire of different gauges within the group of thermocouples.

Where to Position Thermocouples Within the Kiln

Thermocouples should be positioned within the kiln to best serve the purpose of each firing—either to monitor the project's cooling rate throughout the annealing range or to determine how well the kiln is firing.

TO MONITOR THE PROJECT'S COOLING RATE THROUGHOUT THE ANNEALING RANGE

For large slabs of glass, we use a minimum of 2 thermocouples—one above and one below the top and bottom surfaces of the glass. (Figure 1) We position the bottom thermocouple by drilling a small hole in both the bottom of the kiln and the kiln shelf. Then we thread the thermocouple from underneath until it is as close as possible to the bottom surface of the glass without actually touching it. To position the top thermocouple, we drill a hole in the top of the kiln directly above the bottom thermocouple. During firing, when the glass has reached the anneal soak temperature, we loosen the collet and lower the top thermocouple down until it contacts the now-rigid glass surface. This thermocouple then allows us to accurately monitor the temperature of the top surface of the glass.

TO DETERMINE HOW WELL THE KILN IS FIRING

For this process, we typically place one thermocouple above the shelf at the same height as the kiln's control thermocouple and one below the shelf. (Figure 1) Data collected at these points can help to determine how well the kiln is firing and whether or not the control thermocouple is reading accurately. This data can also be used to establish different programs for the top and the bottom of the kiln—if they can be independently controlled—to ensure a uniform temperature within the glass.

How to Position Thermocouples Within the Kiln

Positioning thermocouples within the kiln requires drilling small holes into the kiln, inserting the thermocouples, and securing them in place.

WHEN DRILLING INTO THE KILN

- Measure and mark before drilling.
- The holes should be just large enough to accommodate the thermocouples.
- Avoid damaging the element wires by centering the holes between them. Also, the thermocouples must not contact the element wires. This can result in electrical shock and damage the pyrometer and/or kiln.
- Standard drill bits will penetrate kiln brick and sheet metal.

TO SECURE THERMOCOUPLES IN PLACE

- At Bullseye, we attach collets (keyless chucks, welded to small sheet metal plates) to the outside of the kiln, in line with the drilled holes. The collets can be hand tightened and loosened to secure the thermocouples and/or reposition them, as needed. (Figure 1)
- Collets can be attached to the kiln either with clamps or self-tapping sheet-metal screws.

Where to Find Equipment for Multiple-Point Temperature Monitoring

At Bullseye, we buy our handheld pyrometers from Omega (omega.com). The Omega website has a configuration tool to help you purchase wires, connectors, and thermocouples to match the pyrometer you choose.

- The HH12B: A 2-channel digital thermometer. It has offset adjustment with recessed screws on the front panel, which is very convenient. This model offers no memory or PC connection, so you have to manually record the data during firing.
- The HH309A: A four-channel data logger with internal memory to store readings while you are away, and the ability to interface with a PC running Windows by way of an RS232 connection. Software is included.

Depending upon the pyrometer model you select, you will need to buy either 2 or 4 thermocouples. (The thin-wire thermocouples that come with the pyrometers don't last long.) Purchase thermocouples with these specifications:

- For compatibility: *ungrounded*
- Transition joint: *molded*
- Calibration: *K*
- Sheath material: *Inconel*
- Length: *something that will reach the center of the kiln with a little room to spare*
- Diameter: *1/8 inch*

You will also need connectors for plugging the thermocouples into the pyrometer. Buy one SMP-K-M (sub-mini connector) for each thermocouple. Depending on your setup, you may need to purchase extension-grade wire for the thermocouples.

To purchase pre-mounted collets, contact Paragon Industries (paragonweb.com). The product number is TCCOLLET.

Tip: Coat thermocouple tips with thickened shelf primer to prevent their sticking to glass.

How to Use the Information Gathered

Some pyrometers can record information during firing. Recorded information can be read as data on the pyrometer or as a graph or table on a PC running Windows. (Figures 2 & 3) If your pyrometer cannot record data, you will have to record it manually during firing.

During the annealing phase of a firing, if the temperature difference between thermocouples monitoring the glass is more than 10°F (5°C), the kiln should be adjusted in one of the following two ways:

- If the kiln allows for separate control of elements in the top, side, or bottom zones, these temperatures should be adjusted until the difference is within 10°F (5°C)

OR

- If the kiln does not allow for separate control of zones, the cooling rate should be slowed until the temperature difference is within 10°F (5°C).

General Information About Annealing

If the cooling rates recommended in Bullseye's "Annealing Chart for Thick Slabs" (page 6) are used, and the temperature difference between top and bottom thermocouples is not greater than 10°F (5°C) during the anneal cooling stages, good annealing should result.[1]

As noted on the annealing chart, the recommended firing cycles are "based on a flat slab of uniform thickness that is set up in such a fashion that it can cool equally from top and bottom." It is important to think not only about the thickness of the piece of glass, but also about how it is set up in the kiln. Are there insulating materials surrounding it, or under it, or anything else in the firing chamber with the glass that may impact how uniformly it may cool?

We have found that the best annealing for thicker works is achieved by insulating the perimeter of the glass with ceramic fiberboards, which are often used as dams. Because the perimeter of the work has more surface area per volume than the interior has, it will tend to cool off more rapidly. Insulating the perimeter prevents development of too large a temperature difference between the edges and the interior.

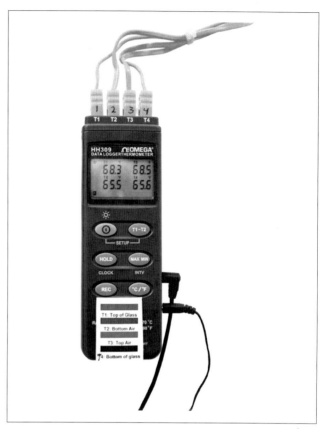

Figure 2: Some Pyrometers can record data.

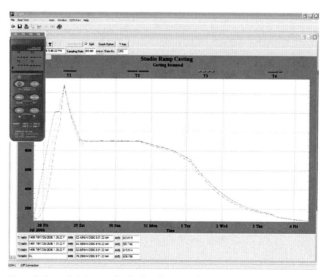

Figure 3: Recorded data can be displayed as a graph on a PC running Windows.

[1] The Bullseye "Annealing Chart for Thick Slabs" was based on trials using a 3" thick block of glass with a thermocouple embedded in the middle, as well as two thermocouples touching the top and bottom of the glass respectively. These thermocouples exhibited less than a 10°F (5°C) temperature difference throughout the annealing range.

Procedure for Verifying That Thermocouples Read the Same

In this procedure, you will insert the thermocouples into a kiln through the peephole; pack them into a partially hollowed length of iron or steel round stock (sometimes called a "core") that is positioned in the center of the kiln; connect the pyrometer; fire the kiln; and adjust the thermocouple readings as necessary. When finished, you will remove the thermocouples from the metal core and transfer them and their extension wires (as assembled) to their working locations. Follow these three steps:

1. SET UP THE CORE AND THERMOCOUPLES (TCS)
- Set the metal core on a kiln post that is centered in the kiln.
- Insert TCs through the peephole and into the hole in the metal core.
- Pack both the core hole and the peephole tightly with fiber.
- Plug TC extensions into the pyrometer and TCs.
- Label TC & extension wire sets with the number of the input they are plugged into. (Figure 4)

> **Note:** If preferred you can use a small kiln with a side or top peephole, such as a Paragon Caldera, for this entire procedure.

2. PROGRAM THE KILN AND FIRE
- Program the kiln to fire as fast as possible (AFAP) to the temperature at which you want the thermocouples to match (the anneal soak temp, for example) and program a hold for 4 hours.
- Example program: AFAP to 900°F (482°C) for 4 hours.
- Start the kiln.

3. ADJUST THE THERMOCOUPLES TO READ THE SAME
- Monitor the multiple-point display until the TCs have stabilized. This will take about 2+ hours.
- Adjust the TCs to match TC1 by turning the offset adjustments on the pyrometer.
- Do not adjust the TCs to match the kiln controller display temperature.
- Turn off the kiln.

When the TCs are cool enough to handle, they can be pulled from the metal core and moved to their working locations. Be sure to keep the assembly as it is, with connectors and extension wires labeled, to ensure maximum accuracy in the working system.

TO DO THIS TEST, YOU WILL NEED
- A pyrometer
- Two or more thermocouples (TCs) with all wire extensions and connectors to be used in the actual working setup
- A 2" (5 cm) length of iron or steel round stock, 2" (5 cm) in diameter, with a hole drilled halfway through. (Order from a machine shop for about $25.)
- Ceramic-fiber-wool scraps
- A kiln post for supporting the round stock
- (Optional) A small kiln, like a Paragon Caldera, with a side or top peephole

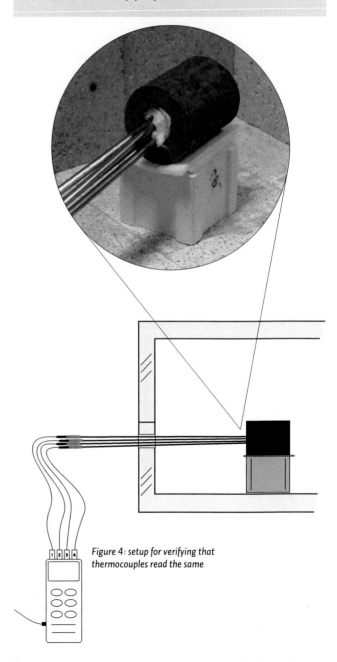

Figure 4: setup for verifying that thermocouples read the same

Annealing Chart for Thick Slabs

This annealing chart has been formulated for use with Bullseye clear glass. It is derived from Corning's method as shown in McLellan and Shand.* It is based on a flat slab of uniform thickness that is set up in such a fashion that it can cool equally from top and bottom. If the piece is not set up in such a fashion that it can cool equally from top and bottom or is anything besides a flat slab of uniform thickness, select an annealing cycle for a piece that is twice the thickness of the thickest area of the piece. Even a very conservative annealing cycle may not work if the kiln is not capable of cooling evenly. For more Bullseye technical and product information see bullseyeglass.com.

THICKNESS	ANNEAL SOAK TIME	INITIAL COOLING RATE	INITIAL COOLING RANGE	2ND COOLING RATE	2ND COOLING RANGE	FINAL COOLING RATE	FINAL COOLING RANGE	TOTAL MINIMUM TIME
inches	@ 900 °F	°F/hr	°F	°F/hr	°F	°F/hr	°F	
mm	@ 482 °C	°C/hr	°C	°C/hr	°C	°C/hr	°C	Hours
0.5 in	2 hr	100	900–800	180	800–700	600	700–70	~5 hr
12 mm		55	482–427	99	427–371	330	371–21	
0.75 in	3 hr	45	900–800	81	800–700	270	700–70	~9 hr
19 mm		25	482–427	45	427–371	150	371–21	
1.0 in	4 hr	27	900–800	49	800–700	162	700–70	~14 hr
25 mm		15	482–427	27	427–371	90	371–21	
1.5 in	6 hr	12	900–800	22	800–700	72	700–70	~28 hr
38 mm		6.7	482–427	12	427–371	40	371–21	
2.0 in	8 hr	6.8	900–800	12	800–700	41	700–70	~47 hr
50 mm		3.8	482–427	6.8	427–371	22	371–21	
2.5 in	10 hr	4.3	900–800	8	800–700	26	700–70	~70 hr
62 mm		2.4	482–427	4.3	427–371	14.4	371–21	
3.0 in	12 hr	3	900–800	5.4	800–700	18	700–70	~99 hr
75 mm		1.7	482–427	3.1	427–371	10	371–21	
4.0 in	16 hr	1.7	900–800	3.1	800–700	10	700–70	~170 hr
100 mm		0.94	482–427	1.7	427–371	5.6	371–21	
6.0 in	24 hr	0.75	900–800	1.3	800–700	4.5	700–70	~375 hr
150 mm		0.42	482–427	0.76	427–371	2.5	371–21	
8.0 in	32 hr	0.42	900–800	0.76	800–700	2.5	700–70	~654 hr
200 mm		0.23	482–427	0.42	427–371	1.4	371–21	

* McLellan and Shand (1984), Glass Engineering Handbook, 3rd Edition, New York, McGraw Hill.

TipSheets

TIP SHEET

Published by Bullseye Glass Co.

Kilncarving
A Simple Kilnforming Technique
Developed by Rudi Gritsch

Figure 1: Underside of kilncarved glass.

"Kilncarving" is a term coined at Bullseye to describe a simple kilnforming process that achieves a bas relief, textured, or sculpted look in glass. The process involves cutting a pattern or design in ceramic fiber paper, then stacking glass on top of the pattern and firing the piece in a kiln. During firing, the underside of the glass conforms to the ceramic fiber paper pattern, assuming its contours and textures. (Figure 1)

Kilncarving is a good beginning technique. In trying it, you can learn how glass reacts with heat at various temperatures, and you can achieve some beautiful shapes and patterns with only minimal glass cutting and fusing.

The two primary materials used in this process are glass and ceramic fiber paper. The primary tool—besides a kiln—is an X-Acto knife. In this TipSheet, we provide some basic information about the materials, tools, and steps involved in kilncarving glass.

GLASS

Different types of glasses react differently when fired in contact with ceramic fiber paper. Some glasses are easier to use for kilncarving than others. Either billets or sheet glass can be used.

Clear and transparent colored glasses: Release more easily from ceramic fiber papers than do opalescent glasses.

Opal glasses: Tend to stick to ceramic fiber papers more than other glasses.

Glasses with an iridescent (irid) surface: The metallic irid surface of Bullseye glasses provides the best release from ceramic fiber paper and creates a very clean fired surface.

Glasses with a dichroic surface: Like the irid surface, the dichroic surface has a thin film that provides excellent separation from ceramic fiber papers.

Pre-fired glass: If a piece of glass has already been fired once, the surface that was previously in contact with the kiln shelf or a ceramic fiber paper will release from the fiber paper pattern more easily than an unfired glass surface.

CERAMIC FIBER PAPER

Ceramic fiber paper is composed of vitreous aluminosilicate fibers and an organic binder. The paper is available in a variety of thicknesses, including 1/16" and 1/8" (1.6 mm and 3.2 mm). The quality of the fiber paper is affected by a number of variables. These include:

Chemical composition: The higher the alumina (Al_2O_3) content of the paper, the less the paper will stick to the glass.

Fiber quality: Tiny glass balls embedded in ceramic fiber paper are a by-product of the manufacturing process. Higher-quality papers contain fewer of these tiny balls, which tend to melt into the surface of fused glass and cause small cracks, due to differences in expansion between the paper and the fused glass.

Surface quality: Surface quality varies, depending on the manufacturer. All ceramic fiber papers have more-or-less textured surfaces. Texture may differ between the front and back sides.

Weave quality: The tighter the weave, the more durable the fiber paper.

Bullseye recommends and carries Lytherm®, the best quality fiber paper we have found for kilnforming.

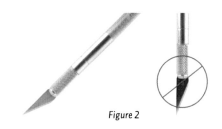

Figure 2

Figure 3a: Positive and negative ceramic fiber paper designs.

Figure 3b: Fiber paper designs stacked with 6 mm pre-fused glass, before kilncarving firing.

Figure 3c: Glass after firing, kilncarved side down.

Figure 3d: Glass after firing, kilncarved side up.

THE KILNCARVING PROCESS

Preparing the fiber paper

To achieve the sculpted look of kilncarving, you can cut and stack patterns from any of the various thicknesses of ceramic fiber paper. When using only a single layer of 3 mm glass, use thinner fiber papers and/or do not stack the paper more than 3 mm high. A single layer of 3 mm glass will stretch in the firing process and may become too thin in certain sections if your pattern is thick.

First, draw your design directly onto your fiber paper—or transfer the design onto the fiber paper using carbon paper.

Cutting ceramic fiber paper will dull the blade of your X-Acto knife rapidly. Two things will help to minimize this:

· Hold the knife at an angle to the cutting surface. Do not hold it straight up and down. (Figure 2)

· Cut only on a penetrable working surface like linoleum, cardboard, or plastic tile. Do not cut on an impenetrable surface like metal or ceramic tile.

If you cut precisely, a single piece of ceramic fiber paper will yield two patterns: a positive and a negative. (Figure 3a)

If you need to glue parts of the fiber papers together, use GlasTac.

To improve the surface of fiber paper and remove tiny glass balls before firing, brush the paper lightly by hand, wearing latex or vinyl gloves, in a well-ventilated space or out of doors.

Consider pre-firing the fiber paper at 1290°F (700°C) before placing the glass on top of it. This will prevent the hazing that sometimes results as the binder burns out. (Be sure your studio is well ventilated.)

Preparing the piece

Once you have prepared your fiber paper pattern, you can then stack one or more layers of sheet glass or a billet on top of it. (Figure 3b)

If you use two layers of 3 mm glass, it is best to fuse the two layers together before kilncarving. You can fuse and kilncarve in the same firing if you take the glass to a full fuse temperature, but you'll risk trapping air bubbles between the glass layers.

Remember that a single layer of 3 mm glass will have a greater tendency than thicker glasses to become thin and ragged ("needlepointed") along the edges.

Firing

The temperature to which the glass is fired will determine the look of the finished piece. The temperatures below work well in our studio kilns and should be useful guides in helping you determine appropriate temperatures for use in your own kiln.

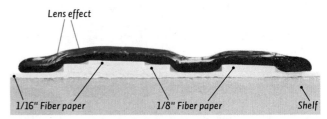

Figure 4: Cross-sectional view of kilnformed glass, fired at 1420°F (~770°C).

At 1420°F (~770°C), the glass will not contact or conform to the sharp edges in the paper pattern, but will gently slope over those edges, creating what we call a "lens effect." (Figure 4)

Figure 5: Cross-sectional view of kilnformed glass, fired at 1490°F (~810°C).

At 1490°F (~810°C)—with a soak of about 5-10 minutes—the glass will pick up the exact texture of the fiber material and will conform more closely to the paper pattern's sharp edges. At this temperature, the upper side of the glass will follow the contour of the fiber paper stencil slightly. The intensity of the color (or color saturation) of a transparent glass will be fairly uniform because the glass thickness will be fairly uniform. (Figure 5)

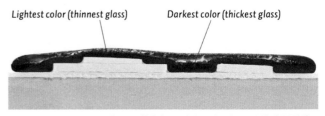

Figure 6: Cross-sectional view of kilnformed glass, fired at 1520°F (~825°C).

At 1520°F (~825°C)—with a soak of about 30 minutes—the glass will conform very closely to the pattern's sharp edges. The upper surface of the glass will begin to level out and different areas of the project will transmit different intensities of color because the glass thickness will vary. (Figures 3c, 6) The soak time and the amount of glass used will depend on how many layers of paper are used.

- Select an annealing cycle that is designed for twice the thickness of the thickest area of the piece. (For more information on annealing cycles, see the *Annealing Chart for Thick Slabs* at bullseyeglass.com.)

For more information on firing in general, see *TechNotes 4: Heat & Glass* at bullseyeglass.com.

Refiring or Slumping

- If the kilncarved piece will be fired a second time (e.g., to slump it), the textured surface can first be altered by sandblasting. If an irid surface was fired against the fiber paper on the first firing, further decoration can be achieved by sandblasting a design onto this surface.

- In refiring or slumping a kilncarved piece with sections of varying thickness, it is important to fire very slowly through the initial heating phase—typically not faster than 200°F (93°C) per hour during initial heat.

WORKING SAFELY WITH CERAMIC FIBER PAPER

When fired, fiber paper will give off a small amount of smoke and aroma from the organic binders. Good ventilation in your studio will ensure that these dissipate quickly.

Ceramic fiber paper can act as an irritant to the skin and respiratory system, particularly after it has been fired and the binders are burned out.

Handle fired fiber paper with care to avoid breathing residual fibers. Be sure to wear proper respiratory protection when removing paper from the glass or sweeping the work area.

43

WORKING DEEP
STACK FIRING FOR IMBEDDED IMAGERY

This TipSheet will introduce you to ways to float imagery and color within thick blocks of clear glass. Historically, thick glass castings have resulted from pours of furnace glass or by kiln-casting glass chunks or frit. The method we call "stack firing" results, instead, from the fusing of multiple layers of clear sheet glass on which are imbedded lines and fields of colored glass. This method is direct, simple, and allows greater control of line quality than is achievable with other techniques. The reader is assumed to have a basic knowledge of glass fusing methods.

The primary technical challenges involved in this working method are:

· Controlling trapped air (bubbles)

· Restraining the glass flow at full fusing temperatures

· Working with extended heating and cooling cycles

· Minimizing coldworking to the finished project

ORIGINS AND EVOLUTION OF THE METHOD
As with most techniques that develop at Bullseye, the methods we will describe evolved from an artist project at the Bullseye factory. Italian artist Silvia Levenson was commissioned to produce a series of large glass blocks for a fountain in Northbrook, Illinois. The extensive equipment and technology required that Levenson engage the services of Bullseye's Research & Education department to produce the work. We, in turn, asked Ray Ahlgren* to develop a method and oversee the production of the fountain blocks.

After the Northbrook project, we scaled down those methods and incorporated them as segments of our beginning and intermediate kilnforming classes. This TipSheet will lead you through two versions of stack firing: Single-Fired Stack and Double-Fired Stack.

---

*   Ray Ahlgren, owner of Fireart Glass in Portland, Oregon, was one of Bullseye's three founders and instrumental in the company's early explorations into kilnformed glass. Fireart (www.fireartglass.com) specializes in larger scale fusing and multiple production methods with an emphasis on architectural and limited-edition lighting.

Figure 1: Silvia Levenson, *Un Mondo Migliore*, 1996. 16 glass blocks for fountain installation, Northbrook, IL. Each block 19 x 35 x 1 3/4 in (483 x 889 x 44 mm).

WHERE YOU'RE GOING: THE FINISHED BLOCK
Whether achieved through one firing or two, the end product will be a solid block of clear glass with internal imagery and color as complex or as simple as your personal style dictates. The bottom and sides of the block will have a faint matte iridescent finish. The top face will be glassy and smooth with a soft bullnosed edge. It will measure about 8" x 8" x 1 3/4" (203 x 203 x 44 mm). These dimensions may be enlarged or reduced by adapting the general guidelines and adjusting the firing schedule.

WHAT YOU NEED TO GET THERE: THE MATERIALS

Glass: Because clarity is essential when working deep, we recommend using a very bright clear—one without a blue, green or yellow tint. Bullseye's Crystal Clear Transparent 3mm double-rolled sheet glass (001401-0030-F) will not muddy or mask your internal colors or lines.

For the bottom and four sidewalls, use Clear Transparent (001101-0037-F). Alternatively you may select colored irid sidepieces to create a contrasting frame around the block. The iridescent finish will give a cleaner release from the fiber paper or shelf separator than will the raw glass, which tends to pick up minute particles of fiber or separator.

The interior imagery will be created out of cut sheet, frit, powder, and stringers of colored glass.

Other Materials: During firing the glass stack will be restrained from flowing outwards by refractory dams. These may be made of mullite clay (sawn-up kiln shelves, for example), vermiculite board, or ceramic fiberboard. The stack will sit on a mullite clay shelf, which may be primed with shelf separator or covered with fiber paper or ThinFire. The upright dam walls will also require fiber paper strips to separate the glass from the refractory dams.

Materials and Cut List

For a block that will measure approximately 8" x 8" x 1 ¾" (203 x 203 x 44 mm) after firing, cut the following:

- Crystal Clear sheet (001401-0030-F):
  13 @ 7 3/4" x 7 3/4" (197 x 197 mm)

- Clear sheet (001101-0037-F), or any colored glass with iridescent finish:
  4 @ 7 7/8" x 1 7/16" (200 x 36 mm)
  1 @ 7 3/4" x 7 3/4" (197 x 197 mm)

- 1/16" (1.5mm) thick fiber paper:
  4 pieces @ 8 3/16" x 1 3/4" (208 x 44 mm)*

- Mullite clay shelf material, ˜5/8" (16 mm) thick or more, or rigidized ceramic fiberboard, ˜3/4" (19 mm) thick or more:
  4 dams @ 9" x 2" (229 x 51 mm) or more

- GlasTac

Consider Your Design

Sketch out your design on tracing paper, using one sheet of paper for each layer of glass that will hold your imagery. Use these as a guide as you build your glass stack.

Remember that less is more in this process. Avoid large amounts of colored sheet glass, frit, or stringer within the interior. The clear block can quickly become muddy and chaotic.

If you use colored sheet glass for your imagery, plan to cut the forms into the clear glass just as you would create the parts for a stained glass window. Avoid laying a colored sheet glass form on top of the clear square. Instead, cut that same form out of the clear square and replace it with the colored form so that each layer is of uniform thickness.

You may include as many or as few layers of imagery in the block as you wish as long as you keep the bottom two (2) and top three (3) layers free of any cut pieces—which will help to control bubbles.

THE PROCESS: SINGLE-FIRED BLOCK

Glass blocks may be created in a single firing, but because of the potential for air entrapment, this method is not recommended for blocks larger than 8" (203 mm) square.

Layering the Image: Avoiding Bubbles

Once you have your design, begin to build the stack.

Place the square of clear irid glass irid side down onto a piece of thin cardboard (slightly larger than the sheet glass) on your worktable. Then place a single layer of clear on top of the irid square. When you later transport your stack to the kiln shelf, the cardboard will allow you to gently slide the stack onto the shelf with minimal jarring of the glass.

Depending on the complexity of your design, you may begin to compose directly on the second layer or stack up a few more squares of the clear glass. Keep the total amount of glass used for inclusions to no more than the equivalent of a single layer of sheet glass. If you add more than that, remove a layer of clear in order to keep the total volume of glass relatively constant at 14 layers – or 1 ¾" (44 mm) – thick.

Finish the stack with at least three full layers of clear. Using fewer layers of full sheets at the top of the stack can result in bubbles rising through and breaking on the surface. Keep these three layers free of cut sheet glass and frit to avoid trapping bubbles.

*Thicker fiber paper such as 1/8" (3 mm) may be used, but will compress more at the bottom of the block in response to the column pressure of the molten glass, resulting in a block that is wider at the shelf than at the top.

As you design each layer, consider how the air will escape out the sides during firing. Avoid encircling areas with "barriers" of sheet glass, frit, or stringer. Plan for "escape routes" by which air can move laterally from the center of the block to the edges.

Any air that does not move out laterally during the first stages of firing will be trapped in the interior and rise up as bubbles during the later stages. These bubbles can break through the surface and eventually erupt as craters on the surface of the block.

Once all layers are composed, tack them in place with GlasTac to secure them for safe transport to the kiln.

Building the Side Walls and Dams: Restraining the Flow

Because glass that is higher than 1/4" (6 mm) will flow outward when fired to a full fuse, the glass stack must be surrounded by a dam of refractory material. At the same time, it must be prevented from sticking to that material.

For dams we use strips of 1" (25 mm) thick rigidized ceramic fiberboard on all four sides. Other refractory materials—strips cut from mullite clay shelves or vermiculite board, soft brick, Bullseye Bricks (008896), or firebrick—may also be used to build your dams. Behind the dams you will need additional support in the form of heavy refractory materials such as Bullseye Bricks or firebricks. Without this additional support, the outward pressure of the melting glass will push out and/or topple the dams.

It is also necessary to put brick or refractory weights on top of the dams. Use one (1) pound per linear foot of dam per inch of thickness (454 grams per 305 linear mm of dam per 254 mm of thickness). Without extra weight, the glass can seep out at the base and side seams.

Use strips of 1/16" (1.5 mm) thick ceramic fiber paper to prevent the glass from sticking to the dam walls. The fiber paper must fit properly at all joints. Sloppy fiber paper joints will also result in glass seepage.

On a level shelf in the kiln, construct the first corner of support bricks, dams, fiber paper, and glass. Check that the irid side of the glass faces towards the fiber paper. (Tip: To avoid sharp corners on the top of the block, consider slightly rounding the top corners of the irid sides with grozing pliers or a diamond hand lap.) Make sure the construction is perfectly square. Then transport your stack to the kiln. Gently slide the glass stack up against the two dam walls. If you've transported it on cardboard it will slide easily onto the shelf and into place.

Consider using ThinFire* on the shelf because it gives the cleanest release and also allows the glass to be gently moved about on the shelf without scratching through the shelf primer.

After positioning the stack into the first corner, construct the two remaining sides with irid strips, fiber paper, dams, and brick supports.

Clean all of the sheet glass in the stack, including any pre-fired layers that may have residual shelf primer on them. Furthermore, it is imperative that the top sheet of clear glass be spotless. Fingerprints, oil smudges or dust on the to top surface may fire into the block.

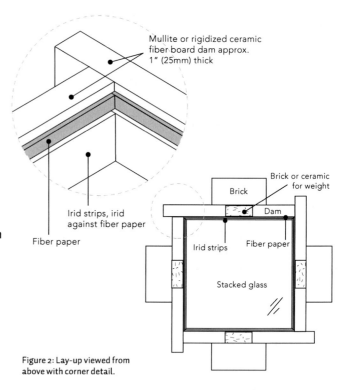

Figure 2: Lay-up viewed from above with corner detail.

Check that the stack is well aligned with all sheets of glass directly above each other. Weight the tops of the refractory dams with pieces of kiln shelf or brick. Fire according to Schedule #1, Single-Fired Block, on page 5.

Top Edge Detail: How to Avoid "The Grind"

After the kiln has finished firing and reached room temperature – and not before! – remove the block. It should have a top surface that rolls cleanly into a bull-nosed edge. This is because the total volume of your interior glass stack was designed to be higher than the upright irid edges by about 5/16" (8 mm). As the glass stack melted, it flowed outwards just enough to meet the upright sides but not flow up against the dams.

*Note that ThinFire can cause pitting on thin irid coatings, such as silver irid. This usually only happens in multiple firings.

Often during the initial lay-up the sheet glass stack will look much too high relative to the irid edges – certainly higher than 5/16" (8 mm). This is because the unfired sheets still have enough texture that there is a significant amount of space between them. In firing, this texture will flatten and most of the air between the layers will be squeezed out. However, unless you have exceeded the recommended amounts of frit, stringer, and cut sheet (the equivalent of one layer) in your design elements, this will not present a problem. The upright irid edges being too high is always more of a problem than their being too low.

THE PROCESS: DOUBLE-FIRED BLOCK

As just shown, it is possible to create the glass block in a single firing. However, you will have more control and fewer problems with trapped bubbles and distorted imagery if you pre-fire your image layers.

Fire to a full fuse, ˜1450°F (788°C) or higher, double layers of clear onto which your cut pieces of thin glass, frit, powder, or stringers have been placed. Keep the decorative parts at least 1/2" (13 mm) away from the edge of the clear sheet to prevent it from flowing out of square.

Fire according to schedule #2, Pre-Fired Layers of Double-Fired Block, on page 5.

Our example shows four fused "design layers" at 1/4" (6 mm) each. This allows for six more layers of 1/8" (1.5 mm) clear sheet glass throughout the stack. We recommend that at least two of these layers be on top.

After creating these initial design layers, try stacking them up different ways to test whether the final piece will work out as you like. The advantage of the double-fired stack is that you have an opportunity to see the piece at this stage and make changes. Furthermore, you can work on the very top layer of the stack, increasing the possibilities for creating depth.

Building the Double-Fired Stack

Build the sidewalls and dams to restrain the flow of the glass in the same fashion as you would for a single-fired stack. The stack of pre-fired layers will be considerably lower than the total stack for your single-fired project. Remember to place the iridized sheet on the bottom of the stack with the irid coating face down against the shelf.

As with your single-fired stack, be sure that all of the glass layers are clean and that the top surface sheet is completely free of film, oil, or dust.

The suggested firing schedule for the second firing is #3, Second Firing of Double-Fired Block, on page 5.

Figure 3: Cross section of single-fired stack.

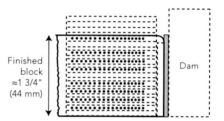

Finished block ≈1 3/4" (44 mm)

Dam

Figure 4: Cross section of single-fired finished block.

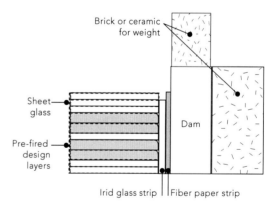

Brick or ceramic for weight

Sheet glass

Dam

Pre-fired design layers

Irid glass strip   Fiber paper strip

Figure 5: Cross section of double-fired stack.

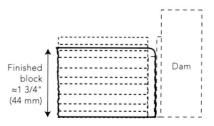

Finished block ≈1 3/4" (44 mm)

Dam

Figure 6: Cross section of double-fired finished block.

FINISHING

The techniques outlined in this TipSheet will result in a finished block with clean, rolled edges and crisp corners. If the block has sharp edges and/or needlepoints, grinding may be necessary. There are many tools and methods available for grinding glass, and they range widely in cost and size. The most basic, a sickle stone, will knock off sharp edges, but will leave a rough, abraded look. A belt sander or lapping wheel will do the job quickly, right up to a polish, but both are large and fairly expensive tools. Diamond hand laps in grit sizes from 60 to 3500 do a wonderful job of everything from a rough grind to close to a polish.

DISPLAY

You may wish to work with a metalworker to fabricate a simple base like the one pictured here (see Figure 7). Smaller blocks can be used as paperweights. Larger blocks work well as tops for end tables. Really large blocks make can function as dividing walls, benches, countertops, and even stair treads!

Figure 7: Jung-Hyun Yoon, *distort*, 2006. Kilnformed and kilncast glass, 8 3/4 x 11 7/8 x 1 7/8 in (222 x 302 x 48 mm).

See next page for project troubleshooting ›

FIRING SCHEDULES

Single Fired Block

SEGMENT	RATE (DPH)*	TEMPERATURE	HOLD
1	400°F (222°C)	1250°F (677°C)	3:00[1]
2	600°F (333°C)	1500°F (816°C)[2]	:20
3	AFAP**	900°F (482°C)	7:00
4	9°F (5°C)	800°F (427°C)	:00
5	17°F (9°C)	700°F (371°C)	:00
6	57°F (31°C)	75°F (24°C)	:00

Pre-Fired Layers of Double-Fired Block

SEGMENT	RATE (DPH)*	TEMPERATURE	HOLD
1	450°F (250°C)	1250°F (667°C)	:45
2	600°F (333°C)	1480°F (804°C)[2]	:10
3	AFAP**	900°F (482°C)	:30
4	210°F (116°C)	700°F (371°C)	:00
5	400°F (222°C)	75°F (24°C)	:00

Second Firing of Double-Fired Block

SEGMENT	RATE (DPH)*	TEMPERATURE	HOLD
1	400°F (222°C)	1250°F (677°C)	1:15[1]
2	600°F (333°C)	1480°F (804°C)[3]	:10
3	AFAP**	900°F (482°C)	7:00
4	9°F (5°C)	800°F (427°C)	:00
5	17°F (9°C)	700°F (371°C)	:00
6	57°F (31°C)	75°F (24°C)	:00

* DPH = degrees per hour

** "As Fast As Possible" will be whatever cooling rate results from the kiln power being cut by the controller. We do not advocate crash cooling. Leave your kiln closed, allowing it to cool naturally to the anneal soak temperature.

1 A longer hold time is necessary for the Single-Fired Block than for the Double-Fired. More time is needed to "squeeze" any trapped air from the interior of the design layers in order to avoid bubbles.

2 Process temperatures and hold times will vary from kiln to kiln.

3 The slightly lower temperature and slightly shorter hold time on the Double-Fired Block compensates somewhat for the heatwork that has already gone into this glass in the pre-firings.

TROUBLESHOOTING

If you have followed the directions given here your fired block will have a smooth top surface, bullnosed upper edges, clean sides, and 90-degree corners (see Figure 8). A block that does not match this perfect profile can result from one or more of the following conditions:

Figure 8: Perfect profile.

Needlepoints–These can occur at the top edge for several reasons (see Figure 9). If you have failed to center the top pieces of sheet glass and they are in contact with the fiber paper along the dams, they will catch along the fiber paper as the glass melts. Needlepointing can also occur when the iridescent sides are too tall in relation to the stack of glass that they surround. Be certain to cut the iridescent sides 5/16" (8 mm) shorter than the total height of your fired stack of glass. For example: 14 layers ≈ 1 3/4" (44 mm) - 5/16" (8 mm) = 1 7/16" (36 mm) irid sides.

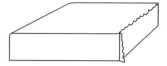

Figure 9: Needlpoints at top edge, flashing at corner.

Flashing at the corner seams–This happens when the fiber sides and/or the dams are not properly sealed in the lay-up process, or when dams are not properly buttressed from behind (see Figure 9). Once again, the molten glass at top temperature has enough force to actually push a dam outwards. Be sure to sufficiently reinforce your dams with firebricks or other weighty materials. Also, if the irid sides have been cut too long, the edges will have a similar problem that is not unlike flashing. Be sure that there are no overhanging edges in the assembled stack.

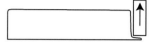

Figure 10: Flashing at bottom edge.

Flashing at the bottom edge–This is the result of the molten glass flowing under the dam (see Figure 10). This typically happens when the dam is not sufficiently weighted from the top. The molten glass actually causes the dam to float upwards, and then flows under the dam.

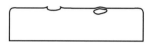

Figure 11: Bubbles under or breaking surface.

Bubbles erupting through the surface – These are often the result of having piles of frit or sheet glass between layers that are closest to the top (see Figure 11). Bubbles may also result when colored sheet glass elements have not been very carefully intercut with clear. When making a block in a single firing, try to have at least three sheets of clear on top of the design layer closest to the top of the stack, and take extra care that cut pieces fit together tightly.

Figure 12: Kiln shelf not level.

Uneven thickness – This is most often the result of a shelf that is not level (see Figure 12). Be certain to level your shelf before you begin building on it, and then check the level after you have completed the stack.

Figure 13: Fiber paper thickness too great. Dams not vertical—finished block won't sit vertically.

A block with inclined sides – This results from improperly braced or non-vertical dams (see Figure 13). Weak bracing will also likely allow the dams to be pushed outward and the block to flow out of square (see Figure 14).

The glass sticks to the shelf – If this happens, it is usually because there was not a sufficient shelf separator such as kilnwash or fiber paper between the glass and the shelf. Never re-use a coat of kilnwash, but rather scrape it off and prepare every shelf anew for each firing. The glass is also more likely to stick to the shelf when it is fired too hot. Try to avoid temperatures in excess of 1500°F (816°C) for times in excess of 20 minutes. For a foolproof clean surface, consider ThinFire paper.

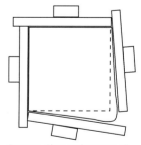

Figure 14: Glass pushing out walls.

The edges of the glass in the stack appear to be "highlighted"–This usually happens because the irid sides were set up with the irid coating facing inward. Make certain that all irid surfaces face outward (toward the fiber paper) when setting up the stack.

TIPSHEET 4

Published by Bullseye Glass Co.

DESIGNING YOUR OWN ART GLASS

BY MARY KAY NITCHIE

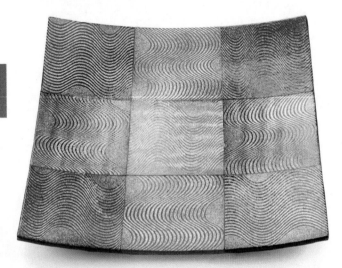

Figure 1: Fused and slumped plate with sgraffito surface, 1.5 x 9.375 x 9.375 in (3.8 x 23.8 x 23.8 cm).

Working with a palette of glass frit, powder, and stringers, you can create unique sheets of art glass to use in stained glass or fusing projects.

Using the materials and techniques described in this TipSheet, you will no longer be dependent on the selection of sheet glass offered by dealers or manufacturers. Rather than searching the globe for a sheet of glass with perfect color transitions, you can create sheet glass to meet the exact requirements of your artwork.

This TipSheet describes how to make a series of sample tiles using the classic elements of design, line, dot, shading, shape, and pattern. Use the same techniques to make larger sheets that can be cut into parts for use in larger projects. As you practice these simple techniques, you will probably be flooded with ideas for unique patterns, colors, and textures of your own.

SKILL LEVEL

You will need basic kilnforming skills: familiarity with basic equipment, firing, and annealing of glass. To learn more about basic kilnforming, visit bullseyeglass.com to watch instructional videos, download free articles, and locate classes worldwide.

GLASS

The base glass for these tiles can be any Bullseye tested compatible sheet. We have specified Clear double-rolled fusible 3mm sheet (001101-0030-F) for most of the tiles here, but other Bullseye clear sheet glass will work, especially:

- Tekta Clear 3mm (001100-0380-F)
- Tekta Clear 4mm (001100-0480-F)
- Tekta Clear 6mm 001100-0680-F)
- Clear fusible 6mm (001101-0060-F)

At Bullseye, we call the following smaller scale non-sheet forms of our glass "accessory glasses."

- **Stringers** are thin threads of colored glass.
- **Frit** is made up of granules of crushed glass. Each color of frit is available in four different grain sizes:
  - *Powder* is the finest size and is easy to sift.
  - *Fine* is the size of sugar grains.
  - *Medium* is the size of very coarse sand grains.
  - *Coarse* is the size of the colored gravel that people put in the bottom of their fish tanks.
- **Confetti** is eggshell-thin, coin-size shards of glass. Imagine a toy balloon made of glass, broken to bits.

KILNS AND TEMPERATURE CONTROL

The thickness of the base glass and the intended process temperature will determine which shelf separator you select. Firing 2-3mm glasses to temperatures above 1425°F (774°C) is best performed on fiber paper to help avoid large bubbles from forming between the shelf and the glass. More information on this phenomenon can be found in *TechNote 5: Volume & Bubble Control* (see www.bullseyeglass.com).

You can fire 4-6mm sheets on ThinFire, fiber paper, or on a shelf prepared with Bullseye Shelf Primer.

Each kiln has its own heating and cooling characteristics. The important thing is to keep records of the firing schedules you try and to make adjustments based on your observations. One firing schedule may produce different results in different kilns. The firing schedule chosen will need to accommodate the thickness of the sheet glass selected.

The "process temperature" is the highest temperature, or peak, of the fusing cycle. The hold time is the amount of time the kiln is kept at the process temperature. If the heating stages and hold time are the same for each of your projects, the surface and texture of each piece can be manipulated by choosing a particular process temperature. The process temperatures typically used for the sample tile projects that follow range from approximately 1300°F to 1500°F (704° C to 816° C). At about 1300°F, fine frits dusted on the sheet will maintain a matte surface and have a sandpapery texture. At about 1500°F, those same fine frits will fire to a smooth glossy shine. Firing to very low temperatures may make the color appear less saturated.

Many of our sample tiles have been fired to relatively low temperatures and, as a result, have bumpy textures. If your ultimate goal is to incorporate them into other works during subsequent firings, you may want fire them to higher temperatures to reduce the likelihood of trapping unwanted air bubbles.

Carefully observing and recording the behavior of glass at different temperatures will give you access to a wide range of surface effects.

Here is an example of a firing schedule for the tiles in this TipSheet:

SAFETY

Good housekeeping and common sense go a long way to ensuring safety in the glass-forming studio.

To keep glass out of your eyes, always wear safety glasses when using frits, powders, sheet glass and stringers. To keep glass dust from irritating your lungs, always use a respirator when using frits and powders. To keep your studio clean, use moist sponges, cloths or mops whenever possible for wiping up counters and floors. For any dry cleanup, use a vacuum with a HEPA filter.

See your local safety supply company for a selection of safety glasses and respirators. For more information, see Bullseye's information sheet entitled "Safety in the Kilnforming Studio."

SETTING UP

To minimize waste, use a large clean piece of paper under the tile to collect any spilled frit or powder. After the tile is removed, the paper can be lifted and used to pour the excess frits or powders into a reclaim jar. To make the tile easy to carry to the kiln shelf, use inverted paper or plastic cups as posts under the corners of the tile. This makes it easier to lift the piece for transport and also allows some light through, for a better view while you are working.

Basic Fuse Firing

SEGMENT	RATE (DPH)*	TEMPERATURE	HOLD
1	400°F (204°C)	1000°F (538°C)	:10
2	600°F (316°C)	Process temp.	:10
3	AFAP	900°F (516°C)	1:00
4	100°F (38°C)	700°F (371°C)	:01
5	AFAP**	Room temp.	:01

* DPH = degrees per hour
**AFAP = as fast as possible (without opening the kiln)
Note: This firing cycle was used for our example pieces, which all have thin, even applications of frit and/or powder. If your project includes application of uneven piles of frit and/or powder, you should slow the rate of heat in Segment 1 to prevent breakage from thermal shock. For instance, try 100°F/hr (55°C/hr).

Figure 2: A proper work setup can help minimize waste and prevent accidental spills.

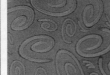

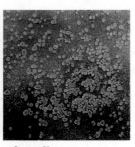

1. Red Sgraffito Square

2. Blue Powder Spiral

3. Yellow Coarse Fading Color Field

4. Blue Powder and Stringer Bits

5. Starry Sky

1. Red Sgraffito Square
Materials
- Red powder (001122-0008F)
- Black powder (000100-0008F)
- Clear double-rolled sheet glass (001101-0030F) cut into an 8" (20.3cm) tile

Tools
- Powder sifter or tea strainer
- 4" (10.2cm) square template (cardboard or glass square)
- Rubber wood-graining tool

Lay-up
Center the template on the tile. Sift a layer of black powder evenly over tile. Use wood-graining tool to make wavy lines. Remove template. Sift a thick layer of red-orange powder evenly over entire tile (including the black areas).

Firing
Try a process temperature of 1315°F (713°C). Hold for 10 minutes.

2. Blue Powder Spiral
Materials
- Deep Cobalt Blue Opal powder (000147-0008F)
- Clear double-rolled sheet glass (001101-0030F) cut into an 8" (20.3cm) tile

Tools
- Powder sifter or tea strainer
- Pencil with an eraser

Lay-up
Sift frit evenly on the tile, holding your sifter at least a foot from the glass. Using the eraser or the pencil point as a stylus, draw spirals (or other designs).

Firing
Try a process temperature of 1325°F (718°C). Hold for 10 minutes.

3. Yellow Coarse Fading Color Field
Materials
- Sunflower Yellow Opal coarse frit (000220-0003F)
- Clear double-rolled sheet glass (001101-0030F) cut into an 8" (20.3cm) tile

Tools
- Paper cup
- Tweezers

Lay-up:
Sprinkle frit in a single even layer across half the tile. Arrange the frit with tweezers to be densely fitted together at one end of the tile, gradually spacing out in the middle, and spaced sparsely at the other end.

Firing
Try a process temperature of 1400°F (760°C). Hold for 10 minutes.

4. Blue Powder and Stringer Bits
Materials
- Deep Cobalt Blue Opal powder (000147-0008F)
- Clear stringers 1mm (001101-0107)
- Black stringers 1mm (000100-0107)
- Clear double-rolled sheet glass (001101-0030F) cut into an 8" (20.3cm) tile

Tools
- Tea strainer
- Tweezers

Lay-up
Break stringers into 1-2 inch (2.5-5 cm) bits. Sprinkle stringer bits on the tile. Use tweezers to arrange any stray bits. Sift a substantial layer of blue powder evenly over the tile.

Firing
Try a process temperature of 1350°F (732°C). Hold for 10 minutes.

5. Starry Sky
Materials
- Midnight Blue powder (001118-0008F)
- Cranberry Pink powder (001311-0008F)
- Black powder (000100-0008F)
- Crystal Clear coarse frit (001401-0003F)
- Clear double-rolled sheet glass (001101-0030F) cut into an 8" (20.3cm) tile

Tools
- Powder sifter or tea strainer

Prep
Create round clear frit balls by sprinkling Crystal Clear coarse frit directly on a primed kiln shelf. Space the grains so that none touches another. Fire the frit grains as fast as your kiln will fire, up to about 1500°F (816°C). Turn off the kiln. Open the door/lid wide. The grains should have formed into little balls. Leave the door/lid open to allow the balls to cool as quickly as possible to room temperature. Remove the balls from the shelf, rinse and allow the balls to dry.

Lay-up
Arrange clear frit balls on the tile. Sift pink powder on the top third of the tile, over the frit balls. Sift blue powder on the rest of the tile, fading into the pink field. Sift a thin fading layer of black powder over the color fields and frit balls.

Firing
Try a process temperature of 1350°F (732°C). Hold for 10 minutes.

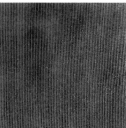
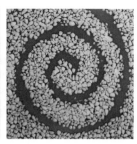
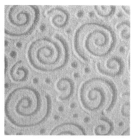

6. Blue Powder Dot Template   7. Black Reeded Texture   8. Yellow and Blue Coarse Spiral   9. Yellow Fine Spiral   10. Orange Powder Fading Color Field

6. Blue Powder Dot Template

Materials
- Deep Cobalt Blue Opal powder (000147-0008F)
- Clear double-rolled sheet glass (001101-0030F) cut into an 8" (20.3cm) tile

Tools
- Powder sifter or tea strainer
- Paper or cardboard dot template
- Jar lid

Lay-up
Place the dot template on the sheet. Use the jar lid as a circle template, placing that on top of the dot template. Sift a substantial layer of blue powder evenly over the tile. Carefully remove the circle template. Carefully remove the dot template.

Firing
Try a process temperature of 1325°F (718°C). Hold for 10 minutes.

7. Black Reeded Texture

Materials
- Black powder (000100-0008F)
- Clear reeded sheet glass (001101-0043F) cut into an 8" (20.3cm) tile

Tools
- Powder sifter or tea strainer
- Light box (optional)

Lay-up
Sift a substantial even layer of powder over the entire tile. Check that the layer is even by viewing the tile over a light box.

Firing
Try a process temperature of 1325°F (718°C). Hold for 10 minutes.

8. Yellow and Blue Coarse Spiral

Materials
- Yellow Opal coarse frit (000120-0003F)
- Deep Cobalt Blue Opal powder (000147-0008F)
- Clear double-rolled sheet glass (001101-0030F) cut into an 8" (20.3cm) tile

Tools
- Paper cup
- Powder sifter or tea strainer
- Pencil with an eraser
- Tweezers

Lay-up
Pour the yellow frit evenly on the tile from the paper cup. Using the pencil eraser as a stylus, draw a big spiral. Use the tweezers to rearrange any stray frits. Sift a thick layer of blue powder evenly over the sheet.

Firing
Try a process temperature of 1400°F (760°C). Hold for 10 minutes.

9. Yellow Fine Spiral

Materials
- Yellow Opal fine frit (000120-0001F)
- Clear double-rolled sheet glass (001101-0030F) cut into an 8" (20.3cm) tile

Tools
- Paper cup
- Pencil with an eraser

Lay-up
Pour frit evenly on the tile from the paper cup. Using the pencil eraser as a stylus, draw spirals and dots.

Firing
Try a process temperature of 1350°F (732°C). Hold for 10 minutes.

10. Orange Powder Fading Color Field

Materials
- Orange Opal powder (000125-0008F)
- Clear double-rolled sheet glass (001101-0030F) cut into an 8" (20.3cm) tile

Tools
- Powder sifter or tea strainer
- Light box (optional)

Lay-up
Sift a thin layer of orange powder evenly over the tile. Sift a second thin layer of orange powder evenly over 3/4 of the tile. Sift a third thin layer of orange powder evenly over 1/2 of the tile. Sift a fourth thin layer over 1/4 of the tile. Repeat steps from the beginning until the powder blends evenly from a thin layer at one end of the tile to a thick layer at the other end. Check that the fade is even by viewing the tile over a light box before firing.

Firing
Try a process temperature of 1325°F (718°C). Hold for 10 minutes.

BULLSEYE BOX CASTING
Reverse-Relief Kilncasting in an Assembled Mold

This TipSheet describes how to create a reverse-relief cast glass object with the optical clarity of a furnace casting, using plaster/silica design elements in an open-faced mold assembled from vermiculite board and other refractory materials. There are several advantages to this process:

- Less waste than traditional kilncasting processes
- The majority of the molds will be reusable
- Molds will be of uniform thickness, allowing for uniform heating and cooling
- Molds will not fail at casting temperature (one of the most common concerns in kilncasting and the reason there is such a boggling array of mold recipes in use)
- Cleaner and more predictable results than kilncasting in most of the traditional methods
- Extremely easy to repeat for the purpose of making editions or production work

Where You Are Going: The Finished Piece
The end result will be a solid block of glass with relief imagery in the back of the piece that when viewed through the flat front creates a nearly holographic image. The top surface of the piece will be glossy and smooth. If carefully planned and executed, the top perimeter will have a soft, bullnosed edge. Occasionally, some coldwork may be necessary or may enhance the finished work. The finished block will measure about 19.5 x 19.5 x 4 cm. These dimensions may be enlarged by adapting the general guidelines and adjusting the firing schedule.

Ted Sawyer, *Speak*, 2003, 19.5 x 19.5 x 4 cm

Ted Sawyer, *Speak* (detail), 2003, 19.5 x 19.5 x 4 cm

Rafael Cauduro, *Tzompantli D*, 2002, 100 x 57 x 5 cm

ORIGINS OF THE METHOD

This method of kilncasting developed as an out-growth of an artist exchange project in our Research & Education department with Mexican artist Rafael Cauduro. Cauduro had originally come to the factory to work in methods known as Painting With Light, but quickly became intrigued with kilncasting and began to make large-scale cast glass sculptures using traditional "monolithic" or one-piece refractory molds. The fabrication, handling, and technical challenges posed by making and firing these molds ultimately led the R&E team, assisted by Ray Ahlgren of Fireart Glass*, to begin researching other ways of building the molds. After the project concluded, the research continued. This TipSheet details the process we subsequently developed.

* Ahlgren was one of Bullseye's founders and instrumental in the company's early explorations of kilnformed glass. Fireart Glass specializes in large-scale fusing and multiple production methods with an emphasis on architectural work and limited-edition lighting. More information at fireartglass.com.

MATERIALS NEEDED

Glass
Because clarity is essential to creating a reverse-relief casting, we recommend using any of Bullseye's casting tints in billet form. Because they have smoother surfaces and less surface area by weight than other forms of glass, billets will trap less air than frit, powders, or sheet glass, and therefore create fewer bubbles in the final piece. Billets are preferable not only for the clarity they produce in the finished casting, but also because they are easy to handle, cut, and load into the mold. Our casting tints are formulated to gradually transition in color saturation as they go from thick to thin, making them ideal for this and other casting processes.

Other materials
- Clay and tools for modeling design elements
- Metric scale
- Metric ruler
- Accu-Cast 880 Alginate Blue or similar moldmaking material
- Mixing containers
- Bucket of water for initial cleanup
- Bucket of water for rinse
- Bullseye Vermiculite Board (8240)
- Stainless steel (deck) screws
- Bullseye Investment (plaster/silica) (8244) or similar refractory investment material
- Fiber paper (7036)
- Petroleum jelly
- Oil-based soap
- 946 ml food storage box, or equivalent
- Garbage can with liner
- Self-lubricating glass cutter
- Hammer

NOTES ON METRIC MEASUREMENTS

For the sake of simplicity, all units of measure in this TipSheet are metric. The decimal format of the metric system and its direct and simple translation from length to volume to weight in water makes it a superior system for studio work.

IN THE METRIC SYSTEM
1 cubic centimeter (cm^3) of water =
1 milliliter (ml) of water =
1 gram (g) of water

If the interior of an empty box measures 20 x 20 x 2.5 cm, then this interior has a volume of 1000 cm^3. 1000 cm^3 of water is equal to 1000 ml of water, which is equal to 1000 g of water. Bullseye glass is 2.5 times denser than water, so it would take 2,500 grams of Bullseye glass to fill this same volume.

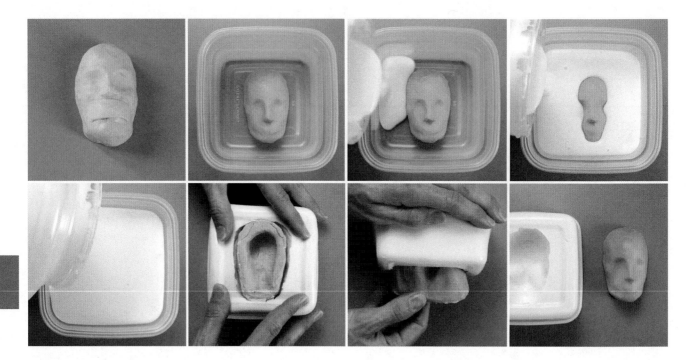

THE PROCESS

MAKING A MOLD FOR MULTIPLE COPIES OF A MODEL

Preparing a model using clay or a found object

Prepare a model no larger than 5 x 5 x 3 cm using either water- or oil-based clay. This model will be used to make the design elements that will create the reverse-relief imagery in the final casting. Water-based clay is usually softer than oil-based clay, can be modeled very quickly, and can be reused and recycled. However, it will dry out over time and will shrink as it does so. Oil-based clay is usually firmer, does not dry out, holds fine detail very well, is reusable, and releases very easily from most mold materials, including alginate, rubber, and silicone.

Found objects may need to be coated with a mold release, such as petroleum jelly or oil-based soap.

For this particular process, the model itself should have minimal undercuts. Undercuts on found objects can be filled in with clay. The very bottom portion of these design elements will end up being submerged in investment material to hold them in place in the final casting process, so plan accordingly.

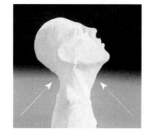

Arrows indicate undercuts.

Preparing to pour a mold

Place the model into a box with a minimum of 15 mm of space all around it; a 10.5 x 10.5 x 9 cm flexible plastic food storage box with a slight draft to the sides works well. The box serves as a containment system into which you will pour the alginate to make the mold. Use petroleum jelly to secure the model to the bottom of the box to keep it from moving or floating when you pour in the mold material.

Types of flexible mold material for casting multiple copies

Accu-Cast 880 Alginate Blue mold compound is a type of alginate that is fairly easy to mix and sets in 5-10 minutes. It is somewhat weak with a short working life and will dry out and shrink over a couple of days, but if kept in a sealed container and treated carefully, it will usually last a few weeks.

RTV Rubber (Room Temperature Vulcanizing) is activated at room temperature but can have long set times and often takes 24 hours to cure into a very durable, very strong material.

For the sake of expediency, we have used Accu-Cast 880 Alginate Blue to illustrate this TipSheet.

Mixing Accu-Cast 880 Alginate Blue mold compound

Measure the containment system—including 1.5 cm above the model in the calculation. For our specific box and model, this is 10.5 x 10.5 x 4.5 cm, which equals 496 cubic cm, which means that it will take 496 grams of water to fill the box to the appropriate level. The manufacturer of Accu-Cast 880 Alginate Blue mold compound recommends mixing it 3 parts water to 1 part Accu-Cast 880 Alginate Blue by weight and adding the mold compound to the water, but we have had success mixing it 4 parts water to 1 part Accu-Cast 880 Alginate Blue by weight and adding the water to the Accu-Cast 880 Alginate Blue. For our project, then, we will need 496 grams of water and 124 grams of Accu-Cast 880 Alginate Blue. We get the best results mixing this with a spatula in a bowl using a folding, not a beating motion, to avoid creating bubbles in the mix. Work in a well-ventilated area and wear a NIOSH-approved respirator whenever working with powdered materials.

Pouring the Accu-Cast 880 Alginate Blue
Be certain that you are working on a flat and level surface. Pour to one side of the object in a flowing motion to keep air from getting trapped on the surface of the model. Vibrate the worktable so that the air bubbles don't get stuck to the model.

Cleanup
Using water immediately makes a mess. Allow the remaining Accu-Cast 880 Alginate Blue to dry in the container and then immerse in a bucket of water for initial clean up. Once cured, it is possible to peel the Accu-Cast 880 Alginate Blue out as a skin. Never pour into a sink.

Removing the mold from the containment system
Turn the box upside down on the worktable and squeeze the flexible walls to let air into the sides until the mold drops out. Turn the mold over again and squeeze and push it carefully to remove the clay model. You now have a flexible mold for pouring multiple copies of your model in another material.

MAKING DESIGN ELEMENTS OUT OF REFRACTORY MOLD MATERIAL

Many different refractory mold (or "investment") materials and recipes exist. We use a simple mixture of 50% #1 Casting Plaster and 50% silica flour (295 mesh), mixed by weight.

Measuring mold material
Measure the original model and overestimate its size. It's better to discard some inexpensive investment than to run out and have to mix more in haste. Our model is roughly 5 x 5 x 5 cm = 125 cubic cm. Referring to the Investment Ratio chart on page 8, we can add together the amounts of material needed for voids of 100, 20, and 5 cubic centimeters to get the proper quantities of water and investment required for our 125 cubic centimeter void. This means that we will need 80 grams of water and

140 grams of investment. Weigh these materials in clean, dry buckets. Remember to work in a well-ventilated area and wear a NIOSH-approved respirator whenever working with powdered materials.

Mixing investment material
Steadily sift all of the required investment into the water. An island of dry material will begin to form once you have sifted most of the material into the water. Allow the investment to become fully saturated. If left alone, the investment can sit for quite some time. Once the mixture is saturated, dip your hand in and break up any chunks. Feel the consistency. It should have a creamy texture. Mix the investment by hand for 3-5 minutes or with an electric mixer/drill for 1-2 minutes. This will cause the plaster to begin to work so that it will subsequently set.

Pouring the mixed investment into the mold
Be certain that you are working on a flat and level surface. If you have a lot of fine detail, begin by brushing some investment mix into the details in the mold, which will break the surface tension so the mix can go into the details. Aim for one place in the mold and pour in a flowing motion to avoid creating bubbles. Once you have finished pouring, vibrate the work surface to make certain that no air is trapped within the details of the mold.

Cleanup
Clean investment mixing buckets right away. Old plaster in mixing buckets, on hands and/or on tools can cause subsequent batches of investment to set before you have a chance to pour them. Use dark colored buckets so you can easily spot old plaster in them. Never pour investment into a normal sink as this will clog the drain. Pour excess investment into a garbage can that has a liner in it. From there, have two buckets of water to use in your cleaning operation: one bucket for cleaning and scrubbing the mixing buckets and one bucket for rinsing them. When these buckets become too filled with waste investment to continue using them, allow them to settle, then pour off the excess water and dispose of the waste investment in garbage bags.

After investment has set up
It usually takes 5-20 minutes for the investment to set. Lightly touch the surface of the investment to test its hardness. Once it has set, the plaster/silica design element can be removed the same way the clay model was. Immediately after setting, the design element will still be a little soft, which means that it can be easily modified with simple clay tools. After the design element hardens, it can still be modified, but you may need to use power tools for the sake of speed.

Store the alginate/Accu-Cast 880 Alginate Blue mold in a closed container for later use, to keep it from drying out.

BUILDING THE BOX MOLD WITH VERMICULITE BOARD

Vermiculite board

Vermiculite has a bad reputation because it is often mined in the same places as asbestos, which can contaminate the vermiculite. Bullseye Vermiculite Board comes from a mine that is certified asbestos free. It is stronger, more durable, and less expensive than most fiberboard and can be cut and tooled like wood or particle board. Work in a well-ventilated area and wear a NIOSH-approved respirator whenever generating dust.

If you want your finished piece to be level and square, it is important to cut the vermiculite boards accurately. Also, pre-drill and countersink screw holes so the board does not bloat or blow out when you screw it together. Use stainless steel screws to put the mold together as they will hold up to repeated firings without flaking. Do not use galvanized steel screws because upon firing, the galvanization will release toxic fumes and the screws will flake and cause contamination in your kiln.

Cut two long side boards at 25.5 x 9 x 2.5 cm, two short side boards at 20 x 9 x 2.5 cm, and one base board at 25.5 x 25.5 x 2.5 cm. Lay the boards out as an open box and pre-drill holes in the flat surface of the long side boards to connect them to the ends of the short side boards using a bit that has a diameter slightly smaller than the diameter of the stainless steel screws. Be sure to drill your holes on center to avoid blowing out the side of the board. Then screw the sidewalls together. Next, set the base board on top of the assembled side boards and pre-drill holes to join it to the sides, and then screw it together. Then take the entire box apart and fire the vermiculite board at a rate of 500°F (278°C) per hour to a temperature of 1580°F (860°C) or about 55°F (30°C) higher than the temperature at which you will cast the glass. Hold at that temperature for half an hour, then crash cool the kiln.

Once the boards are cool, take them out and reassemble the sides using the stainless steel screws. Cut a piece of 3 mm fiber paper at 25.5 x 25.5 cm and set it on the base board, then set the assembled sides on top of the fiber paper, and screw the box together. Line the side walls with 3 mm fiber paper, making sure that it fits tightly, without bowing or leaving gaps in the corners.

AFFIXING DESIGN ELEMENTS WITHIN THE BOX

The design elements must be held firmly in place for the glass casting process. To hold them, a shallow layer (or "bed") of investment is poured into the bottom of the box around the design elements.

Hydrate the plaster/silica design elements by soaking them in water until the bubbles quit rising (5-10 minutes). This helps to keep the plaster/silica bed from sucking in around the design elements due to differences in humidity. Arrange design elements on the interior base of the box. Check once again to make certain that your work surface is flat and level.

Measure the inside of the box to determine the appropriate amount of investment material needed. Our box is 19.5 x 19.5 cm, and we need enough investment to fill it about 0.5 cm deep. Thus, the investment needs to fill a void that is 190 cubic centimeters. The investment (plaster/silica) mixing table on page 8 has a batch listed for 200 cubic cm. This will be more than enough.

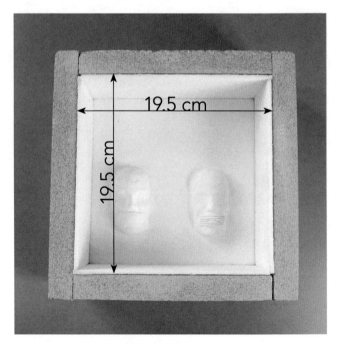

Mix the investment according to the previous directions and pour it quickly and evenly. Avoid pouring the mix directly onto the design elements or the side walls. Vibrate the work surface to assure that the investment levels out.

Set the box mold aside for 24 hours to make sure that all of the plaster/silica components of the mold have cured to an adequate hardness. As with the design elements, you may choose to modify the affixing layer of investment.

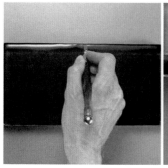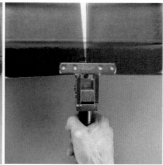

SELECTING GLASS

You may select any form of Bullseye glass to fill the mold (billet, cullet, sheet, frit, etc.), but the form that you select will have a direct impact on the clarity of the casting. The smaller the form of the glass, the more air bubbles in the finished piece, and the less optical clarity. Powders and fine frits will create so many air bubbles that even our Crystal Clear (001401) will appear milky white and opalescent when used at this 4 cm thickness.

Because this is a reverse-relief casting and the intention is to see the imagery created by the design elements through the surface of the finished piece, using billet will give you the desired clarity.

Calculating glass to fill the mold

Measure the inside of the box mold. Then figure out the cubic volume. Use a specific gravity of 2.5 for Bullseye glass to calculate how much glass will be needed to fill the mold to the desired thickness. (Bullseye glass is approximately 2.5 times heavier than water.)

OUR BOX MOLD:
19.5 x 19.5 x 4 cm (desired thickness of casting) =
1521 cm³ 1521 x 2.5 =
3802.5 (grams of glass needed)

This does not account for the displacement of glass caused by the design elements.

If you would like to account for the displacement caused by the design elements, or if you have an irregularly shaped mold, you can use rice for a more precise measurement. Fill your mold with rice to the desired thickness of the casting. Then remove the rice and decant it into a container. Level the rice, and then mark the level. Remove the rice from the container, and weigh the container. Then fill the container with water up to the former level of the rice, and weigh it again. Subtract the weight of the container to get the weight of the water. It will take 2.5 grams of Bullseye for every gram of water.

Cutting the billet

Use a self-lubricating glass cutter to score the billet. It will take about the same amount of pressure required to score 3 mm sheet glass.

It is always easiest to break the score if it is made along the centerline of the piece of glass. In other words, cut the billet in half, then in half again, to get the appropriate sizes to fill the mold.

Hold the billet low and over the table. Find the score line and break with large running pliers. Or hold the billet in a gloved hand and use a hammer to open the score by tapping on the back of the glass underneath the score line. (This does not take a lot of force. A tap exactly under the score line will cause the score to open cleanly.) Always wear eye protection.

Loading the glass into the mold

Clean and dry the glass thoroughly, making sure to remove labels. Any glass that is going to be lower than the thickness of the final piece can be against the mold wall, but be careful not to indent the fiber paper because it will create a bump on the finished glass piece. Stack the rest of the glass into the center of the mold.

Loading the mold into the kiln

Make sure that both the kiln and the mold are level. Set the box mold on kiln furniture/posts, establishing three points of contact at least 2.5 cm from the floor of the kiln. This will allow heat to circulate all around the mold. To intentionally create a wedge shape, set the mold up on an angle. However, make certain that you have enough glass to cover the design elements and that you adjust your annealing schedule to accommodate for the thicker area in the casting. If, for example, you would like a wedge that is 5 cm on the bottom and 2.5 cm on top, you will want to support the end that will be thicker on 2.5 cm kiln furniture, and the thinner end on 5 cm kiln furniture, and then calculate the glass as if you were casting a rectilinear volume with a thickness of 3.75 cm.

FIRING THE PIECE

Vent the kiln at least up to 1100°F (593°C) to make certain that all of the moisture has escaped. Plan to be present when the kiln is at casting temperature, to visually inspect the piece to make sure the casting is going as planned. If unwanted bubbles are present on the surface or just below the surface of the piece, plan to extend the hold at casting temperature until the bubbles have burst and healed.

Firing schedules provided are specific to the Paragon GL24AD kilns used in our Research & Education studio. All kilns fire differently. You may need to adjust the firing schedule for your specific kiln and project.

After the entire firing cycle is complete, we recommend leaving the piece in the kiln at room temperature for at least a day before taking it out to divest it.

CLEANING THE FINISHED PIECE

Remove the piece from the kiln and disassemble the box mold. Remember to wear a NIOSH-approved mask while handling the fired fiber paper and investment materials. Watch out for any sharp points where the glass has clung to the side walls of the mold.

The investment can be removed from the glass with a variety of tools, such as dental instruments, wooden picks, nylon brushes, and wood carving tools. Wooden tools are ideal for carefully removing broad areas of investment, and metal tools should be used delicately to clean fine details. A nylon bristle brush and forced air are also great tools for cleaning areas of residual investment. Most of the investment should be removed from the glass before submerging it in or scrubbing it with water. While water can be used to rinse away residual investment, we have found that scrubbing the glass with vinegar and/or CLR (a household product used for dissolving stains from calcium, lime, or iron oxide deposits) helps to break down the investment material.

Remember that you can create a very different effect if you decide to coldwork and/or polish your piece. The optical qualities can change substantially, especially with coldworking on the edges.

Typical Cycle

STEP	RATE (degrees/hour)	TEMPERATURE	HOLD
1	100°F (55°C)	200°F (93°C)	6:00*
2	100°F (55°C)	1250°F (677°C)	2:00
3	600°F (333°C)	1525°F (830°C)	1:00**
4	AFAP***	900°F (482°C)	6:00
5	12°F (6.7°C)	800°F (427°C)	:00
6	22°F (12°C)	700°F (371°C)	:00
7	72°F (40°C)	75°F (24°C)	:00

* This time can vary. Set the time to ensure you will be in the studio to close the vents, and then be present when the casting reaches process temperature to allow for a visual inspection.
** Visually confirm. The casting may take more or less time to properly form.
*** Allow kiln to cool at its natural rate with the door closed.

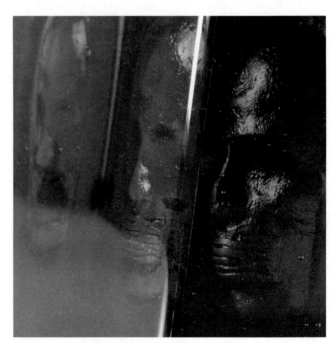

Ted Sawyer, *Speak* (detail), 2003, 19.5 x 19.5 x 4 cm

DIRECTIONS FOR DETERMINING VOID VOLUME

A. Decide your shape (square, rectangle).

B. Set up your coddles. Leave space (about 5 cm) around and above project.

C. Use formulas to find the volume of your void (inside of coddles).

Square & Rectangle
Formula: length x height x width
Example:

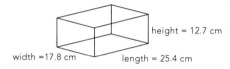

Volume: 25.4 x 12.7 x 17.8 = 5,741.9 cm³

Cylinder
Formula: π x radius² x height
Example:

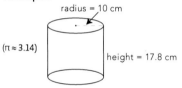

$(\pi \approx 3.14)$

Volume: 3.14 x 100 x 17.8 = 5,589.2 cm³

Notes

· Charts are not equivalent. (10,000 cm³ is significantly less volume than 10,000 in³.)

· Add together any combination of chart listings to best fit your project size.

· The investment recipe we have used is: 50% 295 mesh silica flour + 50% #1 Casting Plaster by weight.

· This chart uses a 1:1.75 ratio (water:investment).

· The investment ratio is suitable for many casting projects.

Imperial Investment Ratio

VOID SIZE	WATER WEIGHT	INVESTMENT WEIGHT
1 in³	0.02 lbs	0.04 lbs
2 in³	0.05 lbs	0.08 lbs
3 in³	0.07 lbs	0.12 lbs
4 in³	0.09 lbs	0.16 lbs
5 in³	0.12 lbs	0.20 lbs
6 in³	0.14 lbs	0.24 lbs
7 in³	0.16 lbs	0.28 lbs
8 in³	0.19 lbs	0.32 lbs
9 in³	0.21 lbs	0.36 lbs
10 in³	0.23 lbs	0.40 lbs
20 in³	0.46 lbs	0.81 lbs
30 in³	0.69 lbs	1.21 lbs
40 in³	0.93 lbs	1.62 lbs
50 in³	1.16 lbs	2.02 lbs
60 in³	1.39 lbs	2.43 lbs
70 in³	1.62 lbs	2.83 lbs
80 in³	1.85 lbs	3.24 lbs
90 in³	2.08 lbs	3.64 lbs
100 in³	2.31 lbs	4.05 lbs
200 in³	4.63 lbs	8.10 lbs
300 in³	6.94 lbs	12.14 lbs
400 in³	9.25 lbs	16.19 lbs
500 in³	11.57 lbs	20.24 lbs
600 in³	13.88 lbs	24.29 lbs
700 in³	16.19 lbs	28.33 lbs
800 in³	18.50 lbs	32.38 lbs
900 in³	20.82 lbs	36.43 lbs
1000 in³	23.13 lbs	40.48 lbs
2000 in³	46.26 lbs	80.96 lbs
3000 in³	69.39 lbs	121.43 lbs
4000 in³	92.52 lbs	161.91 lbs
5000 in³	115.65 lbs	202.39 lbs
6000 in³	138.78 lbs	242.87 lbs
7000 in³	161.91 lbs	283.34 lbs
8000 in³	185.04 lbs	323.82 lbs
9000 in³	208.17 lbs	364.30 lbs
10000 in³	231.30 lbs	404.78 lbs

Imperial: Water weights on this chart are derived by multiplying the size of the void by 0.02313.

Metric Investment Ratio

VOID SIZE	WATER WEIGHT	INVESTMENT WEIGHT
1 cm³	0.64 g	1.12 g
2 cm³	1.28 g	2.24 g
3 cm³	1.92 g	3.36 g
4 cm³	2.56 g	4.48 g
5 cm³	3.20 g	5.60 g
6 cm³	3.84 g	6.72 g
7 cm³	4.48 g	7.84 g
8 cm³	5.12 g	8.96 g
9 cm³	5.76 g	10.08 g
10 cm³	6.40 g	11.20 g
20 cm³	12.80 g	22.40 g
30 cm³	19.20 g	33.59 g
40 cm³	25.59 g	44.79 g
50 cm³	31.99 g	55.99 g
60 cm³	38.39 g	67.19 g
70 cm³	44.79 g	78.38 g
80 cm³	51.19 g	89.58 g
90 cm³	57.59 g	100.78 g
100 cm³	63.99 g	111.98 g
200 cm³	127.97 g	223.95 g
300 cm³	191.96 g	335.93 g
400 cm³	255.95 g	447.91 g
500 cm³	319.94 g	559.89 g
600 cm³	383.92 g	671.86 g
700 cm³	447.91 g	783.84 g
800 cm³	511.90 g	895.82 g
900 cm³	575.88 g	1007.80 g
1000 cm³	639.87 g	1119.77 g
2000 cm³	1279.74 g	2239.55 g
3000 cm³	1919.61 g	3359.32 g
4000 cm³	2559.48 g	4479.09 g
5000 cm³	3199.35 g	5598.86 g
6000 cm³	3839.22 g	6718.64 g
7000 cm³	4479.09 g	7838.41 g
8000 cm³	5118.96 g	8958.18 g
9000 cm³	5758.83 g	10077.95 g
10000 cm³	6398.70 g	11197.73 g

Metric: Water weights on this chart are derived by multiplying the size of the void by 0.63987.

ROLL-UPS: Blowing Glass Without a Furnace

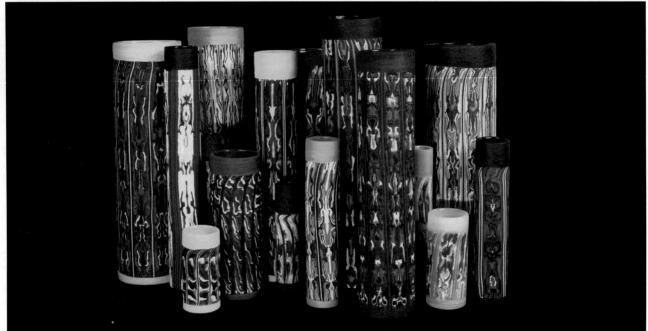

Klaus Moje, *Niijima Series*, 2000. Kilnformed and rolled-up glass, 6" to 23" (152 – 584 mm) high.

A BRIEF HISTORY OF THE ROLL-UP

In 1993, Klaus Moje and Dante Marioni took part in the Connections project at the Bullseye factory in Portland. Together they explored the idea of blowing fused pieces. Moje would make tiles in the kilnforming studio, and Marioni would then pick them up on a bubble of furnace glass in the hotshop. The result was a series of vessels with intense colors and carefully controlled designs that were unlike anything previously achieved through either kilnforming or blowing alone.

While the idea was promising, it still had one major drawback: the furnace and the considerable time and expense associated with maintaining one. Moje continued to explore the technique at the glass workshop he founded at the Australian National University's Canberra School of Art.

In a series of collaborative projects called Latitudes held at Canberra starting in 1995, Moje and glassblower Scott Chaseling adapted the logic of the traditional Venetian murrini-cane pick-up technique. Chaseling and his team picked up Moje's fused tiles on a disc or "collar" of glass at the end of a blowpipe. This collar could be made from sheet glass fired in a kiln, thus eliminating the need for a furnace.

The result has come to be known as the roll-up: blown glass of pure color and carefully controlled design created using only sheet glass, a kiln, a glory hole, and basic hotshop tools. Because furnace glass isn't necessary, the roll-up is accessible to a far broader range of working artists than other blowing methods.

HYBRID PROCESS

This TipSheet describes a hybrid process of fusing and blowing. However, it is not intended to teach anyone how to blow glass. Hotshop and blowing experience are required. We encourage kilnformers to partner with blowers to execute this process.

Tools

- Normal hotshop/blowing equipment, including a glory hole
- At least one kiln that can be used for fusing and pick-ups, and ideally one kiln for annealing
- π divider/calipers
- Ferro(s)
- Pastorale/fork
- Normal kilnforming tools

No furnace required.

Glass

The entire palette of Bullseye compatible colors in sheet glass, frit, stringer, etc., is appropriate for this process. (See notes under Viscosity on page 6 for more information.) In addition, be sure to have some Clear blowing cullet (001501-0066) to make the collar and punty to roll up the kilnformed tile.

THE PROCESS

The Kilnformed Tile

The roll-up begins with a kilnformed tile that measures 8" x 10" (203 x 254 mm) and 3/8" (9 mm) – or three standard sheets – thick. The actual design area is only 6" x 10" (152 x 254 mm), with an 1"-wide (25 mm) strip of clear glass along the top and the bottom edges. This strip of clear will be eliminated in the rolling and blowing process.

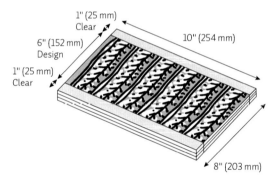

Because glass heated to a full fuse will flow until it reaches a thickness of 6 mm – also known as the 6 mm rule – plan to dam the sides of the tile in the kiln to contain it. Dams can be made from cut-up kiln shelves, soft bricks, vermiculite board, or fiberboard. If using cut-up kiln shelves, coat them shelf primer to keep them from sticking to the glass. After each firing, scrape this material off and reapply it. If working with soft brick, vermiculite, or fiberboard, use strips of fiber paper as gaskets to keep the dams from sticking to the glass.

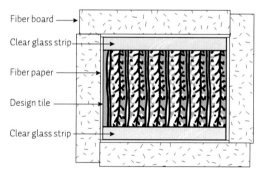

Although all kilns fire differently, we recommend the following full-fuse schedule (for a Paragon GL-24 AD) to fire tiles for rolling up:

Firing Schedule

RATE (DPH)	TEMPERATURE	HOLD
600°F (333°C)	1250°F (677°C)	:30
AFAP[1]	≈1500°F (816°C)	:15
AFAP[2]	900°F (482°C)	:45
100°F (55°C)	700°F (371°C)	:00
AFAP	80°F (27°C)	:00

1 As Fast As Possible – use full power.
2 As Fast As Possible – cut kiln power using controller. We do not advocate crash cooling. Leave the kiln closed, allowing it to cool naturally.

Once the piece is cool and has been at room temperature for 24 hours, bevel the two edges of the tile that will be joined together in the roll-up process. This will ensure that they meet evenly and cleanly for a strong seal. This bevel should be around 30°, but will vary with the size of the piece. The thicker the piece, the more important the bevel will be to properly closing the seam.

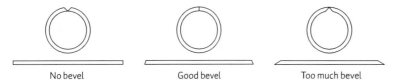

| No bevel | Good bevel | Too much bevel |

Load the beveled tile into a pick-up kiln on a prepared ferro[A] and slowly bring it up to temperature. A front-loading kiln with the shelf at around hip height will be much easier to pull loaded ferros out with the pastorale than a top-loading kiln.

The heat-up schedule for the tiles in the pick-up kiln is:

Heat-Up Schedule

RATE (DPH)	TEMPERATURE	HOLD
350°F (194°C)*	1115°F (600°C)	8:00**

* Thicker tiles will need to be heated at a more conservative rate.

** Hold for at least one hour at 1100°F / 593°C before rolling up the tile. The hold time should correspond with the amount of time it will take to get all of the tiles out of the pick-up kiln.

STARTING THE ROLL-UP

Preparing the Collar

Form a collar of clear glass on the end of a blowpipe.[B] This collar will be used to roll up the kilnformed tile off the ferro. Position the collar just a bit in from the end of the pipe so that heat doesn't close up the hole.

The thickness of the collar should be 1" (25 mm), the same size as the clear glass area on the edges of the kilnformed tile. The diameter of the collar should be the length of the kilnformed tile divided by π (3.14).[C]

Another easy way to determine the diameter of the collar is to use a π divider, or calipers.

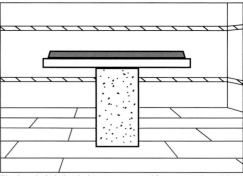

1" (25 mm)

3" (76 mm)

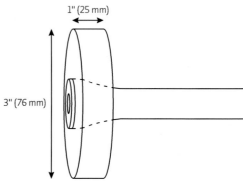

X

Collar diameter = X / π

π Dividers

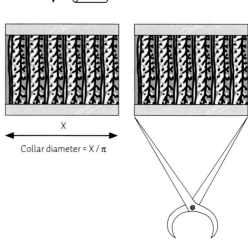

The beveled tile loaded onto a prepared ferro in a pick-up kiln.

A   Traditionally, ferros are made from 1/4" to 3/8" (6 to 9 mm) thick mild steel and prepared with an even layer of fine clay. For the roll-up process, especially when working with tiles thicker than 9 mm, this presents a problem. Invariably, it is difficult to get the kilnformed tile hot enough without also getting the steel ferro so hot that the clay layer spalls off and sticks to the glass. An alternative is to use 1/2" (13 mm) thick kiln shelves. Shelves should be cut so that there is approximately 1/2" of space around the kilnformed tile. For example, an 8" x 10" (203 x 254 mm) tile would require a 9" x 11" (229 x 279 mm) shelf. Mix a batch of separator at 1/3 alumina hydrate, 1/3 china clay, and 1/3 talc by weight and then mix it with water at a 1:5 ratio of separator to water by volume. Apply 5 coats of this mixture to the shelf and then dry it in the kiln at 500°F / 260°C for 20 minutes.

B   If working without furnace glass, you will need to make the collar from cullet. Theoretically, the collar can be made from any glass, because it will be cut off, and therefore need not be made of compatible glass. In practice, however, it should be the same glass as the kilnformed tile because then it will behave in the same way as the rest of the glass on the blowpipe. Have the cullet in a pick-up kiln (this can be the same kiln where the kilnformed tiles are holding at 1115°F / 600°C). Heat the pipe until it is red hot and then pick up a very small chunk of glass. Work that chunk until it is gooey, then use it to pick up a larger chunk of glass on the side of the pipe. Continue in this fashion until you have completed the collar.

C   It is better to err on the small side when making the collar.

When the collar is almost complete, have an assistant remove the kilnformed tile on the ferro from the pick-up kiln with the pastorale and begin to heat it in the glory hole. It is essential that the tile receive even heat, so it may be necessary to pull it out of the glory hole, rotate the ferro 180° on the pastorale, and return it the glory hole. As the tile heats, look for the very beginnings of orange heat and edges that are slightly softened.

At this point, the tile is ready to be rolled up.[D] During repeated heatings in the glory hole, the beveled edges will invariably soften and round-out, losing their angle. Be sure to reestablish the angle of the bevelled edges with a tagliol before attempting to roll up the tile.[E]

Placing the Collar
Roll the tile up along the clear glass that borders the top of the design. Begin about 2.5" (63 mm) in from the beveled edge furthest from your body, rolling the tile towards yourself. Once the collar is 2" (51 mm) from the beveled edge closest to you, stop rolling, lift the piece off the ferro, and bring it to the glory hole to begin heating.

Closing the Seam
After rolling up the tile, heating in the glory hole should be done using a "flipping" technique rather than constant turning. Heat the piece with the open edges of the cylinder face down until it begins to sag and then quickly turn the pipe 180 degrees so that the open edges of the cylinder are face up and the piece begins to sag in the other direction. Continue flipping the piece in this fashion until the piece becomes pliable.

Bring the piece out of the glory hole with the seam facing down, and then flip the seam up when to begin closing the seam. Begin joining the seam at the end furthest from the collar. Use two pairs of pincers to pull the beveled edges together, connecting the inside, front edge first. Then continue to draw the edges together towards the collar to close the seam. Use the back of your pincers or a tagliol to avoid excessive tool marks.

Next heat the piece to a marvering temperature and marver it until the seam is fully incorporated into the body of the vessel. Jacks can be used on the inside of the piece while marvering to smooth the inside seam.

D If the tile is too cold, it will be difficult to roll up and may crack. If the tile is too hot, it will stick to the ferro, or be very sloppy when you roll it up.

E Some practitioners prefer to use very light heats in the glory hole to preserve the beveled edge and to keep the ferro from becoming too hot and sticking to the tile. They rely instead on torching the center of the tile to heat it. This is especially true for thicker Roll-ups.

Process photos taken during development sessions at Bullseye with Klaus Moje, Scott Chaseling and Kirstie Rea. Photographer: Russell Johnson.

Placing the collar...

...and lifting the piece.

Closing the seam.

Closing the Cylinder

Close the cylinder using jacks along the joint between the clear and the design portions of the tile. The clear glass serves both to conserve the design and to hold one end of the cylinder together with a ring of uniform viscosity. Without it, the different glasses in the design can flow at different rates and deform. After the cylinder is closed, cut with diamond shears.

You now have a bubble, and you are blowing glass.

A common alternative to closing the cylinder with jacks is to attach a kilnformed disc to the end of the cylinder to create the bottom of the piece. To do this, the kilnformed disc (on a ferro or shelf) is taken out of the pick-up kiln and heated in the glory hole in essentially the same way that the kilnformed tile was. At the same time, the end of the cylinder is heated so that it will be pliable enough to stick to this disc once it has been adequately heated in the glory hole. Attach by holding the rolled up tile vertically by the blow pipe and then lowering onto the disc. Next, marver the piece to ensure an adequate seal.

Once again, you have a bubble: You are blowing glass.

Annealing

Move the blown pieces to an annealing kiln that is holding at 1000°F (538°C). When you have put away all of the blown work, follow this schedule for pieces rolled-up from 9 mm tiles:

Annealing Schedules

RATE (DPH)	TEMPERATURE	HOLD
AFAP	900°F (482°C)	1:00
75°F (41°C)	700°F (371°C)	:00
AFAP	80°F (27°C)	:00

or

TIME	TEMPERATURE	HOLD
:01	900°F (482°C)	1:00
3:30	700°F (371°C)	:00
:01	80°F (27°C)	:00

A kilnformed disc is taken out of the pick-up kiln...

...heated in the glory hole...

...and attached to the rolled-up tile to close the cylinder.

IMPORTANT CONSIDERATIONS

Viscosity

Different colors of sheet glass have different viscosities. In general, transparent glasses will heat quickly and become very soft, then cool quickly and set up. Opalescent glasses will tend to heat more slowly, but then hold their heat for a longer time. However, Black Opalescent (000100-0030-F) is very soft and responds quickly to heat. To address this, we recommend using Bullseye's Stiff Black Opalescent (000101-0030-F) instead. White Opalescent (000113-0030-F) is stiff and may be slower to respond to heat. Clear (001101-0030-F) will be somewhat stiff, but can be replaced with Clear Blowing Cullet (001501-0066) which is formulated to have a longer working range for blowing.

Glasses of different viscosities will behave differently in the glory hole and in blowing. This can present challenges in terms of controlling shape and form. On the other hand, it can be utilized as a design element (to create a ribbed effect, for example). In the design stage of the tile, before the fusing process, differences in viscosity can be exaggerated or balanced through your choice of glass.

Design

- When you fuse the tile, the side fired against the shelf will appear to be very "tight" and lines will be more straight and crisp than the top surface of the tile. Decide which of these sides you want to be the exterior of the vessel, and lay that side face down on the ferro. Remember that what will eventually be the top of the vessel is the edge along which you will attach the collar and roll up the tile.
- Design with the seam in mind. Many practitioners make the seam a vertical feature in the composition of the roll-up.
- Remember that you may lose a small amount of glass in the beveling process. Furthermore, you may need to vary the angle of the bevel depending on the thickness of your tile.

Yoko Yagi, *Taga Sode III*, 2008. Blown and coldworked murrine glass, 6.5" x 8" x 8".

Marc Petrovic, *Avian Pair*, 2012. Hot sculpted, blown, fused and cold worked glass murrine, 7.75" x 13.75" x 12.75" installed .

Steve Klein, *Exploration* 130, 2009. Kilnformed, blown and cold-worked glass, 6.75" x 16.625" x 17.25" installed.

PLATEMAKING TIPS
FOR WELL-CRAFTED KILNFORMED VESSELS

Plates and platters are popular projects for both advanced and beginning kilnworkers, and platemaking is a perfect way to learn kilnforming's two most frequently used methods: fusing and slumping. The tips shown here are the basic building blocks for more advanced kilnforming methods. Because the object is to make functional plates with smooth surfaces, these notes assume that the first firing will be to full fuse temperatures.

1. Remember the 6 mm rule.

The 6 mm rule states that glass heated to full fuse will flow until it reaches a thickness of 6 mm (1/4"). Therefore, we suggest using two layers of 3 mm glass for your base plate (look for a four-digit suffix of -0030 after the style code). This will keep the overall thickness to about 6 mm (see Figure 1). If you stack higher, the plate will flow out beyond the original footprint (see Figure 2). If you use only a single 3 mm (1/8") base layer, the edges will tend to pull inward (see Figure 3), creating sharp "needle points" around the edge. This setup may also result in the formation of large bubbles if air is trapped between the shelf and the glass. (For more information, see *TechNote 5: Volume and Bubble Control*.)

If you do use a single 3 mm base layer, be sure to completely cover that layer with the equivalent of another layer of glass in some form, such as cut sheet glass, frit, rod, etc. Likewise, you may consider using a 6 mm glass such as Tekta Clear (001100-0680) as your base layer.

Figure 1: Two, 1/8" (3 mm) layers fired to 1500°F (816°C). Notice that the area covered stays the same and the edges are straight.

Figure 2: Five, 1/8" (3 mm) layers fired to 1500°F (816°C). Notice substantial spread in area.

Figure 3: One, 1/8" (3 mm) layer fired to 1500°F (816°C). Notice how the edges pull in.

2. Keep the design elements at least 3/4" (19 mm) from the edge.

Once you have a 6 mm base, use small pieces of thin cut glass, frit, powder, or stringer to create your design. Keep any heavy applications away from the edge. Piling a lot of glass at the perimeter will cause the glass to flow out and distort the shape of your plate at the edge. It may also result in the formation of bubbles between the base layers (see Figure 4). (See also *TechNote 5: Volume and Bubble Control*.)

Figure 4; Stacking glass unevenly and close to edges can result in distortion of the shape of the fired glass.

3. For the cleanest release, use an iridescent glass (coated side down) against the shelf.

Bullseye iridescent glasses (styles with a four-digit suffix of -0031, -0037, or -0038 after the style code) get their metallic sheen from a thin film of tin on the surface. Tin has a higher melting point than glass and on firing will not pick up shelf separators such as primer or the tiny fibers from fiber paper as readily as raw glass. Consider cutting a layer of iridescent glass for your base and using another glass as your top layer. Use a silver iridescent clear (001101-0037-F) base if you do not want the varied coloration of a clear rainbow iridescent (001101-0031-F).

Note that this recommendation applies only when firing on a primed kiln shelf or on fiber paper. We do not recommend firing iridescent surfaces against ThinFire shelf paper. Doing so may result in surface pitting, most frequently in pieces with multiple firings.

4. Master Tip: Put a 45- to 60-minute soak stage into your firing cycle somewhere in the range of 1150-1250°F (621-677°C).

Air bubbles are the most common problem in beginning projects. Soaking your project somewhere in this range allows the top glass to settle onto the bottom glass slowly, pushing any interior pockets of air outward to the edges before they've sealed. You can see this soak segment in the firing schedule shown on page 4.

5. For the sharpest lines and cleanest seams, fire design down.

For the cleanest butt-jointed seams, build your design (of tightly composed pieces) directly onto the shelf or shelf paper and cover with an uncut layer of glass (see Figure 5). The top layer will hold the seams together during firing and leave a virtually invisible seam and crisper lines between colors. The same design laid up on top of the piece will result in softer lines between colors and seams that have pulled apart to reveal the color of the base glass.

Figure 5: The design on the left was fired face down, the design on the right face up. Notice the straight lines between sections of the design on the left.

6. Glass "sandwiches" are recipes for indigestion.

Putting elements of frit, stringer, or cut pieces of sheet between two solid layers of glass will trap air and result in large bubbles (see Figure 6). Instead, place design elements on the top layer of the plate. Or pre-fire them to a sheet glass base, then layer the relatively smooth sheet into your plate. (To learn more, see *Make It Project: Opaline Sushi Set* at bullseyeglass.com).

Figure 6: In firing, the edges of this tile sealed, preventing the escape of air bubbles trapped between stringers.

7. Clean the glass well before firing.

Fingerprints, oil marks and dust fire into the surface of glass and cannot be removed easily after fusing (or slumping). Thoroughly clean the top, bottom, and edge surfaces of the glass before firing. For best results, avoid using cleaners that contain ammonia or detergents.

In this plate, the components are stacked evenly to 6mm (1/4") thick.

8. Place your glass in the middle of your kiln.

Uniform heating is critical. Glass can be heated very quickly if all areas of the glass heat at the same time. But no matter how slowly you heat up your glass, if one edge is right next to an element and the opposite edge is at the (cooler) center of the kiln, you can risk a thermal break. If you must place your glass off-center, or in some fashion in which it will not receive uniform heat treatment, slow the initial rate of heat.

This is the plate after the first, full-fuse firing.

9. Fuse and slump in separate firings.

Full fuse temperatures are much higher than slumping temperatures. If you attempt to fuse and slump in one step by firing to full fuse temperature in a slumping mold, the result will be an extremely misshapen piece of glass with large bubbles or craters. It may also be stuck to the mold (see Figure 8).

The fused plate is placed on the mold prior to the slump firing.

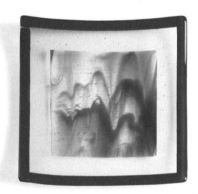

Figure 7: This plate (shown still on the mold) was formed with two separate firings. The first was a full fuse and the second was a slump firing.

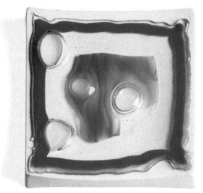

Figure 8: This plate (shown sitting on the mold) was formed with a single firing for both fusing and slumping. This shortcut caused edge distortion and bubbles.

This is the plate after the second, slump firing.

10. Learn from the happy accidents.

Platemaking is simple and can be nearly foolproof if you use Bullseye Compatible glass, conservative firing schedules (see schedules on page 4), and simple designs. But if nothing ever goes wrong, you're not pushing the limits. When you encountering something unexpected, learn from it. Accidents are excellent teachers.

Suggested Firing Schedules

Many variables impact the choice of a firing schedule:

- the heating pattern of the individual kiln
- the accuracy of the temperature recording device
- whether the kiln is top-fired, side-fired or both
- the proximity of glass to the heating elements
- the dimensions and shape of the mold in slump firing

The schedules on this page are provided as starting points and assume that you are working with a 9"-wide (22.8 cm) circle and a kiln that has elements in the ceiling—at least 4" (10 cm) away from the glass during the slump (further on the afuse). These schedules further assume that you work with a programmable controller. They were developed using a Paragon GL24 with top, side, and door elements.

If your plate is larger than 9", or if your kiln's elements are closer than 4" to the glass, or if your kiln heats from the side rather than the top, increase the length of the heating stages (not the hold times). This means slowing the rate of heating. A decrease in rate of 25-50 percent is safe. In the case of your first stage, this means slowing from 400°F (222°C) to about 300°F (167°C) per hour.

Remember, you can always go slower. Firing too fast (i.e., unevenly) can result in breakage from thermal shock.

Slumping should be confirmed visually. Set an alarm for 50°F (28°C) below the process temperature and begin viewing the slumping by occasionally looking through the peephole or door (not the lid!) until the piece is fully slumped. You may need to skip to the next stage or extend the soak to achieve the desired result. Make a note of how long the slumping process took and at what temperature, for use in future firings. Some forms will slump at much lower temperatures than the one that we suggest here. Others may require slightly longer holds at higher temperatures. In general, it is a little better to slump at slightly lower temperatures for slightly longer times, as the glass will be less likely to pick up separators and unwanted details from the mold if it is slumped at a lower temperature.

Additional Resources

Technote 4: Heat and Glass
Mold Tips: Suggested Slumping Schedules

Full Fuse Firing

SEGMENT	RATE (DPH)*	TEMPERATURE	HOLD
1	400°F (222°C)	1225°F (663°C)	1:00
2	600°F (333°C)	1490°F (810°C)	:10
3	AFAP	900°F (482°C)	1:00
4	100°F (56°C)	700°F (371°C)	:00
5	AFAP**	70°F (21°C)	:00

Slump Firing

SEGMENT	RATE (DPH)*	TEMPERATURE	HOLD
1	300°F (167°C)	1225°F (663°C)***	:10
2	AFAP	900°F (482°C)	1:00
3	100°F (56°C)	700°F (371°C)	:00
4	AFAP**	70°F (21°C)	:00

* DPH = degrees per hour
** Allow kiln to cool at its natural rate unless that is greater than 500°F (277°C) per hour.
*** Visually confirm slump.

For more information on firing, see *Technotes 4: Heat and Glass.*

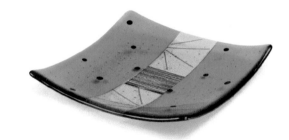

BASIC LOST WAX KILNCASTING

Jim Weiler, *Bullseye Bull*.
Lost wax kilncast glass.

Lost wax kilncasting is a versatile method for making glass pieces in almost any form imaginable. The process involves creating a refractory mold around a wax model. The wax is then removed—or "lost"—creating a cavity. Glass is cast into the cavity, resulting in a fully sculptural finished piece.

What This Tipsheet Covers
This TipSheet covers the steps involved in making a fully sculptural cast glass object using the lost wax process.
- Making a two-layer refractory mold of a wax original
- Steaming out the wax
- Calculating the amount of glass needed
- Curing the mold to ensure better performance
- Preparing the kiln for firing
- Casting the glass into the mold
- Divesting the piece from the mold materials
- Coldworking the finished piece

Measurement Note
All measurements of length, weight, and volume in this TipSheet are metric, a superior system for laboratory work. In measuring volume, 1 cubic centimeter (cm3) of water = 1 milliliter (ml) of water = 1 gram (g) of water. Thus the interior of a container measuring 20 x 20 x 2.5 cm has a volume of 1000 cm3 = 1000 ml of water = 1000 g of water.

The Wax Model
The wax model may be a fully three-dimensional object with undercuts. Ideally, this model is hollow and thus much easier to remove from the mold and less likely to mar or break down the mold. For this TipSheet, we made a wax model of a bull and attached a "funnel" made of wax to the top of the bull's back. During the mold making process, this funnel was at the bottom of the mold. For the kilncasting process, the mold was inverted, the funnel becoming a reservoir into which we loaded the glass. (Figures 1, 9, 10 and footnote 4)

Monolithic vs. Multilayered Molds
Historically, molds for lost wax kilncasting have been "monolithic," or made/poured in one piece. In the Klaus Moje Center for Research and Education (Bullseye's R&E studios), we hand-build molds in two or more layers: a face coat and one or more jacket coats. These multilayered molds are light in weight, with uniform wall thickness around the entire object. This allows for uniform transfer of heat through the mold wall. Multiple layers also create redundancy in the mold: if one layer cracks or fails, there is an intact layer immediately adjacent to it. In contrast, a monolithic mold rarely has uniform wall thickness, requires more material, and introduces more water into the kiln. If a monolithic mold cracks it is more likely to fail completely, allowing glass to flow out of the mold, potentially damaging the kiln.

MATERIALS NEEDED

Glass
Bullseye billets, sheet, or frit

Wax Model
Victory Brown Wax (007064), microcrystalline, paraffin, or beeswax model, preferably hollow

Other
· Rigid plastic sheet, roughly 45.7 x 45.7cm
· Flexible metal rib, available from a ceramics supply store
· Cheap paintbrush
· Bullseye casting investment (1 part 295 mesh silica flour; 1 part #1 Casting Plaster)(008244)
· Bullseye Grog (008770)
· Black plastic investment-mixing buckets
· Lined plastic trashcan
· Bucket of water for initial clean up
· Bucket of water to rinse
· Hairspray
· Wallpaper steamer with steam paddle removed for steaming out wax
· Stand for elevating mold while steaming
· Gloves for handling hot mold
· Metric scale
· Unglazed Italian terra cotta flowerpot with a hole in the bottom (optional)

Figure 1

1. Plasters can be very different in different parts of the world, and this can radically affect the investment recipe and performance.

2. Silica flour expands during firing. This compensates for the plaster, which shrinks during firing.

BUILDING THE MOLD

Preparing the Area
The mold making process involves many steps and is most efficiently executed in a well-organized space. The area for weighing the dry materials should have good ventilation, and you should wear a NIOSH-approved respirator for filtering particulates when working with dry investment.

After reading through this TipSheet to gain perspective on the process, gather the necessary tools.

Affix the wax model to a clean, rigid, plastic sheet and draw a line around it at a distance of about 15 mm from the base. (Figure 1) This line will serve as a guide in making the first layer of the mold, which will be 15 mm thick. A light coating of hairspray on the wax can help the mold material adhere.

Mold Material / Investment Recipes
Kilncasting and mold making are practiced in different ways around the world. There is no one right way to make a mold or one correct recipe for the mold material, or "investment." However, all investment molds for kilncasting are generally composed of three basic ingredients: a binder, a refractory, and modifiers.

A binder is a material used to unite two or more other materials in a mixture. Its principal properties are adhesion and cohesion. At Bullseye we frequently use #1 Casting Plaster as the binder.[1] A refractory is a material that is difficult to melt or work, and that can withstand high temperatures. At Bullseye we use 295-mesh silica flour as our primary refractory material.[2] A modifier is a material used to change the characteristics of the mixture into which it is introduced. Different materials are used as modifiers to serve different purposes. Perlite can be added to a mold recipe to reduce the weight of a large mold. Fiberglass strands are sometimes used to increase the tensile strength of an unfired mold and may allow water to wick out of the mold. Ground up ceramic grog, as an aggregate material, can increase the mechanical strength of the mold. Grog also has refractory properties. At Bullseye, we use grog mixture with particle sizes ranging from 25- to 80-mesh to increase the strength of the outer layer (or layers) of hand-built molds.

We've successfully used the following recipes in Bullseye's R&E studios on a wide variety of cast objects.

The first layer of the mold is called the face coat. The primary purpose of this layer is to pick up as much detail from the wax model as possible. The face coat is composed of a mixture of 50% #1 Casting Plaster and 50% 295 mesh silica flour, by weight. We mix these ingredients with water 70°F (21°C) at a ratio of 1 part water to 2 parts investment, by weight.

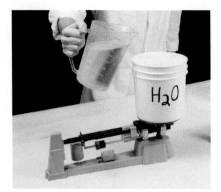

Figure 2   Figure 3   Figure 4

The second layer of the mold is called the jacket coat. Its purpose is to give the mold strength. The jacket coat is composed of the same ingredients (casting plaster and silica powder) plus a mixture of three different sizes of grog at a ratio of 1 part grog mix to 1 part water to 2 parts investment, by weight.

Measuring Investment Material
To determine the amount of investment you need, calculate the dimensions of a box large enough to hold the wax original. This will overestimate the amount you'll actually need, but it's better to have too much than to run out and have to mix more in a rush.

Our model is comprised of two rectilinear forms, the bull and the reservoir, which are roughly 25 x 7 x 12 cm and 15 x 15 x 12 cm respectively, totaling 4800 cubic cm. Divide the number of cubic cm in half and multiply by 0.64 to get the proper quantity of water required: 1536 grams. Multiply this number by 2 to get the proper amount of investment: 3072 grams. Weigh the investment materials in clean, dry buckets. (Figure 2) Be sure to work in a well-ventilated area and wear a NIOSH-approved respirator.

Mixing Investment Material
Steadily sift the investment material into the water. An island of dry material will begin to form once most of the material has been added to the water. Let the investment sit in the water until it is fully hydrated/saturated. Left alone, the investment can sit for quite some time without beginning to set up. After the material has become saturated, break up any chunks by hand. The material should have a creamy consistency.[3] It can then be mixed by hand for 3–5 minutes or with an electric mixer/drill for 1–2 minutes. This mixing will cause the plaster to begin to set.

Applying the Face Coat
Drizzle a thin coating of investment over the wax model and use a paintbrush to pop surface bubbles and work the investment into fine details in the wax. (Figure 3)

After the model has a thin coating over the entire surface, thoroughly clean the brush. This short break will allow the investment to become more viscous as it begins to set.

Building up the first coat to the desired thickness becomes easier as the investment grows more viscous.

Using a flexible metal rib, lift any investment from the work surface back onto the model. Build the face coat out to the line drawn around the base of the wax model. This ensures a thickness of 15 mm. When the investment has become extremely viscous, the first coat should be finished with a rough or toothy texture to which the next layer can readily adhere. (Figure 4) Ideally, the jacket coat is applied soon after the face coat has set. But before mixing up the jacket coat, it is critical to clean the buckets and tools used for making the face coat.

Cleaning Up
The investment buckets and tools and the mold maker's hands should be thoroughly cleaned before the plaster sets and becomes more difficult to remove. Residual plaster on hands and tools will cause subsequent batches of investment to set much more quickly, making it too viscous to capture fine detail. (Tip: black mixing buckets show residual plaster well.) Investment material is never poured into a normal sink, as it will set and clog the pipes. Instead, left-over investment is poured/scooped into a trashcan with a plastic liner. Then two cleaning buckets filled with water are used to clean everything. The first bucket is for scrubbing hands, tools, and buckets completely clean and free of investment. The second bucket is for rinsing them. When these buckets become too filled with waste investment, they are allowed to settle; then the excess water is poured off and the waste investment can be collected in plastic garbage bags.

Mixing Jacket Coat Material
You'll follow the same basic steps as for the first layer of investment, except this coat includes a mixture of ceramic grog for added strength. (See Mold Material / Investment

---

3. Be sure to work with fresh plaster. Plaster has a shelf life after which it may be less effective. If there are hard or sharp chunks in the investment recipe after it has been added to the water, the plaster has likely been exposed to moisture and may not be viable for mold making. If so, discard the plaster and remake the investment with fresh plaster.

Figure 5

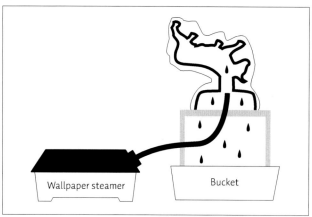

Figure 6

Recipes, page 2.) Blend the grog into the dry plaster/silica mixture before sifting all the dry material into the water. A larger island will form because of the grog, but the material must still become fully saturated before mixing. This investment batch will initially be much thicker than the first batch, but will loosen up and homogenize considerably during mixing.

Applying the Jacket Coat

The second layer can be added much more quickly than the first because the investment material is more viscous and will adhere more readily and because attending to surface detail is no longer necessary. Build this layer up until it covers the first layer by roughly 15 mm all around. Finish the surface by smoothing it with a flexible metal rib. This will make the mold easier to handle and less likely to break. (Figure 5) Clean up as before.

Losing/Removing the Wax

Once the mold is built, you'll remove the wax to leave a cavity into which the glass can be cast. Wait at least one hour after completing the jacket coat before removing the wax. For kilncasting glass, we recommend steaming the wax out with a wallpaper steamer. Elevate the mold with the reservoir facing down and the end of the steam hose inserted into the mold reservoir. (Figure 6) At Bullseye we use a stand that holds the steamer tube in place and allows wax to drip freely. It also provides a view inside the mold. As soon as steam starts coming from the tube, wax will run out of the mold.

The thinner the original wax, the faster the melting process will be. The tube should never touch the surface of the mold, as this could damage the surface and/or drive wax into the investment. Wearing gloves to avoid steam burns, rotate the mold to help wax escape. When no more wax runs out of the mold, remove it from the stand and flush it with water.

Measuring the Mold Cavity Volume

Once the mold is cool to the touch but before it has cured, calculate the volume of the cavity. (Figure 7)

Fill a container with clean water to a level higher than needed to fill the mold cavity to the desired level.[4] Weigh the water and record the weight in grams, then pour water into the mold until it reaches the level of the final casting (and then drain this water into a separate bucket or sink). Weigh the water container again and calculate the difference. The result is the amount of water needed (in grams) to fill the mold to the desired level. To translate the amount of water into glass, multiply this number by 2.5 (the specific gravity of Bullseye glass). The resulting number is how much glass you will need to fill the mold. Write this number in pencil on the lip of the mold reservoir as a reminder.

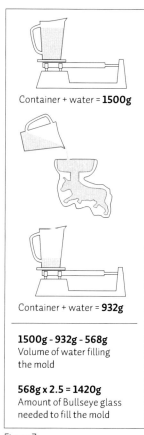

Container + water = **1500g**

Container + water = **932g**

1500g - 932g - 568g
Volume of water filling the mold

568g x 2.5 = 1420g
Amount of Bullseye glass needed to fill the mold

Figure 7

4. At Bullseye, we generally plan to fill the mold so the reservoir will be the thickest area of the casting. This helps reduce the incidence of "suckers," or scars that form when the glass pulls away from the mold forming depressions in the final object. Suckers usually form in the area of the glass that remains the hottest for the longest during the cooling cycle, becoming a focal point for shrinkage in the material. The thickest and/or most heavily insulated area of the casting is usually where the glass remains the hottest during the cooling cycle. Since the reservoir is typically cut off or removed from the finished casting, it is the ideal place for such shrinkage to concentrate, often forming a meniscus. Filling the reservoir with glass to a certain point also has the added benefit of providing increased head pressure that will help glass flow completely into the mold during process temperature.

Figure 8

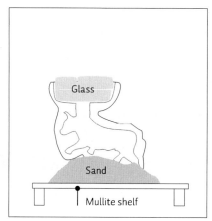

Figure 9

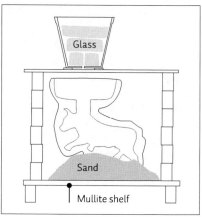

Figure 10

Curing the Mold

Much like concrete, plaster in the investment needs to remain moist while setting up. At Bullseye we wrap our molds in plastic for 24-48 hours, which gives the plaster a chance to cure and increases the green or unfired strength of the mold. (Figure 8)

Drying the Mold

Before the mold is fired, it should be dried either in a mold dryer or ambient conditions. We have observed that this practice often results in a finished casting with an extremely lucid surface. Also, firing wet molds releases a lot of water that will attack/rust the structure of the kiln and deposit contaminants on the glass. If there is not sufficient time to dry the mold before loading it into the kiln, incorporate the drying step into the firing program.

SELECTING THE GLASS

You can cast with any form of Bullseye glass (billet, cullet, sheet, frit, etc.), but the form selected will have a direct impact on the clarity of the casting.

Powders and fine frits trap large numbers of air bubbles—so many that even our Crystal Clear (001401) will appear milky white and opalescent when cast. Billets, on the other hand, trap fewer air bubbles and result in castings of greater clarity and transparency.

Color is another major consideration when selecting glass. Most of Bullseye's original transparent colors were developed to have their full color intensity at thicknesses of 3–6 mm. Many of these colors, when used at full strength in thicker works, appear very dark. Others, such as Yellow (001120), Red (001122), and Orange (001125), may opalize during the longer hold times at higher temperatures required for kilncasting.

Our 001800 and 001900 series of casting tints were specifically developed to create colors that would be of lighter saturation and greater stability at these thicknesses and temperatures. Or our standard palette can be used to tint Clear (001101) as described in our technical article *Frit Tinting* (available on bullseyeglass.com).

FIRING THE MOLD AND GLASS

Loading the Kiln

To aid in uniform heating and cooling, place the mold on a 15-mm-thick mullite shelf elevated on 50-mm posts nestled in a mound of sand. The sand will stabilize the mold and make it easier to level. Once the mold is level, it is ready to be loaded with glass. (Figure 9) The height of some kilns makes it difficult to load the mold once it is in the kiln. In that case, load the glass outside the kiln and then level the mold in the kiln. The glass should be thoroughly cleaned before loading.

An alternative to loading glass directly into the mold is to load it into a crucible above the mold. (Figure 10) An unglazed US- or Italian-made terra cotta flowerpot makes an ideal, affordable crucible.[5] Before loading the pot with glass, use a rattail file to enlarge the hole in the bottom to about 16 mm. Remove small shards that could flow into the casting, and wipe the pot with a damp cloth to remove dust. A portion of glass will inevitably stick to the crucible, so you'll need to increase the amount of glass by 10 percent.

The advantage of casting through a crucible is that it keeps the glass away from the mold during the heating process, when water vapor is being driven out of the mold. Contaminants in this vapor can seed devitrification or cause the glass to haze. It can also change the surface tension of the glass, making it flow more slowly or not at all. Furthermore, glass is heavy and may have sharp edges. Loading glass directly into a mold (especially if freshly made) can damage details and break off small pieces of

---

5. Mexican terra cotta flowerpots have repeatedly failed when used for this purpose and are not recommended.

mold material that can become trapped in the finished casting. The primary disadvantages of working with a crucible are the loss of some material in the crucible and the added height required in the kiln.

At Bullseye, we have successfully cast objects using both the crucible and non-crucible methods.

Firing

There are three major considerations when developing a firing cycle for lost wax kilncasting:

- Glass and kiln conditions
- Mold materials
- Timing the firing

Glass and Kiln Conditions

The firing cycle as it relates to glass and kiln conditions is covered in depth in *TechNotes 4: Heat and Glass*. We recommend reviewing that article.

One additional consideration area not fully addressed in *TechNotes 4*, however, is the issue of "charging," or adding glass to a hot mold. This is sometimes necessary if you aren't able to load all of the glass at the beginning of the firing. The primary concern here is that certain glasses—such as Ruby Red Tint (001824) and other gold-bearing glasses—if heated too rapidly, will develop a sapphirine quality instead of their intended color. If you need to charge such a glass into the mold, it should be preheated in a separate kiln to 1225°F (663°C), held for two hours, and transferred hot into the mold or crucible.

Mold Materials

The firing cycle as it relates to the mold materials involves four basic tasks.

1. Removing interstitial water. This task occurs from room temp to 212°F (100°C). During this phase of the firing, you're trying to drive water out without boiling it. Boiling the water may create small fractures throughout the mold, causing it to weaken and potentially fail when the glass is flowing and exerting outward pressure on the mold wall. Boiling also seems to degrade the mold in general, producing a rougher surface in the finished casting. To avoid boiling the water, hold at 200°F (93°C) (below the boiling point) until you're confident all of the interstitial or free water has been driven from the mold. Vent the kiln during this phase and through 1100°F (593°C) to make certain that water vapor can easily escape the kiln and will not attack the kiln's frame (causing rust) or deposit contaminants on the glass.

2. Removing chemically bound water. This task occurs from 212°F (100°C) to around 350°F (177°C). During this phase of the firing we are trying to drive out chemically bound water, again without boiling it. To avoid boiling, fire at a slow rate of 100°F (55°C) per hour from 200°F (93°C) to 1225°F (663°C).

3. Heating evenly through the quartz inversion zone. This occurs at about 1100°F (593°C). At this point in the firing the silica and the grog (and possibly other modifiers in the mold) suddenly expand in size. It is important that all of these materials go through this sudden change at the same time. If not, strain can develop that may result in the mold cracking. Again, fire at a slow rate of 100°F (55°C) per hour to achieve uniform heating.

4. Employing a low process temperature. The plaster loses much of its integrity above 1100°F (593°C), making the mold progressively weaker the hotter it's fired. Also, the hotter the mold is fired the more likely it is to stick to the glass. Finally, though it seems somewhat counterintuitive, firing to temperatures higher than 1550°F (843°C) can, in some instances, actually make the glass flow more slowly. This is because the hotter the mold and the glass are fired, the more they react with one another. This reaction can cause the surface tension of the glass to increase.

Timing the Firing

In timing the firing, plan to be present at the following key times.

1. At 1100°F (593°C), close the vents. Up to this point, the vents will need to be open to allow water and organic materials burning out of the mold to exit the kiln.

2. At 1225°F (633°C), confirm that the mold is stable and no cracks have formed. To do this, open the kiln enough to take a quick look, then close the door and think about what you've seen (holding the door open for a long time could thermal shock and crack the mold). Check the mold several times at this temperature. If it remains stable and no cracks have formed, it is safe to proceed to the casting/process temperature. If the mold is cracking, however, it may fail at casting/process temperature, and you may need to consider aborting the firing at this point.

3. At process temperature, confirm:

   - The integrity of the mold. If the mold fails seriously at this temperature you have limited time to halt the firing to prevent the glass from flowing out of the mold. This could potentially damage or destroy your kiln. Again take quick looks, close the door, and think about what you have seen.
   - That the glass has flowed and filled the mold cavity.
   - That any unwanted visible bubbles have risen, popped, and healed.

4. Throughout the annealing process, to monitor and record multiple thermocouples and make adjustments. For more information see *TechNotes 7: Monitoring Kiln Temperatures for Successful Annealing*.

Typical Cycle

STEP	PURPOSE	RATE (degrees per hour)	TEMPERATURE	HOLD
1	Initial heat, remove physical water	100°F (55°C)	200°F (93°C)	6:00
2	Initial heat, remove chemical water, Quartz Inversion, pre-rapid heat soak	100°F (55°C)	1250°F (677°C)	2:00
3	Rapid heat, process hold	600°F (333°C)	1525°F (830°C)	3:00*
4	Rapid cool and anti-sucker soak	AFAP**	1150–1250°F (596–677°C)	4:00***
5	Anti-sucker cool, anneal soak	50°F (27.7°C)	900°F (482°C)	6:00
6	1st anneal cool	12°F (6.7°C)	800°F (427°C)	:01
7	2nd anneal cool	22°F (12°C)	700°F (371°C)	:01
8	Final cool	72°F (40°C)	70°F (21°C)	:01

* Visually confirm process hold time.

** "As Fast As Possible" Specifically: allow the kiln to cool at its natural rate with the door closed. Do not crash cool by opening the kiln door.

*** The anti-sucker processes can be performed in a variety of methods and through a range of temperatures; however, the most important aspect of this step is to cool the glass uniformly while it is experiencing its most dramatic rate of shrinkage/contraction.

Divesting and Cleaning the Glass

Once the entire firing cycle is complete, we recommend leaving the piece in the kiln at room temperature for at least a day before divesting. Remove it from the kiln carefully. After firing, the mold will be considerably weaker and no longer structurally sound.

Be sure to wear proper safety equipment, including a respirator to protect you from the plaster and silica particles. Ideally, you should divest the casting in an area with local ventilation, as many of the finer dusts generated may remain airborne for hours. Safety glasses and gloves will protect you from the jagged edges that can result from glass hanging up as it flows into the mold from the reservoir.

You can remove the investment material with a variety of tools, including dental instruments, wooden picks, nylon brushes, and wood carving tools. (Figure 11) We recommend wooden or hard plastic tools. Metal tools should be used carefully, as they can scratch or chip the casting. A nylon bristle brush and forced air are also great tools for cleaning areas of residual investment. Most of the investment should be removed from the glass before submerging it in or scrubbing it with water. (Figure 12) While water can be used to rinse away residual investment, we have found that scrubbing the glass with vinegar and/or CLR[6] breaks down residual investment material.

6. Calcium Lime Rust, commonly known as CLR, is a household product used for dissolving calcium, lime, and iron oxide deposits.

Figure 11

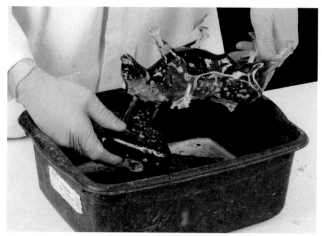

Figure 12

Coldworking

If the cast glass object includes a reservoir that needs to be removed (Figure 13), this can be taken off with a wet tile saw with a diamond blade, or it can be ground off using rotary tools.

Coldworking presents a myriad of possibilities, but first a word of caution: the casting should be at room temperature for a day before attempting any coldworking. A casting that feels cool on the exterior may be considerably warmer on the interior. If subjected to cold water, the exterior will contract around the interior, which will not be able to yield, and the piece may crack.

Figure 13

Studio Tips

⊚ Annealing Thick Slabs (Celsius, rates in degrees per hour)

This annealing chart has been formulated for use with Bullseye clear glass.* It only applies to flat slabs of uniform thickness positioned to cool evenly from top and bottom. If your work is not positioned to cool evenly from top and bottom or is anything besides a flat slab of uniform thickness, select the annealing cycle listed for pieces twice the thickness of your work's thickest area. Please note, however: even the most conservative annealing cycle may fail if the kiln cannot cool the work uniformly. For more information, see TechNotes 7: Monitoring Kiln Temperatures for Successful Annealing at www.bullseyeglass.com.

ANNEALING PIECES OF UNIFORM THICKNESS (RATES IN DEGREES PER HOUR)

THICKNESS	RATE	TEMP	ANNEAL SOAK TIME	HOLD	1ST COOLING RATE	TEMP	HOLD	2ND COOLING RATE	TEMP	HOLD	FINAL COOLING RATE**	TEMP	HOLD	TOTAL
6mm	AFAP	482	1:00	:00	83	427	:00	150	371	:00	500	21	:00	~3:00
12mm	AFAP	482	2:00	:00	55	427	:00	99	371	:00	330	21	:00	~5:00
19mm	AFAP	482	3:00	:00	25	427	:00	45	371	:00	150	21	:00	~9:00
25mm	AFAP	482	4:00	:00	15	427	:00	27	371	:00	90	21	:00	~14:00
38mm	AFAP	482	6:00	:00	6.7	427	:00	12	371	:00	40	21	:00	~28:00
50mm	AFAP	482	8:00	:00	3.8	427	:00	6.7	371	:00	22	21	:00	~47:00
62mm	AFAP	482	10:00	:00	2.4	427	:00	4.3	371	:00	14.4	21	:00	~70:00
75mm	AFAP	482	12:00	:00	1.7	427	:00	3.1	371	:00	10	21	:00	~99:00
100mm	AFAP	482	16:00	:00	0.94	427	:00	1.7	371	:00	5.6	21	:00	~170:00
150mm	AFAP	482	24:00	:00	0.42	427	:00	0.76	371	:00	2.5	21	:00	~375:00
200mm	AFAP	482	32:00	:00	0.23	427	:00	0.42	371	:00	1.4	21	:00	~654:00

*This chart is derived from Corning's method as shown in McLellan and Shand (1984), Glass Engineering Handbook, 3rd Edition, New York, McGraw Hill

**Your kiln may cool more slowly than this rate, and if so it may display an FTC (Failed To Cool) or FTL (Firing To Long) error message. These messages do not affect the firing.

HOW TO READ THIS CHART IN 5 STEPS

1. Choose a chart from either side of this form based on your preference for units used to express cooling times: Rates in Degrees Per Hour or Rates in Time to Temperature.
2. Calculate the final post-fired thickness of your slab.
3. Match that thickness with the size options listed in the chart's far left column.
4. Focus on the row to the right of your piece's listed thickness. This is now your focal row; it contains all information necessary to successfully anneal your slab.
5. Notice the chart's top row. The boxes in the top row explain the information in the columns below them. Intersect your focal row with the top row to interpret the chart.

As an example expressed in Bullseye's standard chart style, a 50mm slab of uniform thickness would follow this annealing cycle:

Rate	Temperature	Hold
AFAP	482°C	8:00
3.8	427°C	:00
6.7	371°C	:00
22	21°C	:00

Annealing Thick Slabs (Celsius, rates in time to temperature)

This annealing chart has been formulated for use with Bullseye clear glass.* It only applies to flat slabs of uniform thickness positioned to cool evenly from top and bottom. If your work is not positioned to cool evenly from top and bottom or is anything besides a flat slab of uniform thickness, select the annealing cycle listed for pieces twice the thickness of your work's thickest area. Please note, however: even the most conservative annealing cycle may fail if the kiln cannot cool the work uniformly. For more information, see *TechNotes 7: Monitoring Kiln Temperatures for Successful Annealing* at www.bullseyeglass.com.

ANNEALING PIECES OF UNIFORM THICKNESS (RATES IN TIME TO TEMPERATURE)

THICKNESS	RATE	TEMP	HOLD/ ANNEAL SOAK TIME	1ST COOLING TIME	TEMP	HOLD	RATE/2ND COOLING RATE	TEMP	HOLD	RATE/FINAL COOLING RATE**	TEMP	HOLD	TOTAL MINIMUM TIME
6mm	AFAP	482	1:00	0:40	427	:00	0:22	371	:00	0:42	21	:00	~3:00
12mm	AFAP	482	2:00	1:00	427	:00	0:33	371	:00	1:03	21	:00	~5:00
19mm	AFAP	482	3:00	2:13	427	:00	1:14	371	:00	2:20	21	:00	~9:00
25mm	AFAP	482	4:00	3:42	427	:00	2:02	371	:00	3:53	21	:00	~14:00
38mm	AFAP	482	6:00	8:20	427	:00	4:32	371	:00	8:45	21	:00	~28:00
50mm	AFAP	482	8:00	14:42	427	:00	8:20	371	:00	15:22	21	:00	~47:00
62mm	AFAP	482	10:00	25:15	427	:00	12:30	371	:00	24:14	21	:00	~70:00
75mm	AFAP	482	12:00	33:20	427	:00	18:30	371	:00	35:00	21	:00	~99:00
100mm	AFAP	482	16:00	58:49	427	:00	32:15	371	:00	63:00	21	:00	~170:00
150mm	AFAP	482	24:00	133:20	427	:00	76:55	371	:00	140:00	21	:00	~375:00
200mm	AFAP	482	32:00	238:05	427	:00	131:34	371	:00	252:00	21	:00	~654:00

*This chart is derived from Corning's method as shown in McLellan and Shand (1984), Glass Engineering Handbook, 3rd Edition, New York, New York, McGraw Hill.

**Your kiln may cool more slowly than this rate, and if so it may display an FTC (Failed To Cool) or FTL (Firing To Long) error message. These messages do not affect the firing.

HOW TO READ THIS CHART IN 5 STEPS

1. Choose a chart from either side of this form based on your preference for units used to express cooling times: Rates in Degrees Per Hour or Rates in Time to Temperature.
2. Calculate the final post-fired thickness of your slab.
3. Match that thickness with the size options listed in the chart's far left column.
4. Focus on the row to the right of your piece's listed thickness. This is now your focal row; it contains all information necessary to successfully anneal your slab.
5. Notice the chart's top row. The boxes in the top row explain the information in the columns below them. Intersect your focal row with the top row to interpret the chart.

As an example expressed in Bullseye's standard chart style, a 50mm slab of uniform thickness would follow this annealing cycle:

Rate	Temperature	Hold
AFAP	482°C	8:00
14:42	427°C	:00
8:20	371°C	:00
15:22	21°C	:00

◎ Annealing Thick Slabs (Fahrenheit, rates in degrees per hour)

This annealing chart has been formulated for use with Bullseye clear glass.* It only applies to flat slabs of uniform thickness positioned to cool evenly from top and bottom. If your work is not positioned to cool evenly from top and bottom or is anything besides a flat slab of uniform thickness, select the annealing cycle listed for pieces twice the thickness of your work's thickest area. Please note, however: even the most conservative annealing cycle may fail if the kiln cannot cool the work uniformly. For more information, see TechNotes 7: Monitoring Kiln Temperatures for Successful Annealing at www.bullseyeglass.com.

ANNEALING PIECES OF UNIFORM THICKNESS (RATES IN DEGREES PER HOUR)

THICKNESS	RATE	TEMP	ANNEAL SOAK TIME	1ST COOLING RATE	TEMP	HOLD	2ND COOLING RATE	TEMP	HOLD	FINAL COOLING RATE**	TEMP	HOLD	TOTAL
0.25"/6mm	AFAP	900	1:00	150	800	:00	270	700	:00	900	70	:00	~3:00
0.5"/12mm	AFAP	900	2:00	100	800	:00	180	700	:00	600	70	:00	~5:00
0.75"/19mm	AFAP	900	3:00	45	800	:00	81	700	:00	270	70	:00	~9:00
1"/25mm	AFAP	900	4:00	27	800	:00	49	700	:00	162	70	:00	~14:00
1.5"/38mm	AFAP	900	6:00	12	800	:00	22	700	:00	72	70	:00	~28:00
2"/50mm	AFAP	900	8:00	6.8	800	:00	12	700	:00	41	70	:00	~47:00
2.5"/62mm	AFAP	900	10:00	4.3	800	:00	8	700	:00	26	70	:00	~70:00
3"/75mm	AFAP	900	12:00	3	800	:00	5.4	700	:00	18	70	:00	~99:00
4"/100mm	AFAP	900	16:00	1.7	800	:00	3.1	700	:00	10	70	:00	~170:00
6"/150mm	AFAP	900	24:00	0.75	800	:00	1.3	700	:00	4.5	70	:00	~375:00
8"/200mm	AFAP	900	32:00	0.42	800	:00	0.76	700	:00	2.5	70	:00	~654:00

*This chart is derived from Corning's method as shown in McLellan and Shand (1984), Glass Engineering Handbook, 3rd Edition, New York, McGraw Hill.

**Your kiln may cool more slowly than this rate, and if so it may display an FTC (Failed To Cool) or FTL (Firing To Long) error message. These messages do not affect the firing.

HOW TO READ THIS CHART IN 5 STEPS

1. Choose a chart from either side of this form based on your preference for units used to express cooling times: Rates in Degrees Per Hour or Rates in Time to Temperature.
2. Calculate the final post-fired thickness of your slab.
3. Match that thickness with the size options listed in the chart's far left column.
4. Focus on the row to the right of your piece's listed thickness. This is now your focal row; it contains all information necessary to successfully anneal your slab.
5. Notice the chart's top row. The boxes in the top row explain the information in the columns below them. Intersect your focal row with the top row to interpret the chart.

As an example expressed in Bullseye's standard chart style, a 2" slab of uniform thickness would follow this annealing cycle:

Rate	Temperature	Hold
AFAP	900°F	8:00
6.8	800°F	:00
12	700°F	:00
41	70°F	:00

◎ Annealing Thick Slabs (Fahrenheit, rates in time to temperature)

This annealing chart has been formulated for use with Bullseye clear glass.* It only applies to flat slabs of uniform thickness positioned to cool evenly from top and bottom. If your work is not positioned to cool evenly from top and bottom or is anything besides a flat slab of uniform thickness, select the annealing cycle listed for pieces twice the thickness of your work's thickest area. Please note, however: even the most conservative annealing cycle may fail if the kiln cannot cool the work uniformly. For more information, see TechNotes 7: Monitoring Kiln Temperatures for Successful Annealing at www.bullseyeglass.com.

ANNEALING PIECES OF UNIFORM THICKNESS (RATES IN TIME TO TEMPERATURE)

THICKNESS	RATE	TEMP	HOLD/ ANNEAL SOAK TIME	1ST COOLING TIME	TEMP	HOLD	RATE/2ND COOLING RATE	TEMP	HOLD	RATE/FINAL COOLING RATE**	TEMP	HOLD	TOTAL MINIMUM TIME
0.25"/6mm	AFAP	900	1:00	0:40	800	:00	0:22	700	:00	0:42	70	:00	~3:00
0.5"/12mm	AFAP	900	2:00	1:00	800	:00	0:33	700	:00	1:03	70	:00	~5:00
0.75"/19mm	AFAP	900	3:00	2:13	800	:00	1:14	700	:00	2:20	70	:00	~9:00
1"/25mm	AFAP	900	4:00	3:42	800	:00	2:02	700	:00	3:53	70	:00	~14:00
1.5"/38mm	AFAP	900	6:00	8:20	800	:00	4:32	700	:00	8:45	70	:00	~28:00
2"/50mm	AFAP	900	8:00	14:42	800	:00	8:20	700	:00	15:22	70	:00	~47:00
2.5"/62mm	AFAP	900	10:00	25:15	800	:00	12:30	700	:00	24:14	70	:00	~70:00
3"/75mm	AFAP	900	12:00	33:20	800	:00	18:30	700	:00	35:00	70	:00	~99:00
4"/100mm	AFAP	900	16:00	58:49	800	:00	32:15	700	:00	63:00	70	:00	~170:00
6"/150mm	AFAP	900	24:00	133:20	800	:00	76:55	700	:00	140:00	70	:00	~375:00
8"/200mm	AFAP	900	32:00	238:05	800	:00	131:34	700	:00	252:00	70	:00	~654:00

*This chart is derived from Corning's method as shown in McLellan and Shand (1984), Glass Engineering Handbook, 3rd Edition, New York, McGraw Hill.

**Your kiln may cool more slowly than this rate, and if so it may display an FTC (Failed To Cool) or FTL (Firing To Long) error message. These messages do not affect the firing.

HOW TO READ THIS CHART IN 5 STEPS

1. Choose a chart from either side of this form based on your preference for units used to express cooling times: Rates in Degrees Per Hour or Rates in Time to Temperature.
2. Calculate the final post-fired thickness of your slab.
3. Match that thickness with the size options listed in the chart's far left column.
4. Focus on the row to the right of your piece's listed thickness. This is now your focal row; it contains all information necessary to successfully anneal your slab.
5. Notice the chart's top row. The boxes in the top row explain the information in the columns below them. Intersect your focal row with the top row to interpret the chart.

As an example expressed in Bullseye's standard chart style, a 2" slab of uniform thickness would follow this annealing cycle:

Rate	Temperature	Hold
AFAP	900°F	8:00
14:42	800°F	:00
8:20	700°F	:00
15:22	70°F	:00

GLASS CLEANING BASICS

Cleaning glass before firing it removes problem-causing contaminants like glass-cutting fluid, oils, minerals, salts, dusts, fibers, sticker residues, fingerprints, and pen marks. If these substances are not washed from glass before it is fired, they may be visible in the finished glass or may cause devitrification—the growth of crystalline structures on the glass.

TIPS FOR CLEANING GLASS
Cleaning agents
It is important to use a cleaning agent that will loosen oils, minerals, and organic materials without depositing a problematic residue. Detergents, ammonia, and denatured alcohol all leave behind residues that can cause devitrification. Household products that contain these ingredients—such as dish soaps, multi-purpose cleaners and some window cleaners—should not be used to clean your glass.

At Bullseye, we clean all of our glass with Spartan Window Cleaner (008236).* Other window cleaners may work for you. Always test off-the-shelf products to make sure they clean glass well and do not cause devitrification. Conduct separate tests on transparent and opalescent glasses, as they may react to products differently.

Towels
For wiping glass clean, we recommend using kitchen towels made of lint-free cotton. White is a good color choice because it shows dirt well. Keep an ample supply on hand so you can change towels often as you work. Always use towels that are clean to avoid smearing dirt and residues from one part of the glass to another.

At Bullseye, we do not clean glass with paper towels because they can lack durability, contain problematic additives, and waste natural resources.

Process
Start the cleaning process by washing away sticker residues and pen marks. These substances are especially problematic and easy to smear on the glass. Spray glass cleaner on sticker and pen residues and allow the puddles to sit for a minute or two. Wipe away the loosened debris with a towel that is designated for this step in the process only. (Do not use this towel to clean the rest of the glass.) Check the glass from several angles against light and dark backgrounds to be sure you've completely removed glue and pen debris from the top, bottom, and edge surfaces. If residues remain, clean the glass again, applying more pressure.

Next, spray the entire bottom surface of the glass with cleaning agent. Wipe it vigorously with a clean towel, taking care that your bare fingers and hands do not touch the glass. Once you have cleaned the bottom surface of the glass in this fashion, buff it dry with a fresh, dry towel. (Buffing removes residual glass cleaner, which can cause devitrification.) Repeat these steps to clean the top and edge surfaces of the glass. When finished, inspect the glass from a variety of angles. If residues remain, clean the glass again, applying more pressure.

Coldworked edges can be especially difficult to clean because abraded surfaces tend to trap contaminants. Edges that are coldworked to a smooth or polished finish are easier to clean.

KEEPING GLASS CLEAN
If possible, load clean glass directly into the kiln to protect it from dust and other contaminants. If you must leave your cleaned glass outside the kiln for several hours before firing, protect it with a cover.

When loading glass into the kiln, handle only the edges. Be sure that your hands are clean. When we use disposable gloves at Bullseye, we put them on and then wipe them clean with glass cleaner and a towel prior to handling glass because they can be covered with powders that cause devitrification.

It is easier to keep glass clean if your studio is clean. Take care to vacuum and wipe work surfaces regularly, controlling problem-causing particles as well as you can. Isolate dusts from ceramic work, mold making, and shelf preparation. The same goes for metal shavings, sawdust, and particles from fiber paper and ThinFire.

LAUNDERING TOWELS
Detergents, fabric softeners, and dryer sheets contain compounds that can promote devitrification. When laundering studio towels, use detergent that is free of perfumes and dyes, and be sure to rinse thoroughly. Do not add fabric softener. Do not dry the towels with dryer sheets or in an appliance in which dryer sheets are used regularly. Do not wash studio towels with your regular laundry. Mixing these could contaminate your regular laundry with glass shards and your studio towels with laundry residues.

*For sale as a concentrate through Bullseye Glass Co. and other distributors

◎ 12 Ways to Improve Your Cutting

1. **BUY THE BEST CUTTER YOU CAN AFFORD.**
   If it helps you to cut accurately and comfortably, it will save you money in the long run. Look for a cutter with a comfortable handle and a high-quality, long-lasting wheel made of carbide steel. Inexpensive cutters designed for scoring float glass have neither of these features.

   A handle with a rest for the index finger will let you apply pressure down onto the score. A wide housing will allow your middle finger to guide the wheel. (*Figure 1*)

2. **ALWAYS USE A CUTTING LUBRICANT.**
   Cutting oil is the best lubricant. Use it to fill a self-lubricating cutter, dip your cutter into the oil, or apply the oil with a brush. (*Figure 2*) Remember to clean away the oil completely before firing the glass because any residue can cause devitrification. Some kilnworkers prefer to use mineral spirits for lubrication because it's easier to clean than oil. However, cutting oil is a smoother lubricant and is not difficult to clean. Oil is also less harmful to skin and doesn't smell.

3. **USE THE CORRECT WHEEL FOR THE GLASS.**
   The size of the wheel determines how much pressure you need to penetrate the surface of the glass. The smaller the wheel, the less pressure is needed. Small wheels with a diameter of about 1/10th of an inch (like those on the Silberschnitt 2000 and Toyo cutters) are best for thin and standard thickness art glass.

   The angle of the wheel also affects the pressure needed. For cutting most glasses up to 10mm (≈ .375") thick, we recommend the versatility of 135° angle. For 2mm (.0625") thin sheets a 120° is excellent. For glasses thicker than 10mm, a 160° angle is appropriate. (*Figure 3*)

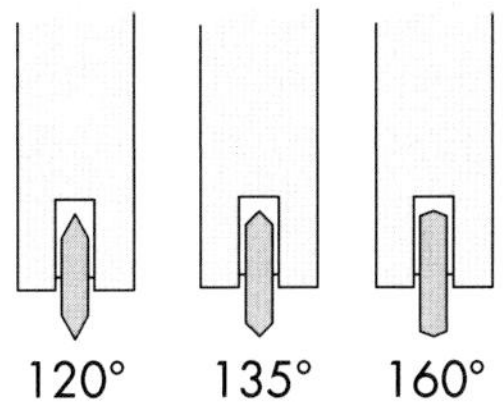

4. **MAKE SURE THE TEMPERATURE OF YOUR GLASS IS OPTIMAL FOR CUTTING.**
   When glass is cold, it can become more difficult to cut. Comfortable room temperature conditions are favorable. If your glass is cold, consider warming it up before attempting to cut it.

5. **WORK WITH YOUR FULL BODY.**
   For the most uniform score, stand up and away from the worktable. Keep the cutter wheel perpendicular to the glass with the handle held upright or slightly angled back toward your body. Then move your whole body—not just your arm or hand—for the most uniform score. (*Figure 4*)

   When scoring severe curves, work at the corner of your worktable and move around the table as you cut.

6. **SCORE THE SMOOTHER SIDE OF YOUR GLASS.**
   With art glass, often one side is smoother than the other. You'll find that scoring on the smoother surface is easier and leads to cleaner breaks.

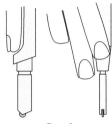

Figure 1

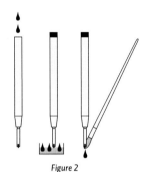

Figure 2

Figure 3

120°   135°   160°

Figure 4

7. **IF POSSIBLE, POSITION YOUR SCORE SO THAT THERE IS AN EQUAL MASS OF GLASS ON EITHER SIDE OF THE SCORE.**

    Otherwise, the break below the scoreline will naturally tend to move to the side where there is less glass, resulting in an edge that flares out from your score on the bottom side of the sheet. (*Figure 5*)

    If you're cutting numerous thin strips, start with a piece that is four times as wide as the strips you need. Cut it exactly in half. Then cut each half in half. (*Figure 6*) By always keeping an equal amount of glass on each side of your score line, you can get perfect strips that are as narrow as the glass is thick.

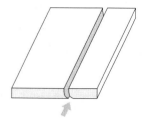

Figure 5

8. **CONCENTRATE ON APPLYING UNIFORM PRESSURE AND USING CONSISTENT SPEED.**

    Listen for a smooth consistent sound as you score. It should not be scratchy. However, when scoring opalescent glasses with the correct amount of pressure, you may hear no sound at all.

    Want to compare the pressure needed for different cutters or different glasses? Try putting your glass on a scale while you score. (*Figure 7*) Notice the difference in "weight" required.

Figure 6

9. **NEVER SCORE TWICE OVER THE SAME PATH.**

    If you make a bad score, do not re-score the same line on the same side of the glass. You'll dull the cutter wheel and lessen your chances for a clean break.

    If you absolutely must break the glass along a line that is poorly scored, turn the glass over and very carefully score along the same line. Then break it as usual.

10. **WHEN CUTTING CURVES, CONSIDER RUNNING YOUR SCORE FROM THE INTERIOR OF THE SHEET.**

    Consider how glass naturally breaks when you start to run a score. It tends to run as directly as possible to the edge of the piece. Therefore, if possible, when cutting complex shapes, start running your complex curves or circles away from the edge. (*Figure 8*)

Figure 7

11. **AVOID TAPPING WHENEVER POSSIBLE.**

    Tapping almost always leaves a jagged edge. But if you must, tap directly under the score line to minimize flared edges. (*Figure 9*)

12. **BREAK OUT YOUR GLASS IMMEDIATELY AFTER SCORING.**

    If allowed to sit too long, a scoreline will begin to develop fractures radiating along its entire length. Such fractures make it nearly impossible to run the score cleanly.

These tips are courtesy of Rudi Gritsch of the Glasfachschule in Kramsach, Austria. Rudi is a former Director of Research at Bullseye Glass Co. and a world-class glasscutter.

Figure 8

Figure 9

◎ Pre-Firing Your New Kiln

Before using a new kiln for glass projects, you will need to pre-fire it. This burns out binders, moisture, and other residue left over from the manufacturing process.

New shelves can be slow to take on primer, so we recommend pre-firing them, too. To do this, coat your new kiln shelf with Bullseye Shelf Primer. (See *Using Bullseye Shelf Primer* for mixing instructions.) After the pre-firing, be sure to thoroughly scrape and re-prime the kiln shelf before firing any glass on it.

Pre-Firing Process

Place the primed shelf and kiln posts in the kiln and program it with the three-segment schedule below.

To allow moisture to escape during the first segment, vent the kiln until it reaches 700°F (an opening 3 mm wide is plenty). Once the kiln reaches 700°, close the kiln.

The top temperature (in Segment 2) is 1520°F or at least 20°F higher than the top process temperature you'll be using for glass projects.

Note that curing paint or oil on the kiln's elements can produce an odor. This is usually gone after a few firings but you may want extra ventilation at first.

See the Paragon User Manual for more info on safely setting up and operating your kiln.

Pre-Firing Schedule

Segment	Rate	Temperature	Hold
1	400°F / hour	1250°F	1:00
2	AFAP	1520°F (or at least 20°F higher than intended top process temp for glass projects)	1:00
3	400°F / hour	70°F (room temperature)	—

Get the Most From Your Kiln With These Bullseye Video Lessons

· *Bringing Home Your New Kiln*
· *Kiln Operation*
· *Kiln Shelves and Furniture*
· *Preparing Kiln Shelves*
· *Recommended Annealing Cycle for Bullseye Glass*

Each included with a $45 subscription to Bullseye Kiln-Glass Education Online video lessons. Subscription gives you access to the complete video library—more than 120 so far. Each 10-15 minute lesson is designed by Bullseye instructors and appropriate for everyone from beginners to advanced kilnformers.

Sign up today!
videos.bullseyeglass.com

◎ Bullseye Kiln-Glass Project

Project _____

Description

Date Fired _____ Firing # _____

Target Dimensions _____

Glass Used (style # and production date from glass label; sheet #)

_____

_____

_____

_____

_____

_____

_____

_____

Mold Type _____

Kiln_____

Firing Schedule

Process (full fuse, slump, etc.)

_____

	Rate	Temperature	Hold Time
1.	____	____	____
2.	____	____	____
3.	____	____	____
4.	____	____	____
5.	____	____	____
6.	____	____	____
7.	____	____	____
8.	____	____	____
9.	____	____	____

Double Check Program Review   Contents Review

Process Review   Kiln Turned On

Shelf   Mullite   Fiberboard

Other _____

Shelf Release   Primer   Fiber   ThinFire

Other _____

Sketch

Notes on Results (success, devitrification, cracking, ideas for future firings, etc.)

Post-Firing Dimensions _____

Safety in the Kiln-Glass Studio

GENERAL CONSIDERATIONS

Good housekeeping and common sense go a long way toward ensuring safety in the kilnforming studio. Ventilate your studio well, keep dust to a minimum, and confine hazardous materials to a limited area.

Avoid eating and drinking in the studio. Toxins and dusts are easily ingested when you handle food and kilnworking materials in the same space.

Wash your hands upon leaving the studio. If you can't change clothes, wear a smock or apron while you work. To avoid tracking dusts and toxins to other locations, consider dedicating a pair of shoes to studio use only.

Remember that your physical condition and lifestyle choices can be factors when working with certain hazardous materials. For example, smoking has been proven to increase the rate at which many toxins are ingested. Pregnant women, children under twelve years of age, and people taking certain forms of medication may have increased susceptibility to some chemicals.

The table on the following page covers hazards specific to kilnforming glass.

SAFE KILN USE

Thoroughly read the manual and other information provided by the manufacturer.

Operate your kiln in a well-ventilated area. Full-fuse firings of glass on primed shelves will not release fumes, but firings that involve fibers, enamels, glazes, and other materials can.

Avoid burns by wearing protective clothing. Use heat-resistant gloves whenever opening a hot kiln.

Always turn off the power before reaching into a hot kiln (for example, during glass combing or other manual forming).

Protect your eyes. Looking into a hot kiln for prolonged periods of time exposes your eyes to potentially damaging infrared light. Excessive exposure can cause cataracts. Wear safety glasses with protective ANSI shade 1.7 lenses. Didymium glasses used for flameworking **DO NOT** provide protection from infrared light.

BASIC SAFETY EQUIPMENT

- Safety glasses: Make sure they have side shields.
- Respirator: NIOSH-approved for specific process: fume, vapor, or dust- trapping.
- Heat-resistant gloves: Non-asbestos Zetex or Kevlar.
- Lightweight cotton gloves: These protect skin from irritating dusts or fibers.
- Bandages: Cuts are almost inevitable when handling glass. However, they are usually clean and rarely serious.

SAFETY RESOURCES

- Bullseye Forum: Post questions about safety on our forum. It's a great way to tap into the advice of Bullseye technicians and experienced artists and craftspeople working in their own studios. *bullseyeglass.com/forum*
- Glass Artist Health & Safety: A helpful webpage with information on safety for artists working in glass. Compiled by Greg Rawls, an artist, industrial hygienist, and certified safety professional. *gregorieglass.com/Health_Safety.html*
- Material Safety Data Sheets (MSDS): These are available online or from the product suppliers or manufacturers. They are particularly important when using a material that is either new or unfamiliar to you.
- National Institute of Occupational Safety and Health (NIOSH) *cdc.gov/niosh*
- Your local safety supply store may be able to provide assistance in the proper fit of safety gear and additional advice on personal protective equipment, apparel, first aid supplies, and environmental protection.

MATERIAL	HAZARD	PRECAUTION
Sheet glass, cullet, billets	a) Cuts during scoring and breaking. b) Chips in the eyes during scoring and breaking. c) Dust and powder created during grinding. This may irritate the eyes, skin, and respiratory system. If glass is ground extremely fine, the hazard depends on the solubility of any toxic metals it contains.	a) Gloves provide some protection against cuts but often hamper dexterity. Glass cuts are generally clean. Flush with hydrogen peroxide and bandage. Wear gauntlets when handling sheets over eight square feet. b) Always wear eye protection. Safety glasses should have side shields. Goggles are recommended during grinding. c) Use water when grinding or polishing to keep tools and glass cool and to keep dust down. Clean up ground glass slag while it is still wet to prevent it from becoming airborne. When dealing with dry glass dust and powder, wear a NIOSH-approved respirator and replace the filter cartridge regularly. Use local ventilation.
Glass frit and powder	See notes above on dust and powder. Be cautious with frit from lead-bearing glass, as it may be both irritating and toxic.	When working with dry glass powder, always wear a NIOSH-approved respirator and replace the filter cartridge regularly. Use local ventilation.
Shelf primer and kiln wash	Silica dust. Inhaling can cause respiratory irritation. Long-term exposure may cause silicosis.	Wear a NIOSH-approved respirator when mixing dry powder or scraping fired shelves clean. Use local ventilation.
Ceramic fiber products	Fibers can irritate eyes, skin, and respiratory system, particularly when cut or torn. After firing, fiber products readily release dusts that may be dangerous to breathe.	Avoid contact with skin. Wear a respirator designed to filter particulates. Clean residual fibers from glass with running water. Dispose of used materials in a sealed plastic bag.
ThinFire Shelf Paper	When fired, disintegrates into a dusty tissue that can irritate eyes, skin, and respiratory system.	See precautions above for ceramic fiber products. Avoid breathing residual dust. Vacuum kiln using a High Efficiency Particulate Air (HEPA) filter vacuum, or remove dust by saturating it with water and collecting in a plastic bag.
Wax	Overheated and burning wax produces acrolein and aldehydes, which are respiratory irritants and suspected human carcinogens.	Avoid overheating wax. No respirator filters out all of the hazardous components present in wax vapors. Steam wax out of molds rather than burning it out.
Plaster	Skin, eye, and respiratory irritant. Contains mild alkalis and can produce burns.	Wear safety goggles and a NIOSH-approved respirator while mixing investment or divesting molds and use local ventilation. Wear gloves and/or use a protective cream on hands.
Silica	Irritates respiratory system. Long-term exposure may cause silicosis.	Wear a NIOSH-approved particulate respirator and use local ventilation.
Talc	Respiratory irritant. Dusts may irritate the eyes.	Wear safety goggles and a NIOSH-approved respirator and use local ventilation.
Enamels	May contain heavy metals.	Wear protective gloves. Do not wash down drain. Consult MSDS for further information.

Make It Projects

Make It Projects

Make It: Dilution Solution

Glass

2 sheets:
- White, 3 mm, 10" x 10" (000113-0030-F)

1 sheet each:
- Sea Blue, 3 mm, 10" x 10" (001444-0030-F)
- Khaki, 3 mm, 10" x 10" (001439-0030-F)
- Tekta, 4 mm, 5" x 10" (001100-0480-F)

1 piece:
- Clear rod, 7–9 mm (001101-0876)

Tools & Supplies
- 3M Diamond Hand Lap 120 grit (7220)
- Basic glass cutting tools
- Bullseye Shelf Primer (8220) or Bullseye ThinFire Shelf Paper (7089)
- GlasTac (8234)
- Neo GC Cutter (7162)
- Nylon scrub pad
- Square Slumper A, 10.5 inch Slumping Mold (8634)
- Square Slumper B, 5.375 inch Slumping Mold (8997)
- Square Slumper A, 4.625 inch Slumping Mold (8636)
- Tweezers, Pointed (7212)

Helpful Resources
- Glass Cleaning Basics
- Improve Your Glass Cutting
- TechNotes 5: Volume & Bubble Control
- TipSheet 7: Platemaking
- Tips for Using Bullseye Slumping Molds
- Video Lesson: Dilution Solution (subscription required)

View articles and videos at bullseyeglass.com

HOW THIS PROJECT WORKS

Significant amounts of clear sheet and rod are fired over a palette of medium-saturation sheet to displace the material directly underneath. This creates lighter areas by diluting the color to reveal more of the white base layer.

Lay-up: White base capped with Sea Blue and Khaki. Clear design elements are placed on top.

This project produces one 9" x 9" (23 x 23 cm) plate, two 5" x 5" (13 x 13 cm) plates, and two 4" x 4" (10 x 10 cm) plates (plus rod and sheet left over for future projects).

PREPARE THE CLEAR DESIGN ELEMENTS

1. Cut three 1" x 1.5" pieces of Tekta.

2. Cut six 1" lengths of rod. Look for a relatively clean break on the ends for similar volume in each piece. In this design, these pieces are fired lengthwise and are prone to roll if not secured properly. Option: Pre-fire the rod pieces to create a flat spot along one side, eliminating the need for holding agent. Fire the clean rod pieces on a primed kiln shelf with a little space around each one. (See Pre-Fire Firing schedule.)

3. Cut six 8 mm lengths of rod. These will be placed on-end, so select pieces with relatively flat and smooth cross-sections. Cut a few extra so you can select the best. A Neo GC Cutter works well.)

PREPARE THE SHEET GLASS

See the cutting charts on the next page. Following the numbered order of operations will ensure an accurate yield of cut pieces for the project. Ideally, the pieces will be close fitting, with minimal gaps at the seam. Use a wet diamond pad to remove any flared edges preventing a tight seam. You will also need to cut one 9" x 9" sheet of White.

ASSEMBLE THE DESIGNS & FUSE

9" x 9" plate: Clean and assemble the pieces on inverted cups or blocks for easy handling. Place the White sheet glass smooth side up, then cap with the larger Sea Blue and Khaki pieces (also smooth side up). Clean the three Tekta rectangles. Starting about 1" (3 cm) from the perimeter, place the pieces over the seam, leaving about 0.5" between them. Overlap about one-quarter of each rectangle over the Sea Blue side.

5" x 5" plates: Clean and assemble the components, again checking for a tight seam on the top layer. Arrange three of the 1" sections of Clear rod over the seam with an overlap of about one-third over the Khaki side. The lower-most section is about 0.75" from the closest edge. Leave the thickness of about one rod between each piece. If using GlasTac, be sure to wait until it is set before transferring it to a prepared firing surface. Or assemble the piece directly on a prepared firing surface.

4" x 4" plates: Clean and assemble components with the rod pieces placed on end, centered over the seam, about 0.5" from the edge, spaced about 0.25" apart.

Fire the pieces on a prepared kiln shelf using the firing schedule provided.

SLUMP FIRING

Prior to slumping, remove any sharp points or edges with a wet diamond pad. Note: Separator materials like primer are more likely to adhere to opalescent styles than transparent or iridized glasses. Remove residue with a green scrub pad and water.

Clean the pieces and load them onto primed molds. Elevate molds to promote even heating and cooling. Fire the pieces using the Slump Firing schedule provided.

NOTES FOR FUTURE PROJECTS

Using Clear glass for dilution and displacement has great design potential. Firing Clear directly over opalescent glasses creates yet another effect, forming pools of clear with a visually recessed surface design. When exploring this technique, leave space around each clear design element to allow for the glass to flow.

SUGGESTED FIRING SCHEDULES

Greater heatwork than our standard full fuse gives the top design elements a better chance to fuse deeply into the base layer.

PRE-FIRE FIRING (SEE STEP #2)

	RATE*	TEMPERATURE	HOLD
1	500°F (278°C)	1350°F (732°C)	:05
2	Vent kiln to cool AFAP.		

FUSE FIRING

	RATE*	TEMPERATURE	HOLD
1	300°F (167°C)	1225°F (663°C)	:45
2	600°F (333°C)	1500°F (816°C)	:10
3	AFAP**	900°F (482°C)	1:00
4	100°F (56°C)	700°F (371°C)	:00
5	AFAP**	70°F (21°C)	:00

SLUMP FIRING

	RATE*	TEMPERATURE	HOLD
1	300°F (167°C)	1225°F (663°C)	:05
2	AFAP**	900°F (482°C)	1:00
3	100°F (56°C)	700°F (371°C)	:00
4	AFAP**	70°F (21°C)	:00

* Degrees per hour
** As Fast As Possible. Allow kiln to cool at its natural rate with the door closed.

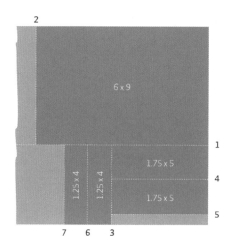

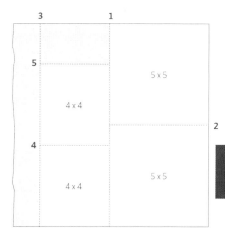

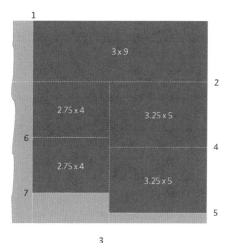

Follow this order to cut the smaller pieces of colored glass. From top: Sea Blue, White, and Khaki.

Make It: Inline Plate

Glass

1/2 tube each:
- Burnt Orange Stringer, 2 mm (000329-0072)
- Butterscotch Stringer, 2 mm (000337-0072)
- Petal Pink Stringer, 2 mm (000421-0072)
- Opaque White Stringer, 2 mm (000013-0072)
- Clear Stringer, 2 mm (001101-0072)

4 sheets:
- Clear Tekta, 3 mm, 10" x 10" (001100-0380)

Produces one 9" x 9" and one 8" x 8" plate.

Tools
- Basic glass cutting tools
- Neo GC Cutter
- Square Slumper Mold A (8634)

Non-Glass Items
- GlasTac
- Bullseye Shelf Primer (not ThinFire or shelf paper)
- Butcher or kraft paper to use as a clean workspace

Other Handy Items
- Ultra fine point Sharpie® pen
- Small cups or blocks to elevate the piece during the design phase
- 120 grit diamond pad

Optional Coldworking Equipment
- Wet belt sander

Recommended Reading
- Improve Your Glass Cutting
- Glass Cleaning Basics
- TipSheet 7: Platemaking
- Tips for Using Bullseye Slumping Molds

Recommended Viewing
- Slumping Basics
- Working with Stringer
- Inline Plate Project (12/2013)
- Coldworking with the Wet Belt Sander

Articles and videos can be found at www.bullseyeglass.com/education

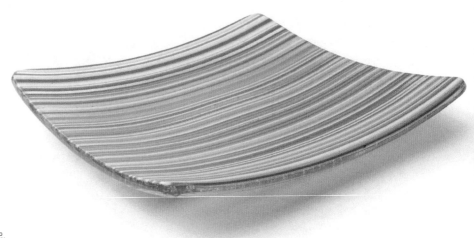

PREPARE THE SHEET GLASS

1. Cut two pieces of 3 mm Clear Tekta to 9" x 9".

2. Clean one of them and trace its border with a pencil on a piece of butcher paper to serve as a template and clean workspace. Set the sheet glass aside.

PREPARE THE STRINGER

3. Set out enough stringers to cover the 9" x 9" template you have drawn. It takes approximately 116 2 mm stringers to cover a 9" x 9" square end to end (an average of 23 stringers or about a half-tube of each color). Don't worry about color placement just yet.

4. Measure, mark, and cut all of the stringers in the same step to make sure they are uniform in length and have "clean" ends. Start by aligning the stringers so that 1/4" or less hangs over one edge of the template. (Full-length stringers will overlap the opposite side of the template by about 8 1/4".) Using the template as a guide, place the 9" x 9" piece of clean Tekta on top of the stringers. Next, run an ultra fine point Sharpie® pen along the edge of the sheet glass, leaving a cutting mark on each stringer. Before marking the stringers on the other side of the Tekta, move the Tekta over ever so slightly to cover the first row of marks. This will produce a more accurate measurement. Remove the Tekta sheet. Now your stringers are ready to cut.

Set materials on your paper template from Step 1

Tekta

Trace the sheet glass edge to mark your stringers

Note: If using stringers that already have one nicely cut end, set the "clean" ends flush with one side of the template instead of cutting them.

5. Cut the stringers, using the marks as a guide. A disc nipper like the Neo GC will work well.

CREATE THE DESIGN (SET THE STRIPES)

6. Set a single piece of clean Tekta (rough side up) on small inverted cups or blocks—to elevate it from the work surface. The slight elevation will make handling and moving the piece much easier.

7. Place a drop of GlasTac at each corner and set down a few stringers to determine the ends.

8. Fill in with the remainder of the stringers, arranging them to your liking. You'll know the surface is covered when you can't add a stringer without another one falling off. Keep an eye out for stringers that might need to be re-cut. Adjust stringers to make them flush with the edge of the sheet glass.

9. Once your design is complete and all of the stringers are in place, draw at least three beads of GlasTac across the stringers, making contact with each one. While the GlasTac is still wet, gently press down on the stringer layer to make sure it is only a single stringer deep and that all of the stringers are touching the sheet glass underneath. It is important for Glastac to flow between the stringers to the sheet glass.

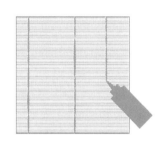

10. Allow the GlasTac to dry completely. Minimally, it should be left to dry overnight. This is very important, as you will see when you get to the next step.

ASSEMBLE THE LAYERS & FUSE

11. Once the piece is dry, turn it over and transfer it to a primed kiln shelf—a very delicate maneuver. Holding the edges that run parallel to the stringers, gently pick the piece up, turn it over, and place it with the stringer layer touching the shelf. This is best done in close proximity to the firing surface, spending minimal time holding the inverted piece. If the GlasTac is not set and dry, the stringers will slide off, taking you back to step 7. Be gentle in both handling and placing the piece, leaving the primed shelf surface even and free of scratches. (Keep in mind that with this design, the shelf side becomes the front of the piece.)

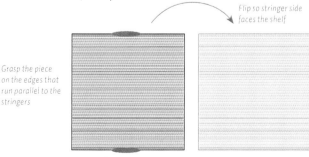

Grasp the piece on the edges that run parallel to the stringers

Flip so stringer side faces the shelf

12. Cap the piece with the other 9" x 9" sheet of Tekta. The Tekta should be clean and placed with the smoother side facing up (to create a smooth-to-rough interface with the base sheet).

Tekta cap *Stringer layer faces the shelf*

Shelf

13. Now you are ready to program the kiln, double-check everything, and fire the piece. (See Fuse Firing schedule below.)

SLUMP FIRING

14. Prior to slumping, address any sharp points or edges with a wet diamond pad or wet belt sander to remove material from the edges for a cleaner-looking edge.

15. Clean the piece thoroughly and load it onto Mold 8634 with the shelf-side texture facing up. Elevate the mold to promote even heating and cooling.

16. Now you are ready to program the kiln, double-check everything, and slump the piece. (See Slump Firing schedule below.)

NOTES FOR FUTURE PROJECTS

Consider using a single piece of 6 mm Clear (001100-0680-F) instead of 2 layers of 3 mm sheet glass for fewer bubbles and greater clarity.

SUGGESTED FIRING SCHEDULES

Fuse Firing

	RATE*	TEMPERATURE	HOLD
1	400°F (222°C)	1225°F (663°C)	:45
2	600°F (333°C)	1490°F (810°C)	:10
3	AFAP**	900°F (482°C)	1:00
4	100°F (56°C)	700°F (371°C)	:01
5	AFAP**	70°F (21°C)	:00

Slump Firing (with mold # 8634)

	RATE*	TEMPERATURE	HOLD
1	300°F (167°C)	1225°F (663°C)	:05
2	AFAP**	900°F (482°C)	1:00
3	100°F (56°C)	700°F (371°C)	:01
4	AFAP**	70°F (21°C)	:00

* Degrees per hour
** As fast as possible. Allow kiln to cool at its natural rate with the door closed.

Make It: Linear Reaction

Glass
Partial tube each:
- Turquoise Blue Stringer, 2 mm
  (001116-0272)
- Turquoise Blue Stringer, 1 mm
  (001116-0107)
- Clear Stringer, 2 mm
  (001101-0272)
- Clear Stringer, 1 mm
  (001101-0107)

2 sheets:
- Tekta, 3 mm, 10" x 10"
  (001100-0380-F)

1 sheet:
- Reactive Cloud Opal, 3 mm, 10" x 10"
  (000009-0030-F)
- Reactive Ice Clear, 3 mm, 10" x 10"
  (001009-0030-F)

Produces two 9" x 9" finished pieces, with stringers left over for future projects.

. . . .

Tools
- Basic glass cutting tools
- Neo GC Cutter (7162)
- Slumping Mold (8634)

Non-glass Consumables
- GlasTac (8232, 8234)
- Shelf primer, ThinFire, or shelf paper

Other Handy Items
- Small cups or blocks to
  elevate the piece during
  the design phase
- Tweezers (7211)
- 120 grit diamond pad (7220)

Professional-style Options
- Coldworking equipment /
  grinder / belt sander

Recommended Reading
- Bullseye Reactive Glass
- Improve Your Glass Cutting
- Glass Cleaning Basics
- TipSheet 7: Platemaking
- Tips for Using Bullseye
  Slumping Molds

Articles can be found at bullseyeglass.com

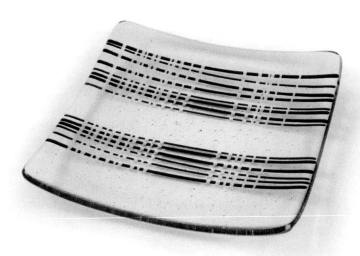

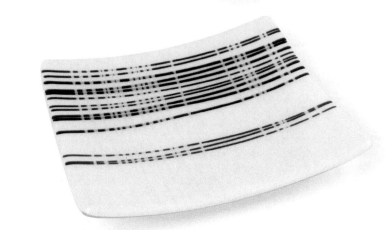

WHY THIS PROJECT WORKS

Clear stringers act as a barrier (or resist) between the reactive sheet glass and copper-bearing Turquoise. Wherever the Turquoise stringers overlap Clear, a Turquoise spot remains. Through the firings, the remainder of the Turquoise stringers react and develop to values of deep red. (For the latest information on reactive glasses, www.bullseyeglass.com/education.)

PREPARE THE SHEET GLASS & ASSEMBLE THE LAYERS

1. Cut one of the reactive sheet glass styles to 9" x 9". Note that the color of Reactive Ice Clear, viewed on edge, often has a blue to green tint. This tint will help you differentiate Reactive Ice Clear from non-reactive Clear, knowledge that is crucial in the lay-up of this piece.

2. Cut Tekta clear to match, 9" x 9".

3. Clean both sheets and place them on inverted cups or blocks (for easier handling). Place Tekta first (smooth side facing up), then cap with reactive glass (also smooth side up).

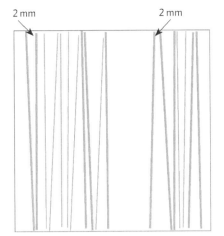

2 mm   2 mm

Step 4: Span the square with a single layer of Clear 1 and 2 mm stringers, starting and ending with 2 mm pieces.

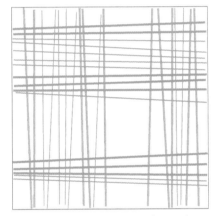

Step 5: Span the square again with a single layer of Turquoise 1 and 2 mm stringers in the opposite direction, forming a grid.

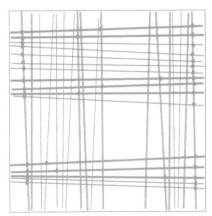

Step 7: Apply beads of GlasTac to key intersections of 2 mm Clear and Turquoise.

CREATE THE DESIGN & FUSE

4. Cut several lengths of Clear 1 and 2 mm stringers to span the square and arrange them in a single layer. In the samples, stringers were placed in a loose zigzag design with a random arrangement of 1 and 2 mm thicknesses. Placement and balance of the Turquoise stringers (step #6) will be easier if there are 2 mm Clear stringers towards the edges.

5. Use a small amount of GlasTac to hold the stringers in place. Tip: Handle stringer lengths from the middle (tweezers may be useful) and dip the ends in a small amount of GlasTac. Then set in place.

6. Cut several lengths of Turquoise 1 and 2 mm stringers to span the project. Gently place them across the the Clear stringers in a perpendicular configuration to make an asymmetric grid—leaving bands of solid clear or white.

7. Using a short piece of 2 mm stringer as a tool, apply beads of GlasTac to key intersections of 2 mm Clear and Turquoise. Just dip the tool-stringer into a cup of GlasTac and touch it to each Turquoise stringer where the GlasTac will flow and connect it to the Clear stringer underneath. Do not move the project until the GlasTac is set.

8. Once the GlasTac is set, transfer the piece to a prepared firing surface.

9. Now you are ready to program the kiln, double-check everything and fire the piece. (See fuse firing schedule.)

SLUMP FIRING

10. Prior to slumping, address any sharp points or edges with a wet diamond pad. Professional-style option: remove material from the edges/coldwork for a cleaner-looking edge.

11. Clean the piece and load it onto (primed) Mold 8634. Elevate the mold to promote even heating and cooling.

12. Now you are ready to program the kiln, double-check everything and fire the piece. (See slump firing schedule.)

NOTES FOR FUTURE PROJECTS

Experience other types of reactions with Reactive Cloud Opal and Reactive Ice Clear by working with silver foil and copper leaf. Get the latest information on Bullseye's reactive glasses at www.bullseyeglass.com/education.

SUGGESTED FIRING SCHEDULES

FUSE FIRING

	RATE*	TEMPERATURE	HOLD
1	400°F (222°C)	1225°F (663°C)	:30
2	600°F (333°C)	1490°F (810°C)	:10
3	AFAP**	900°F (482°C)	1:00
4	100°F (56°C)	700°F (371°C)	:01
5	AFAP**	70°F (21°C)	:00

SLUMP FIRING (WITH MOLD 8634)

	RATE*	TEMPERATURE	HOLD
1	300°F (167°C)	1225°F (663°C)	:05
2	AFAP**	900°F (482°C)	1:00
3	100°F (56°C)	700°F (371°C)	:01
4	AFAP**	70°F (21°C)	:00

* Degrees per hour
** As Fast As Possible. Allow kiln to cool at its natural rate with the door closed.

Make It: Opaline Sushi Set

Glass

- 3 sheets of Opaline Opalescent, 3 mm, 10" x 10" (000403-0030-F)
- 1 sheet of Canary Yellow Opalescent, 3 mm, 10" x 10" (000120-0030-F)
- Partial sheet of Fuchsia Transparent, 3 mm, 10" x 10" (001332-0030-F)
- Partial tube of Charcoal Gray Stringer, 1 mm (001129-0107)

Tools & Supplies

- 3M Diamond Hand Lap 120 grit (7220)
- Basic glass cutting tools
- Bullseye Shelf Primer (8220)
- GlasTac (8234) or GlasTac Gel (8268)
- Square Slumper A 10.5" Mold (8634)
- Square Slumper B 6.25" Mold (8996)
- Square Slumper B 3.5" Mold (8998)
- Tweezers, Serrated Tip (7211)
- Ultra Fine Point Sharpie

Optional

- Coldworking equipment / grinder / belt sander

Helpful Resources

- Glass Cleaning Basics
- Improve Your Glass Cutting
- TechNotes 5: Volume & Bubble Control
- TipSheet 7: Platemaking Tips
- Tips for Using Bullseye Slumping Molds
- Video lesson: Designing with Part Sheets, 1 & 2 (subscription required)
- Video lesson: Opaline Overlays (subscription required)

View articles and videos at bullseyeglass.com

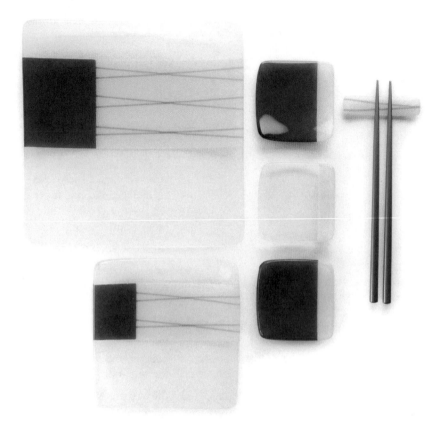

HOW THIS PROJECT WORKS

Opaline Striker transforms Canary Yellow and Fuchsia into an exciting, modern palette with unique effects in both reflected and transmitted light. Through multiple firings, you'll embed a stringer design between the layers (without trapping lots of bubbles).

This project produces one 9" x 9" (23 x 23 cm) plate, one 6" x 6" (15 x 15 cm) plate, three 3.25" x 3.25" (8 x 8 cm) plates, and multiple chopstick rests.

PREPARE & FUSE THE PART SHEET

The stringers are pre-fired to a base, forming a relatively smooth sheet that layers well in subsequent firings. Cutting through this part sheet facilitates a cleaner-looking design.

1. Trim the rolled edge from the Canary Yellow sheet. Then cut a 0.75" strip from the same side and cut it into three 3.25" lengths. Set these pieces aside to complete the smaller dishes. The remaining piece will be approximately 8.75" x 10". Clean the sheet and place it smooth side up on inverted cups or blocks for easy handling.

2. Break 14 of the stringers into 9" lengths. Place 7 of these on the Canary Yellow base parallel and equidistant to one another (about 1.125-1.25" apart) and at an angle. Use GlasTac on the ends to hold them in place.

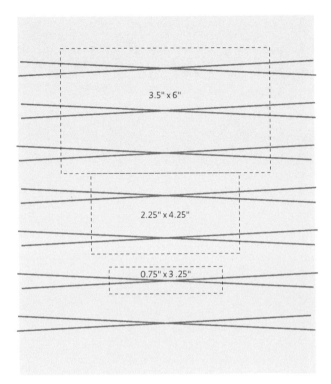

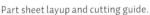

Part sheet layup and cutting guide.

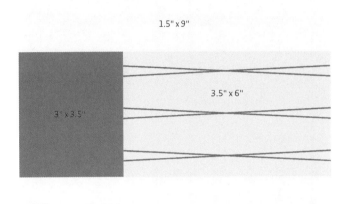

Base layup for 9" x 9" piece. Cap with Opaline.

3. Place the remaining 7 stringers across the first layer at the opposing angle, forming a wide X with intersections along the center of the sheet. Apply GlasTac where the stringers touch the sheet and at the center of the X.

4. Once the GlasTac is set, transfer the piece to a prepared firing surface. We recommend a primed kilnshelf because the edges of the sheet will pull in as the material responds to the heat.

5. Program the kiln according to the Part Sheet Firing schedule on page 4 and fire the part sheet.

PREPARE THE SHEET GLASS

For the 9" x 9" plate

1. Cut a 9" x 9" square of Opaline for the top layer. (If the removed piece is 1" wide, save it for the 6" x 6" project.)

2. Cut a 9" section from a second piece of Opaline Striker. From that piece, cut two pieces: 1.5" x 9" and 4" x 9".

3. Cut a 3" strip from the Fuchsia sheet. Then cut it to 3" x 3.5".

4. Using an Ultra Fine Point Sharpie pen, mark a 3.5" x 6" section on the part sheet and center three of the X formations. (Remember: a 2.25" x 4.25" piece will be cut later.) To cut the part sheet, a well-lubricated score is crucial. Consider brushing a thin layer of oil to the path prior to scoring. The relatively smooth, flat top surface of the part sheet is appropriate for scoring.

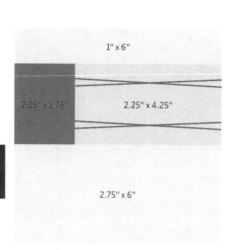

Base layup for 6" x 6" piece. Cap with Opaline.

Base layup for 3.25" x 3.25" pieces. Cap with Opaline.

Base layup for chopstick rest. Cap with Opaline.

For the 6" x 6" plate

1. Cut a 2.25" x 4.25" part sheet section. Center two X formations.

2. Using the third 10" x 10" of Opaline Striker, cut a 6" section. From that piece, cut two pieces: 6" x 6" and 2.75" x 6".

3. Using the strip of Fuchsia left over from Step 3 of the 9" x 9" plate, cut a piece that is 2.25" x 1.75".

4. Cut a 1" x 6" strip of Opaline Striker from the 1" strip left over from Step 1 of the 9" x 9" plate. If that strip is not wide enough, cut it from one of the remaining pieces.

For three 3.25" x 3.25" plates

1. From the remaining pieces of Opaline Striker, cut: three 3.25" x 3.25" pieces for the top layers, one 2.5" x 3.25" (bottom layer + Canary Yellow)

2. From the remaining pieces of Fuchsia, cut two 2.5" x 3.25" (bottom layer + Canary Yellow)

3. Use the three 0.75" x 3.25" Canary Yellow strips from step 1 of Prepare & Fuse the Part Sheet.

Chopstick rests (variable amount)

Layer two pieces that are 1" x 3.25". To slump, use the center of Square Slumper B 3.5" mold (8998).

ASSEMBLE THE LAYERS & FUSE

We recommend assembling these projects directly on a prepared firing surface.

1. Clean the base layer pieces and place them smooth side up, with minimal sliding. If necessary, use a diamond hand lap to remove material for a better fit.

2. Clean and set the caps in place with the smooth sides up. If firing several projects, leave at least 0.5" between them.

3. Program the kiln according to Fuse Firing schedule Program the kiln and fuse the pieces.

SLUMP THE PLATES

1. Before slumping, remove any sharp points or edges with a wet diamond hand lap. Optional: Coldwork edges for a cleaner-looking edge.

2. Clean the pieces and load them onto primed slumping molds. Elevate the molds to promote even heating and cooling.

3. Program the kiln according to Slump Firing schedule and slump the pieces.

NOTES FOR FUTURE PROJECTS

Layering with Opaline makes an entire new palette of colors possible. Experiment and document. Before using the remaining part sheet, remove about 0.5" from the rounded edges. This area is thicker, which makes it difficult to lay-up next to 3 mm sheet glass and may also cause bubbles if capped.

SUGGESTED FIRING SCHEDULES

PART SHEET FIRING

	RATE*	TEMPERATURE	HOLD
1	400°F (222°C)	1225°F (663°C)	:15
2	600°F (333°C)	1480°F (804°C)	:10
3	AFAP**	900°F (482°C)	:45
4	150°F (83°C)	700°F (371°C)	:00
5	AFAP**	70°F (21°C)	:00

FUSE FIRING

	RATE*	TEMPERATURE	HOLD
1	400°F (222°C)	1225°F (663°C)	:45
2	600°F (333°C)	1490°F (810°C)	:10
3	AFAP**	900°F (482°C)	1:00
4	100°F (56°C)	700°F (371°C)	:00
5	AFAP**	70°F (21°C)	:00

SLUMP FIRING

	RATE*	TEMPERATURE	HOLD
1	300°F (167°C)	1225°F (663°C)	:05
2	AFAP**	900°F (482°C)	1:00
3	100°F (56°C)	700°F (371°C)	:00
4	AFAP**	70°F (21°C)	:00

(With mold 8634, 8996, and 8998)

* Degrees per hour
** As Fast As Possible. Allow kiln to cool at its natural rate with the door closed.

◎ Make It: Tint Tone Plate

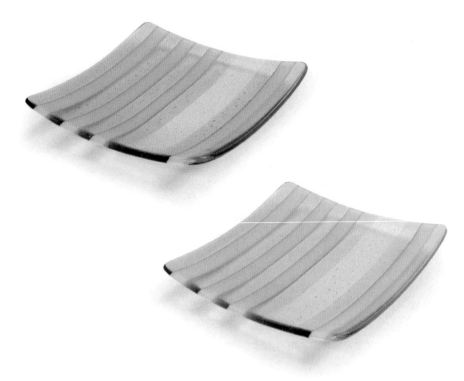

Glass

2 sheets each:
- Olivine Tint, 3 mm, 10" x 10"
  (001877-0030-F)
- Brown Topaz Tint, 3 mm, 10" x 10"
  (001819-0030-F)

1 sheet each:
- White, 3 mm, 10" x 10"
  (000113-0030-F)
- Tekta, 3 mm, 10" x 10"
  (001100-0380-F)

*Produces the two 9" x 9" finished
pieces shown.*

. . . .

Tools
- Basic glass cutting tools
- Slumping Mold (8634)

Non-glass Consumables
- Shelf primer, ThinFire or shelf paper

Other Handy Items
- Ultra Fine Point Sharpie pen
- 120 grit diamond pad (7220)

Professional-style Options
- Coldworking equipment/grinder/
  belt sander

Steps 3 & 4: Follow this order to run your scores.

WHY THIS PROJECT WORKS

This design is tailor-made for transparent glass styles with light color saturation like Bullseye Tints. Combining layers of the same tint with White and clear Tekta creates a pleasing, monochromatic palette.

PREPARE THE SHEET GLASS

1. Choose one of the tint styles to work with and cut one of the 10" x 10" sheets down to 9" x 9" to use as the top layer in this project.

2. Take the second sheet of that same tint style and cut off the rolled edge, leaving a 9" x 10" piece. This is the first step toward creating a series of 9" strips.

3. Using an Ultra Fine Point Sharpie pen, make marks for cutting six strips that measure 0.75" x 9". Score all of the strips. To run the scores, follow a particular order to best ensure success. First, run the score that separates the strips from the larger sheet. Next, run the two scores that divide the piece into thirds. Lastly, run the remaining scores right down the center, leaving you with six even strips of material. Learn about the principle behind this approach in *Improve Your Glass Cutting* (see Recommended Reading).

4. Cut four strips of White, also 0.75" x 9", using the same method described in steps 2 and 3. You may generate more scrap by cutting off the rolled edge, leaving a 9" section, but this step generally makes the cut components more consistent in length and saves having to measure and cut individual strips down to 9". (To complete both projects, you will need eight 0.75" x 9" pieces.)

5. Cut a single piece of 1.5" x 9" from the 10" x 10" piece of Tekta. (To complete both projects, you will need two 1.5" x 9" pieces.)

ASSEMBLE THE LAYERS & FUSE

6. For this project, it is best to build directly on a prepared firing surface. Glass pieces should be placed smooth side face-up, with minimal sliding, especially when using a primed shelf. First clean and load the base layer of stripes—starting with a tint, alternating with White, until seven pieces are placed. Then place the wide piece of clear Tekta, finishing with one more set of tint – White – tint.

Step 6: Place glass pieces, smooth side up, in this order.

Tekta

7. Clean the 9" x 9" piece and use it to cap the base layer, making slight adjustments to align the ends of the stripes with the edge of the top layer. This top layer should be placed with the smooth side facing up.

8. Now you are ready to program the kiln, double-check everything and fire the piece. (See fuse firing schedule.)

SLUMP FIRING

9. Prior to slumping, address any sharp points or edges with a wet diamond pad. Professional-style option: remove material from the edges/coldwork for a cleaner-looking edge.

10. Clean the piece and load it onto (primed) Mold 8634. Elevate the mold to promote even heating and cooling.

11. Now you are ready to program the kiln, double-check everything and fire the piece. (See slump firing schedule.)

NOTES FOR FUTURE PROJECTS

Many Bullseye tint glasses will be effective in the same general lay-up, as will light transparents like 001414, 001437 and 001408.

SUGGESTED FIRING SCHEDULES

Fuse Firing

	RATE*	TEMPERATURE	HOLD
1	400°F (222°C)	1225°F (663°C)	:30
2	600°F (333°C)	1490°F (810°C)	:10
3	AFAP**	900°F (482°C)	1:00
4	100°F (56°C)	700°F (371°C)	:01
5	AFAP**	70°F (21°C)	:00

Slump Firing (with Mold 8634)

	RATE*	TEMPERATURE	HOLD
1	300°F (167°C)	1225°F (663°C)	:05
2	AFAP**	900°F (482°C)	1:00
3	100°F (56°C)	700°F (371°C)	:01
4	AFAP**	70°F (21°C)	:00

* Degrees per hour
** As fast as possible. Allow kiln to cool at its natural rate with the door closed.

Recommended Reading
· Improve Your Glass Cutting
· Glass Cleaning Basics
· TipSheet 7: Platemaking
· Tips for Using Bullseye Slumping Molds

Articles can be found at
bullseyeglass.com/education

Quick Tips

◎ Quick Tip: A Riot of Effects

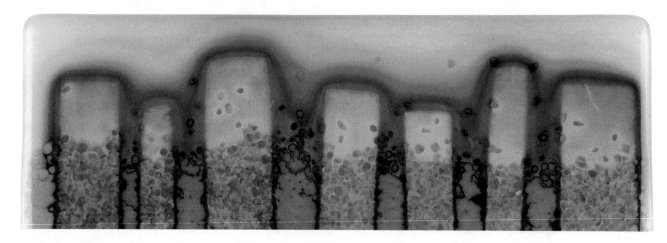

Simple layup + reactions = a riot of effects

What's going on in this glass? Our piece may look complex, but the colorful effects resulted from just allowing and preventing two types of reactions: sulfur + copper and sulfur + silver.

The layup was simple: A base of Tekta Clear sheet (001100-0380) topped with French Vanilla sheet (000137-0030); strips of Silver Foil (7217) placed on the French Vanilla sheet; and Light Aquamarine Blue medium frit (001408-0002) layered over the bottom 2/3 of the silver strips, spilling onto the French Vanilla sheet. We fired to a full fuse.

Firing

We've had success firing this layup with an initial heat range of 200-400°F in the first segment of a full fuse. If using larger pieces of silver, slow this rate to 100 degrees per hour to prevent thermal shock.

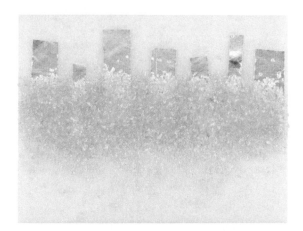

Here's what happened:

1. Copper-bearing Aquamarine frit reacted with sulfur-bearing French Vanilla sheet.

2. Silver foil reacted with sulfur-bearing French Vanilla sheet. Uncapped and unrestrained, the reaction spread out (fumed) toward the edge of the piece.

3. Copper-bearing Aquamarine frit did not react with silver foil. Instead, it capped the foil, confining the reaction between silver and French Vanilla to the border.

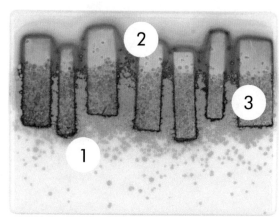

Because uncapped metal foil reactions can spread out and travel, they may contaminate the kiln shelf and affect future firings, even if the shelf is properly scraped and reprimed. Shelf contamination may or may not be visible and can even occur through ThinFire or fiber paper. Contamination is not permanent, but several firings may be needed to adequately burn it out. Consider designating a shelf specifically for firing metal foils.

◎ Quick Tip: Alchemy Metallic Palette

Create gold & bronze hues by capping silver foil with Bullseye's Alchemy Clear styles. Adding Clear to the mix expands the palette to three handsome metallics.

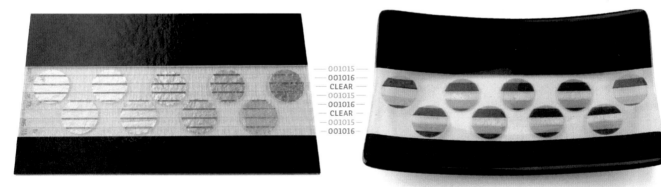

— 001015 —
— 001016 —
— CLEAR —
— 001015 —
— 001016 —
— CLEAR —
— 001015 —
— 001016 —

Design
Place silver foil elements on a base of 3 mm Tekta Clear. Make the top layer with strips of both Alchemy Clears (Silver to Gold, Silver to Bronze) and any 3 mm Clear (Tekta or standard) with seams and transitions in the Clears over the silver. For contrast and drama, we framed the design with Black. Fire to a full fuse. Expect variation with Alchemy Clears.

Tips
- Whether cutting with scissors or a paper punch, sandwich silver foil between pieces of office paper or thicker paper, like cover stock for a crisp edge.
- To minimize potential shelf contamination, keep silver 0.75" (2 cm) away from the perimeter.

Firing Considerations
We've had success firing this 7" x 12" (18 x 30 cm) layup with an initial heat rate of 300°F in the first segment of a full fuse. If you plan to use larger pieces of silver or experiment with base colors other than Clear, slow this rate to 100-200 degrees per hour. This will minimize the potential for thermal shock.

Materials
- Any 3 mm Clear: Tekta (001100-0380) or standard (001101-0030)
- Alchemy Clear, Silver to Gold, 3 mm (001015-0030)
- Alchemy Clear, Silver to Bronze, 3 mm (001016-0030)
- Black Opalescent, 3 mm (000100-0030)
- Silver Foil (7217)

◎ Quick Tip: Color Line Dot Bowls

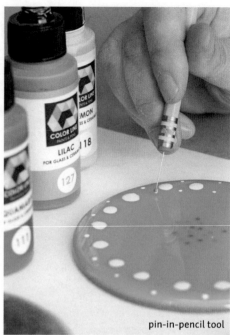

pin-in-pencil tool

Make these sweet dotted bowls with Color Line Paints and the simplest of tools!

To get started, layer two 4.75˝ circles of colorful 3mm sheet combinations and fire to a full fuse. For a slightly thinner, lighter bowl, swap the top 3mm layer for thin (-0050). The thinner top layer will contract just enough to form a narrow border of the base color along the bowl's rim. Once your blanks are ready, let the fun begin!

Using pins, toothpicks, and Color Line's affixable tips, add dots and flourishes of Color Line Paint in organic patterns. Explore the diversity of colors and the bold-to-whimsical mark-making range that these ready-to-use, lead-free enamels make possible. Easily mixable, they're also great for developing your own custom colors.

Fuse the Color Line enamels to a gloss by firing the painted blanks, then slump in a Ball Surface mold (firing schedules below). Firing Color Line reds often requires a little extra attention. (Visit **bit.ly/CLPaints** for details.)

Materials & Supplies
Color Line Paints, all colors
Turquoise Blue Opalescent (000116-0030, -0050)
Mink Opalescent (000119-0030, -0050)
Orange Opalescent (000125-0030, -0050)
Sunflower Yellow Opalescent (000220-0030, -0050)
White Opalescent (000113-0030, -0050)
True Blue Transparent (001464-0030, -0050)
Ball Surface Slumping Mold (008746)
Color Line Tip Set (008472)
Mark-making tools: pins, paperclips, toothpicks, pencils, etc

Fuse the Blank

Rate (DPH)*	Temperature	Hold
300°F (167°C)	1225°F (663°C)	1:00
600°F (333°C)	1490°F (810°C)	:10
AFAP**	900°F (482°C)	1:00
100°F (56°C)	700°F (371°C)	:00
AFAP**	70°F (21°C)	:00

Dry and Fuse Color Line Paint

Rate (DPH)*	Temperature	Hold
200°F (111°C)	200°F (93°C)	:20
300°F (167°C)	1000°F (538°C)	:20
600° (333°C)	1425°F (774°C)	:10
AFAP**	900°F (482°C)	1:00
100°F (56°C)	700°F (371°C)	:00
AFAP**	70°F (21°C)	:00

Slump in Ball Surface Mold

Rate (DPH)*	Temperature	Hold
300°F (167°C)	1220°F (660°C)	:20
AFAP**	900°F (482°C)	1:00
100°F (56°C)	700°F (371°C)	:00
AFAP**	70°F (21°C)	:00

*DPH = degrees per hour.

**As Fast As Possible.
Allow the kiln to cool at its natural rate with the door closed.

◎ Quick Tip: Circles from Squares

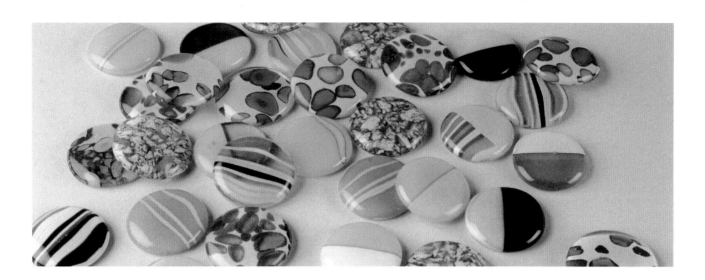

You can create nicely rounded cabochons from stacks of 0.75" (20 x 20 mm) squares, thanks to heat, gravity, and the 6 Millimeter Rule. But be careful, they're addictive!

The Stack
Top (6 mm): A "lensing" layer of Clear. This layer will stretch considerably.
Middle (3-4 mm): This "design" layer will stretch and be visible through the top layer. Use part sheets or pieces of 3 mm sheet glass.
Bottom (6 mm): Typically not visible from the front. This layer will stretch the least.

Tips
- 6 mm Tekta Clear is a natural for this project. It's more efficient, with fewer pieces to cut, clean and assemble! Measure and score a grid of 0.75" squares, then run them using the Rule of Halves. Two layers of 3mm will also work.
- A dab of GlasTac Gel will keep the stack together before firing.
- The stacks flow out to about 1.25" (32 mm) in diameter, so give them room.
- For the cleanest release, we recommend firing on ThinFire.

Cabochon Firing Schedule

	Rate	Temperature	Hold
1	400°F (222°C)	1225°F (662°C)	:30
2	600°F (333°C)	1525°F (829°C)	:30
3	AFAP	900°F (482°C)	1:00
4	100°F (56°C)	700°F (371°C)	:00
5	AFAP	70°F (21°C)	:00

Note: This heatwork goes beyond what the glass is tested for. Some styles may opalize and/or shift in compatibility. Test before making multiples.

Some Design Layer Possibilities
- Blue/Vanilla part sheet: Scatter Steel Blue Opalescent coarse frit (000146-0003) onto a base of 3mm Clear sheet glass, then sift a heavy layer of French Vanilla powder (000137-0008) over the top to cover. Fire to a full fuse. Maximize depth by arranging the Clear side toward the top of the stack.
- River Rock Reaction (See Quick Tip: River Rock Reaction)
- Pieces of Citronelle Opalescent (000221-0030) and Turquoise Blue Opalescent (000116-0030).

◎ Quick Tip: Fibonacci Fade Plate

Combine mathematics and metallics to create this handsome design!

What is the Fibonacci sequence?

The Fibonacci sequence is a numbering system found in nature, from flower petals and pinecones to seashells. It's pleasing to the eye (even if you're not aware of it) and a versatile design tool. It starts with a one (or a zero), followed by a one. Each subsequent number is equal to the sum of the preceding two numbers:

$$F(1) = 1, 1, 2, 3, 5, 8, 13, 21...$$

For this project, we've translated the beginning of this Fibonacci sequence into centimeters and arranged them to transition from one color to another.

Materials
- 3mm Medium Amber, Gold Irid (001137-0038)
- 3mm Light Silver Gray, Silver Irid (001429-0037)
- 3mm Tekta Clear (001100-0380)
- Channel Plate Mold 17" (8944)

Directions
1. Cut a 12cm wide strip of Medium Amber, Gold Irid that will yield all of the strips, (which total 20cm). Then score & break out strips in the following dimensions.
- 1cm x 12cm (x 2)
- 2cm x 12cm
- 3cm x 12cm
- 5cm x 12cm
- 8cm x 12cm
2. Repeat with Light Silver Gray, Silver Irid.
3. Arrange the strips to transition from one color into the next. See sequence example.

4. Measure and cut 3mm Clear to fit, approximately 12cm x 40cm.
5. Clean and load the strips with the iridescent coating face down on a primed kiln shelf. Cap with Clear and fire to a full fuse.
6. Coldwork the perimeter prior to slumping for crisp and clean edges.
7. Slump with the irid layer facing up. (Note: This plate only uses a portion of the mold.)

For firing schedules, see Tip Sheet 7, Platemaking Tips (Basic Fuse Firing) & Mold Tips: Suggested Slumping Schedules.

Sequence example

◎ **Quick Tip:** Fine Lines

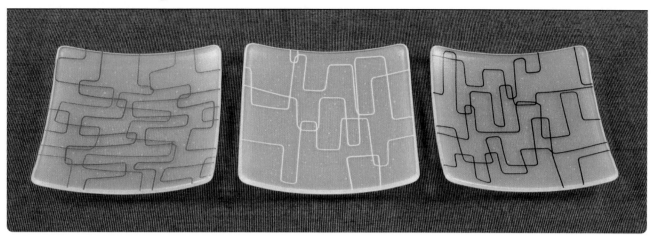

Candle-bent Fine Line stringers bring a lean line quality to this Mid-Century inspired design.

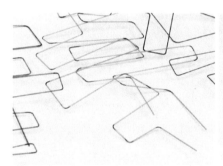 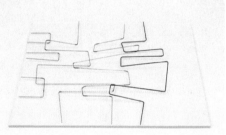 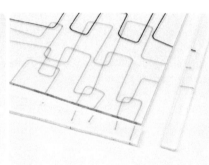

Bend the Stringer

Holding the stringer with thumbs and forefingers, place the spot you want to bend in the tip of a candle flame (tea lights work well). Apply a light pressure until you feel the glass soften. Lift the stringer out of the flame to cool and set the angle. Keep the stringer relatively flat as you move on to the next bend. Carbon will burn off in the kiln, so there's no need to clean.

Safety tips: Wear eye protection—stringers can snap. Allow the bent area to cool before touching.

Make a Part Sheet

Arrange the bent stringers on a 7.5" (190 mm) square of 3 mm Clear. Trim the ends to fit on the sheet, although they don't need to be perfect. Centering the design will make trimming the part sheet simpler. You can also break off sections and use them to carry the line work to the edge of the sheet. When you're satisfied with the design, fire the part sheet following the schedule below.

Design suggestions: Mix and match different colored stringers. Play with density of pattern and negative space.

Part Sheet Firing Schedule

Rate	Temperature	Hold
300°F (167°C)	1000°F (538°C)	:20
600°F (333°C)	1460°F (793°C)	:10
AFAP	900°F (482°C)	1:00
100°F (56°C)	700°F (371°C)	:00
AFAP	70°F (21°C)	:00

Compose, Fire, and Slump

The fired part sheet will be smooth enough to score on either side. Trim it to a 6" (152 mm) square, then clean it and place the stringer side against the kiln shelf. Cap with a 6" square of Opaline and fire to a full fuse. Finally, flip the shelf side up for a slump firing in a Square Slumper mold (8996).

Materials

SHEET
Clear (001101-0030-F) or
Tekta Clear (001100-0380-F)
Opaline (000403-0030-F)

FINE LINE STRINGER
Stiff Black (000101-0507)
Red (000124-0507)
Deep Cobalt Blue (000147-0507)
Sunflower Yellow (000220-0507)
Cranberry Pink (001311-0507)

MOLD
Square Slumper B (8996)

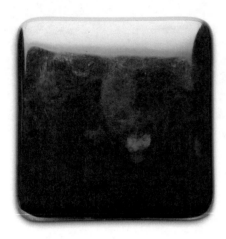

The growth of crystals on glass, aka devitrification, aka devit, is not that common or easy to create. But if devit does appear on your fired glass, there are several ways to remove it. One simple way, for glass that's flat, is to sift a very thin layer of Clear powder (2 grains thick) over the entire piece until the surface appears white. Then re-fire at 1425°-1450°F (774°-788°C) for about ten minutes, depending on the kiln and thickness of the glass. The resulting piece, like our tile on the right, will have a clean appearance. This method is similar to working with overglazes, but Clear powder has advantages: it contains no lead, it fires quickly, and a very small amount will get the job done.

Quick Tip: Fresh Color

New color palettes bring freshness to artwork. You can discover professionally curated, current color combinations to make your own in magazines and websites about design, interiors, and even fashion. An article about bedroom makeovers inspired these striped tabletops—color to live with!

Standout color discoveries

1. Shades of gray bring out brightness in other colors, but still keep the palette sophisticated.

2. Using Light Peach Cream (000034) as a neutral: combined with other warm whites it softens the palette.

3. Mink (000119) brings a more contemporary feel to a traditionally neutral palette of brown, cream, and rose.

Tabletop composition: We arranged stripes of 3 widths – 0.5, 1.5 & 3 inches – then capped with Clear and fired design-down to a full fuse. Using the shelf-side as the top not only showcases the color but also makes for a flat surface.

Tip: Placing the same color on both ends unifies the object.

Glass cutting tips

- See *12 Ways to Improve Your Glass Cutting*. Number 7 is especially helpful for cutting multiple half-inch strips: position your score so that there is an equal mass of glass on either side (also known as the "Rule of Halves").
- If cutting on the smooth side of an opalescent sheet proves challenging, turn it over and score the underside. A very thin layer of transparent glass migrates to this side of the sheet in the forming process and may yield a better result.

Products

TABLETOP 1
000227-0030 Golden Green
000403-0030 Opaline Striker
000236-0030 Slate Gray
000920-0030 Warm White
000206-0030 Elephant Gray

TABLETOP 2
000225-0030 Pimento Red
000034-0030 Light Peach Cream
000148-0030 Indigo Blue
000208-0030 Dusty Blue
000420-0030 Cream

TABLETOP 3
000119-0030 Mink
001419-0030 Tan
000139-0030 Almond
000305-0030 Salmon Pink
000920-0030 Warm White

TABLE BASES
8621 Accent Table Base, Black
8622 Accent Table Base, Nickel
8623 Accent Table Base, Recessed, Black
8624 Accent Table Base, Recessed, Nickel

◎ Quick Tip: Frit Balls

Easy to make and fun to use

Scatter pieces of coarse frit (-0003) on a freshly primed kiln shelf and adjust them with tweezers, leaving space around each piece. Fire hot enough to round out the pieces, which will pull up slightly during the firing as they conform to the Six Millimeter Rule. We recommend firing as fast as possible to 1500°F (816°C) with a 20-minute hold. There's no need to anneal. Open the kiln and voila, you'll find frit balls: rounded bits of glass with a small flat spot where they formed on the shelf.

Once they're cool, bulk rinse the whole lot with water and glass cleaner and rub dry to remove primer dust. A mesh sieve and a lint-free towel are handy items to have around for this procedure. Once they're clean, the frit balls are ready to use as design elements or for building larger forms.

A few recommendations

We recommend making frit balls with transparent styles, as they release cleanly from the primed shelf. Opalescent styles generally pick up a significant amount of primer, which is challenging and tedious to remove. One noteworthy exception is Opaline (000403), which behaves like a transparent, releasing cleanly from the primed shelf.

The frit balls shown above were made with Opaline frit, which should be fired on the cool side to achieve a pleasing translucent quality: 1480°F (804°C) with a 15-minute hold. Get Opaline frit working notes, available at bullseyeglass.com.

Consider skimming the upper portions of one- or five-pound jars of coarse frit to work with larger pieces.

Try tack fusing frit balls to a flat full-fused piece to create a bumpy dot texture, as shown at right. They'll remain bumpy through a slump firing.

Making an opaline frit ball bowl

To make the opaline frit-ball bowl shown above, first create a dam by cutting a 5.5" circle in a sheet of 1/8" fiber paper, leaving the border intact. Place the dam on a primed kiln shelf and load it up with about five ounces of frit balls. This approach essentially creates a new material that is a few frit balls thick with a network of tiny connection points. Nestle them into place and fill in any large gaps or thin spots. Tack them together by firing at a rate of 300°F (167°C) per hour to 1375°F (746°C) for 10 minutes. Slump the piece in a separate firing using mold 8746. We recommend annealing in both firings.

◎ Quick Tip: Fritfetti

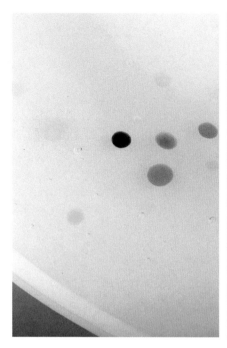

Say yes to sprinkles!

Steps (4 firings)
· Make frit balls with Medium Frit. See Quick Tip: Frit Balls.
· Cut 7" (approx. 18cm) circles. You'll need 3 circles of Clear and one of each opalescent style to make the set.
· Clean and layer the sheet glass. Use an opal style for the base and cap with Clear.
· Brush a thin layer of GlasTac onto the clear sheet, sprinkle the frit ball mix and adjust to your liking. Don't worry about finding the flat sides of the frit balls.
· Fire to a full fuse. See Tip Sheet 7: Platemaking Tips.
· You will likely notice a little haze around the dots. Fix this surface flaw and gloss up the project by firing a fresh layer of Clear Powder to the top surface. It's worth it! See Quick Tip: Fix Surface Flaws.
· Center on Drop Out Ring Mold (008632), place directly on a kiln shelf and slump. See Mold Tips: Suggested Slumping Schedules.

Making Mini Frit Balls
The secret to the small dots is to make them with Medium (-0002) Frit. Guidelines include firing on a primed kiln shelf and using transparent frit. The larger grains of -02 are a little easier to manage here. These smaller grains can be fired with a little less heatwork than when making frit balls with Coarse Frit; firing as fast as possible to 1490°F (810°C) for 10 minutes usually does the trick. Include a two hour hold at 1225°F (663°C) on the way up for color development in gold-bearing pinks.

Transparent, Medium Frit
· Light Orange (001025-0002)
· Turquoise Blue (001116-0002)
· Yellow (001120-0002)
· Red (001122-0002)
· Light Pink (001215-0002)
· Light Aquamarine Blue (001408-0002)

Sheet Glass/Supplies
· Light Peach Cream Opalescent (000034-0030)
· White Opalescent (000113-0030)
· Warm White Opalescent (000920-0030)
· Tekta Clear (001100-0380)
· Bullseye GlasTac, 4oz (008234)
· Clear, Powder (001101-0008)
· Drop Out Ring Slumping Mold, 8.9" (23 cm) (008632)

Quick Tip: Get the Look with Stripes & Dots

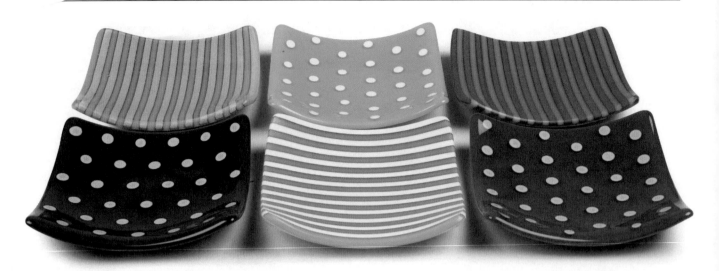

Rods are a natural choice for easy stripes and dots. We found this summer-themed nautical palette of opalescents fresh and irresistible for mixing and matching.

Stripes

Use a complete layer of rods as the base, then cap with 3 mm Clear and fire to a full fuse. The shelf side has a smooth, semi-matte finish, while the top has glossy goodness. Slump with either side up! (Coldworking may be necessary to smooth edges before slumping.)

Dots

Nip rods into 3-5 mm sections—we used a Neo-GC Cutter (7162)—and arrange them on a sheet of 3 mm Clear. Place this on a base of 3 mm opalescent and fire to a full fuse.

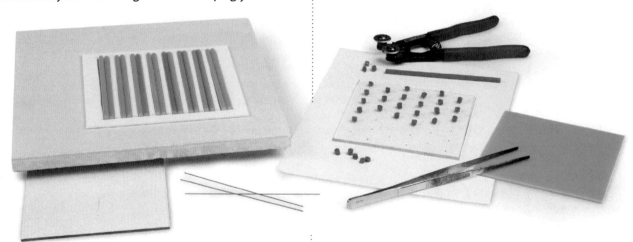

Tips

- Make a square frame from 1/16" fiber paper (7037) to ease set up and prevent rods from rolling.
- For variation in line width, place stringer in the low spot between rods. Stringers will stay perfectly straight through the fuse.
- To cut rods in bulk, secure a bundle with rubber bands and use a wet tile saw.

Tips

- Cut rod into a container with a towel draped over it to prevent bits of rod from flying.
- Position the attached pattern template under the sheet of Clear to guide dot placement.
- To maintain a square footprint and control volume, use shorter snippets closest to the perimeter.

Rod: Light Cyan (000216-0576-F), Golden Green (000227-0576-F), Tomato Red (000024-0576-F), French Vanilla (000137-0576-F). Any fusible (or F grade) rod is suitable for kilnforming. **Sheet:** Light Cyan (000216-0030-F), Indigo (000148-0030-F), Tomato Red (000024-0030-F), Clear (001101-0030-F). **Mold:** Square Slumper Mold (8997)

Gold and silver irid + clear powder = shimmering glass

In the tiles above, powdered and exposed iridescent surfaces catch and reflect light differently, producing subtle glimmering effects.

To make the tiles, we sifted Clear powder (001101-0008) onto Silver (000100-0037) and Gold (000100-0038) iridized sheet glass, using bits of foliage as stencils. Select foliage that's flat and rigid enough to support some powder, then adhere tabs made of tape so you can remove the stencil without spilling.

Elevate the sheet glass on blocks for ease of moving to the kiln later on. Position the stencil and, wearing a NIOSH approved respirator, sift on a uniform layer of powder, about 1/16 inch (1.5 mm) thick. For even distribution, hold the sifter 14-16 inches above the sheet glass and apply multiple light taps to the handle.

When finished, carefully remove the stencil and place on top of a 3 mm base sheet. Fire to a full fuse.

◎ Quick Tip: Gold-Bearing Pink Tints

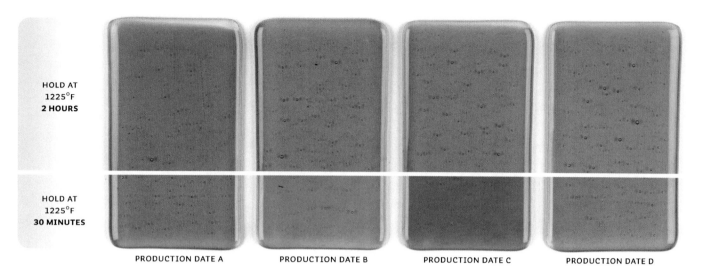

HOLD AT
1225°F
2 HOURS

HOLD AT
1225°F
30 MINUTES

PRODUCTION DATE A   PRODUCTION DATE B   PRODUCTION DATE C   PRODUCTION DATE D

Samples of Ruby Red Tint (001824-0030-F) from various production dates.

To consistently reach target color when firing our gold-bearing striking glasses, Bullseye advises a pre-rapid heat soak of 2 hours at 1225°F (663°C) on the way up to process temperature. This applies to all forms of these glasses: sheet, billet, rod, frit, etc.

However, we've discovered something interesting in the process of testing our 1800 series of gold-bearing tint styles. It's possible to produce a variety of hues by firing these styles with a shorter pre-rapid heat soak hold of 30 minutes. Testing is required, since the color development varies in different production runs, and within a single production run.

Note that firing these styles with the 30-minute pre-rapid heat soak permanently affects color development. You may be able to continue developing color by firing again with a longer soak, but this will not push the glass to its target color.

1800 Series of Gold-Bearing Tints
Ruby Red Tint 001824-0030-F
Ruby Pink Tint 001831-0030-F
Burnt Scarlet Tint 001823-0030-F

Suggested Schedule for Gold-Bearing Glasses

Rate	Temperature	Hold
*	1225°F (663°C)	2:00
600°F (333°C)	1490°F (810°C)	:10
AFAP	900°F (482°C)	**

Shortened Pre-Rapid Heat Soak Schedule

Rate	Temperature	Hold
*	1225°F (663°C)	:30
600°F (333°C)	1490°F (810°C)	:10
AFAP	900°F (482°C)	**

* The initial rate of heat is not a critical factor in successfully striking gold-bearing glasses. Choose an initial rate of heat appropriate to the scale and design of the project that you are firing.

** Remainder of cycle depends on the thickness of the piece. Consult the *Bullseye Annealing Chart for Thick Slabs.* For color-sensitive projects, we recommend testing the cycle you plan to use by fusing a small sample of a similar setup in the same kiln as the project to best predict final color results.

◎ Quick Tip: Holiday Punch

Holiday punch plate, 8" x 13", slumped on Rectangular Slumper, Mold 8929.

For a festive feel, break out the punch!

(The paper punch, that is.) Combine punched silver foil design elements with Tomato Red Opalescent for something truly festive.

The Details

Arrange silver foil (7217) punches on Tomato Red (000024-0030-F). You can use GlasTac (008232-GLUE) to keep them in place. Cap with 3 mm Clear (001101-0030-F) and invert the whole layup so that the clear sheet is against the shelf and the Tomato Red is the top layer—or arrange the foil on the Clear and cap with Tomato Red.

The pieces shown here were fired "design down," so the side facing the shelf in the fuse becomes the front of the piece. To achieve an effortless semi-matte finish, slump with the shelf-side up.

In addition to Tomato Red (left), try Red Opalescent (000124-0030-F) and Deep Red (000224-0030-F).

Hint: Sandwich silver foil between sheets of paper before punching out shapes (or cutting them with scissors). This creates a toothy structure that cuts cleanly and keeps the foil from tearing. Be sure to remove all traces of paper before firing.

Firing

We've had success firing this layup with an initial heat range of 200-400°F in the first segment of a full fuse. If using larger pieces of silver, slow this rate to 100 degrees per hour to prevent thermal shock.

Remember Reactivity

A dark reaction will develop around foil elements as a result of a silver-sulfur reaction with Red Opalescent. Reactions near the edge of the piece may "feather" because there's more airflow there. Some yellowing between Clear and silver may develop (this is called silver stain). Expect variation. It's part of the beauty of this combination.

Firing with silver foil between layers of glass usually contains the silver. To protect your kiln shelf from silver contamination, place the foil elements at least 3/4" from the outer edge of the project. If firing with silver on the perimeter, keep it within the footprint of the base without any overhang.

Enjoy the punch!

Samples shown were placed on an additional 3 mm sheet and fired to a full fuse.

Combining GlasTac (008234-GLUE) and Aventurine Blue powder (001140-0008) is the perfect way to make saturated, gestural brush strokes in kilnforming. Think of sumi-e and other East Asian styles of brush painting and calligraphy.

Here's how it works: Using a brush, create your design in GlasTac on clean, dry 3 mm sheet glass, then sift Aventurine Blue powder over the wet area. Tilt the sheet vertical, give it a swift tap to remove excess powder, and you're ready to head for the kiln. It's that simple!

Further considerations

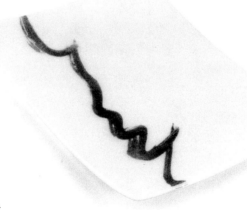

- Aventurine Blue is a color-saturated indigo, so even a small amount can have an impact. Consider the tiny sparkles found in this style a bonus!

- Working on a sheet of paper makes it to easy to reclaim excess powder.

- For greater versatility in line quality, choose a brush that tapers to a point.

- Allowing the design to dry makes light editing easier but isn't required. We've successfully fired both wet and dry works.

- If you're not satisfied with the design, wipe the powder away to a container or surface and let it dry out. Once you break up the clumps, it's ready to be used again.

- GlasTac is clear when applied. To better see the wet brush strokes, work with side lighting set up at a low angle.

Grab a brush and try this technique today!

Quick Tip: Iridescent Squares

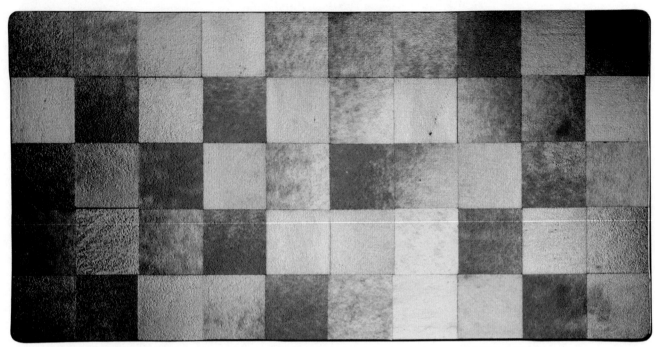

7.5 x 15 inch (190 x 380 mm) tile composed of pieces from a single sheet of Black with Rainbow Irid coating (000100-0031-F).

You can transform a single sheet of Rainbow Iridescent glass into a shimmering design by cutting it into squares and reconfiguring the pieces.

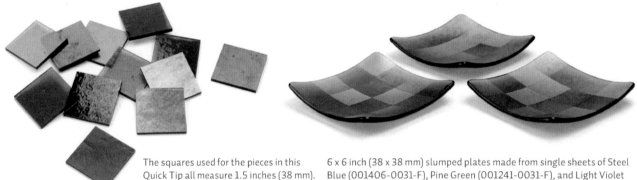

The squares used for the pieces in this Quick Tip all measure 1.5 inches (38 mm).

6 x 6 inch (38 x 38 mm) slumped plates made from single sheets of Steel Blue (001406-0031-F), Pine Green (001241-0031-F), and Light Violet (001428-0031-F).

The Details

Start with a 3 mm sheet of a saturated transparent color (or black) with a Rainbow irid coating. Find a section with a range of color and cut it into squares. Arrange the pieces with an eye to both color contrast and color transitions at the seams. Clean the pieces and carefully transfer them to a primed shelf with the irid coating face down.

Make sure the squares fit tightly. If there are gaps, the glass will flow to close them but the irid coating won't, leaving spaces where the base color shows through the metallic surface.

Cap with a single sheet of 3 mm Clear and fire to a full fuse. Flip the piece over to slump it. Note that this brings the glossy side in contact with the slumping mold, where it can pick up the texture of the mold. To minimize this, choose gently sloped mold profiles that require less heatwork.

Note: When used in direct contact with iridized glass, ThinFire may cause a reaction resulting in surface pitting.

Quick Tip: Keen On Green

How to make green from other colors of Bullseye glass.

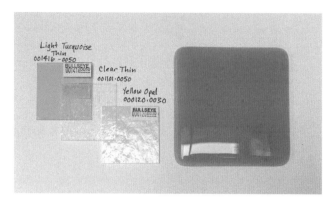

Top: Light Turquoise Blue Thin 001416-0050
Middle: Clear Thin 001101-0050
Base: Canary Yellow Opal 000120-0030. Requires Clear Thin between colors to prevent a dark color reaction.

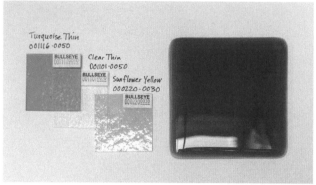

Top: Turquoise Blue Thin 001116-0050
Middle: Clear Thin 001101-0050 **Base:** Sunflower Yellow Opal 000220-0030. Requires Clear Thin between colors to prevent a dark color reaction.

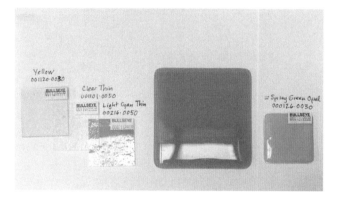

Top: Yellow 001120-0030
Middle: Clear Thin 001101-0050 **Base:** Light Cyan Opal Thin 000216-0050. Requires Clear Thin between colors to prevent a dark color reaction.

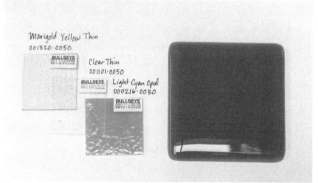

Top: Marigold Yellow Thin 001320-0050
Middle: Clear Thin 001101-0050 **Base:** Light Cyan Opal 000216-0030. Requires Clear Thin between colors to prevent a dark color reaction.

Top: Yellow 001120-0030
Base: Periwinkle Opal 000118-0030

Top: Marigold Yellow Thin 001320-0050
Base: Cobalt Blue 000114-0030

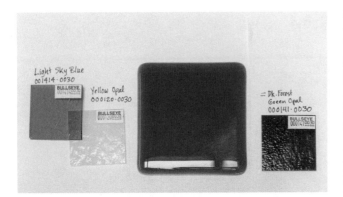

Top: Light Sky Blue 001414-0030 **Base:** Canary Yellow Opal 000120-0030

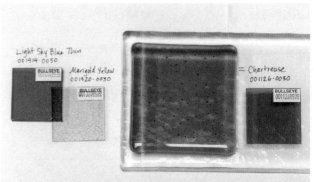

Top: Light Sky Blue Thin 001414-0050 **Base:** Marigold Yellow Opal 001320-0030. (Tile shown elevated on a Clear billet for light transmission.)

Top: Medium Amber 001137-0030 **Middle:** Clear Thin 001101-0050 **Base:** Light Turquoise Thin 001416-0050. Requires Clear Thin between colors to prevent a dark color reaction. (Tile shown elevated on a Clear billet for light transmission.)

Top: Light Sky Blue 001414-0030 **Base:** Medium Amber 001137-0030. (Tile shown elevated on a Clear billet for light transmission.)

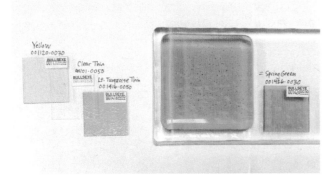

Top: Yellow 001120-0030 **Middle:** Clear Thin 001101-0050 **Base:** Light Turquoise Thin 001416-0050. Requires Clear Thin between colors to prevent a dark color reaction. (Tile shown elevated on a Clear billet for light transmission.)

Top: Light Amber 001437-0030 **Middle:** Clear Thin 001101-0050 **Base:** Light Turquoise Thin 001416-0050. Requires Clear Thin between colors to prevent a dark color reaction. (Tile shown elevated on a Clear billet for light transmission.)

◎ Quick Tip: Kilncarved Billet

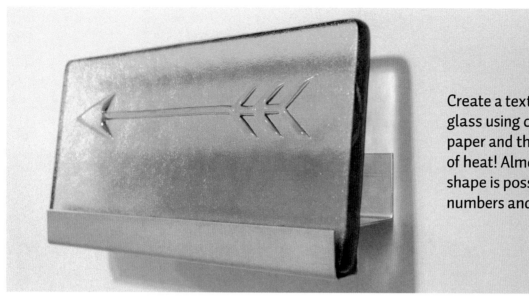

Create a textured block of glass using ceramic fiber paper and the right amount of heat! Almost any shape is possible: letters, numbers and more.

Design with texture:
In the kiln, the billet conforms to your fiber paper design. Note that the glass will take on the texture of the fiber paper and the kiln shelf.

Color considerations:
Any billet will work, even Curious billets. Lighter saturation styles are a good choice to display with the smooth side facing out.

1
Plan a design based on the billet dimensions, approximately 10" x 5" x 0.75" (127 x 254 x 19 mm).

2
To make this design, we started with an image on paper and cut it out to make a stencil.

3
Trace the design onto 1/8" fiber paper (7036) and cut it out using an X-Acto knife. For a raised design, oversize the fiber paper by 0.5" on each side to keep the billet from flowing over the edge.

4
Arrange the fiber paper on a primed kiln-shelf. Clean the billet and load it on the fiber paper. Fire with the schedule below.

Rate	Temperature	Hold
150°F (83°C)	1000°F (538°C)	:30*
600°F (333°C)	1375°F (746°C)	:10
AFAP	900°F (482°C)	3:00
45°F (25°C)	800°F (427°C)	:00
81°F (45°C)	700°F (371°C)	:00
270°F (150°C)	70°F (21°C)	:00

*For color development in gold-bearing styles (1823, 1824, 1831), we recommend a 2:00 hold at 1225°F (663°C).

5
Be sure to wear respiratory protection as you peel away the fiber paper. Remove any residue with a scrub pad or nylon brush and water.

Image at the top: A kilncarved billet in a wall-mounted Glass Bracket (8619). Kilncarving results in various thicknesses, so you may need to add Bumpons (8402) for a better fit.

◎ Quick Tip: Kilncast and Slumped Bowl

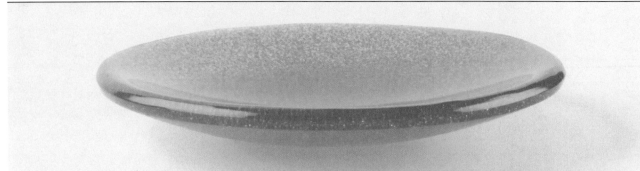

Get experience in volume calculation, frit tinting, and more as you create a kilncast disc from a frit-and-powder mixture, coldwork the edges, and slump it into this graceful bowl.

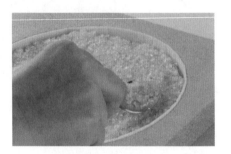

Prepare the Dam

Cut a 2.5 cm strip of 1.6 mm Fiber Paper (7037) to line a Bullseye Circle Dam (8848). For a precise fit, cut it slightly longer than needed, press it against the wall and trim the excess. Note: Always prefire a new Circle Dam.

Calculate the Glass

To find the volume of a disc 1 cm thick: height x π x radius^2 = volume. Or:
1 cm x 3.14 x 9.75 cm^2 = 298cm^3

Next, multiply the volume by 2.5 (the specific gravity of Bullseye glass) to find out how many grams of glass you'll need. In this case, the total is 745 grams of glass.

Frit Tinting

Frit tinting creates color blends by adding colored glass powder to Clear frit. It broadens the palette immensely and makes it possible to achieve colors—red, yellow, orange—that are often difficult in casting.

To make this vibrant orange, we tinted damp Medium Clear Frit (001101-0002) with Pimento Red powder (000225-0008) at 3%—specifically 723 g of Clear frit and 22 g of powder. For complete mixing instructions, see our technical document *Frit Tinting*.

Place the mold on a primed kiln shelf. Fill the center with the damp frit mixture and compact the material into a uniform layer. With the back of a spoon, create a v-shaped gap between the frit and the fiber paper. Go about

two-thirds of the way down. This will develop a rounded profile when fired and minimize needlepointing.

After firing, and coldworking the edge, slump in a Ball Surface Mold (8736).

Fusing Schedule

Rate	Temperature	Hold
400°F (222°C)	1225°F (663°C)	:30
600°F (333°C)	1500°F (816°C)	:30
AFAP	900°F (482°C)	2:00
100°F (56°C)	700°F (371°C)	:00
AFAP	70°F (21°C)	:00

Slumping Schedule

Rate	Temperature	Hold
300°F (167°C)	1215°F (657°C)	:05
AFAP	900°F (482°C)	2:00
100°F (56°C)	700°F (371°C)	:00
AFAP	70°F (21°C)	:00

⊚ Quick Tip: Little Wisp Bowls

Wisps of white and clear let the color shine through

Create your own streaky color palette. Layer Clear and White Streaky sheet glass over transparent tint glass styles. Slump in the Cone Bowl mold to upturn the edges and achieve luscious color at the rim. We're making bowls for days!

Materials
· Clear, White Streaky (002130-0030)
· Pale Yellow Tint (001820-0030)
· Coral Orange Tint (001834-0030)
· Purple Blue Tint (001948-0030)
· Cone Bowl Mold (8943)

Steps
· Cut 4.5" (approx. 11.5cm) circles. You'll need 3 circles of Clear, White Streaky sheet glass and one of each tint style to make the set.
· Clean & layer. Use a tint style for the base and cap with Clear, White Streaky sheet glass.
· Fire to a full fuse. We recommend the schedule from Tip Sheet 7.
· Slump into Cone Bowl mold (8943). See Mold Tips: Cone Bowl Molds for additional notes.

Tips
· Clear, White Streaky sheet glass may become more translucent upon firing.
· Remove any needlepointed edges with a diamond pad prior to slumping.
· A clean Small Suction Lifter (7196) is handy for minor adjustments of the flat, fused blank in the mold, as well as removing the slumped dish from the mold.

SLUMP FIRING CONE BOWL 8943

	Rate (Degrees/Hour)	Temperature	Hold
1	300°F (167°C)	1200°F (649°C)	:30
2	300°F (167°C)	1225°F (663°C)	1:30*
3	AFAP**	900°F (482°C)	1:00
4	100°F (56°C)	700°F (371°C)	:00
5	AFAP	70°F (21°C)	:00

* If possible, visually confirm the slump.
** As Fast As Possible. Allow the kiln to cool at its natural rate with the door closed.

◎ Quick Tip: Making a Chevron Design

Making this chevron plate is a snap with Bullseye's Cascade sheet glass.

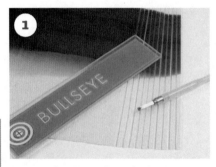

Start with a Cascade style sheet, cut into quarter inch strips. Keep your strips in order as you go.

Slide the strips up or down into the pattern you like.

Once you settle on a pattern, decide on your dimensions and mark a top and bottom line with Sharpie.

Score along these lines. You can score the strips all at once, being careful to keep consistent pressure throughout your score.

Run your score lines. You can run multiple strips at once by sliding a section to the edge of the table and using the table to snap the score lines.

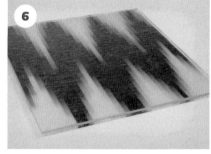

Cap with Clear to keep your lines tight.

Glass/Tools: Cascade style sheet glass, 3 mm Clear sheet glass, glass cutter, Sharpie, and a straightedge.

Tip: Make quick and effi cient work of creating those strips with the G-Manu Glass Cutting system, an elegantly simple yet powerful tool developed by Rudi Gritsch.

Suggested Fusing Schedule

Rate	Temperature	Hold
300°F (167°C)	1225°F (663°C)	1:00
600°F (333°C)	1490°F (810°C)	:10
AFAP	900°F (482°C)	1:00
100°F (56°C)	700°F (371°C)	:00
AFAP	70°F (21°C)	:00

Suggested Slumping Schedule

Rate	Temperature	Hold
300°F (167°C)	1170°F (632°C)	:05
AFAP	900°F (482°C)	1:00
100°F (56°C)	700°F (371°C)	:00
AFAP	70°F (21°C)	:00

◎ Quick Tip: Multitasking Molds

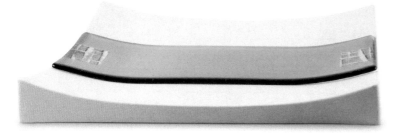

There's more than meets the eye with some slumping molds. They can certainly be used to form pieces that utilize the entire surface, but consider the options when slumping pieces that only make use of a portion of the mold. In our studios, we've found Rectangular Slumper mold (8929) and Round Slumper mold (8629) to be particularly versatile.

Rectangular Slumper mold (8929)

The central lengthwise portion of the Rectangular Slumper produces an elegant form with upturned corners, as seen with this 5 x 17" centerpiece.

Slumping a 9 x 14" blank in the center of the same mold produces a piece with gently elevated edges.

Round Slumper mold (8629)

A 9" diameter circle in the 12" Round Slumper has a gently sloped rim with a flat base, which is right at home as a first course or generous dessert plate. Tip: An 11" diameter round blank in Plain Plate mold (8721) makes for a lovely companion dinner plate.

Check your studio for these and other possibilities. Ready, set, slump!

Transparents transform with on-edge strip construction

Cut 3mm sheet glass into 1cm wide strips, turn those on edge, and—presto!—color saturation increases. In the pairings below, notice how the 1cm thick on-edge samples (right) are darker than the thinner 3mm flat sheet samples (left), producing new depths of color. Your palette just multiplied!

Indigo Tint (001818-0030)

Light Sky Blue (001414-0030)

Deep Royal Blue (001114-0030)

Aqua Blue Tint (001808-0030)

Light Aquamarine Blue (001408-0030)

Aquamarine Blue (001108-0030)

On-edge strip construction samples

Sample tiles are made from 3mm sheet glass (color and any clear) cut into strips, dammed, and fired on edge. Narrowest color bands are one strip; wider bands are two or three. Making samples with this technique allows you to gauge how a project's thickness will affect its color saturation. Just look at the dramatic transformation in those tint styles! You'll love having these valuable design tools to reference in your studio.

Additional resources

- Video: <u>On-Edge Strip Construction</u>
- Video: <u>Kiln Shelves and Furniture</u>
- Video: <u>Glass Cutting Basics (Free)</u>
- Tip Sheet: <u>Working Deep</u>

Quick Tip: Opaline Overlays

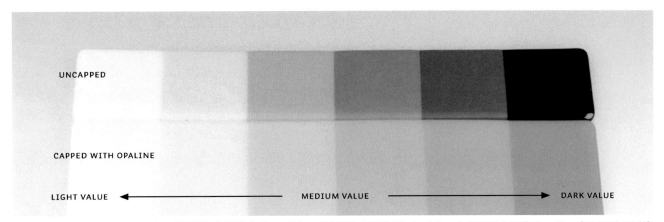

UNCAPPED

CAPPED WITH OPALINE

LIGHT VALUE ◄————— MEDIUM VALUE —————► DARK VALUE

Style codes for glasses above: White (000113-0030), Driftwood Gray (000132-0030), Elephant Gray (000206-0030), Deco Gray (000136-0030), Slate Gray (000236-0030), Black (000100-0030)

Opaline sheet glass. Amazing on its own—also a great tool to expand your color palette in kilnforming, creating new colors with distinct properties.

As an overlay, expect subtle changes when fired over light value styles and more dramatic effects over dark values.

The small tiles are uncapped, fired on a clear base. The large tiles are capped with Opaline (000403-0030). All shown in reflected light, unless noted.

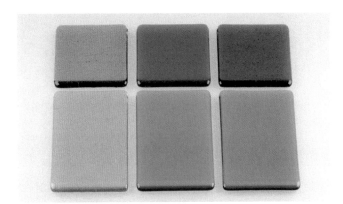

Medium Value Transparent: Medium Amber (001137-0030), Light Sky Blue (001414-0030), Light Plum (001405-0030)

Medium Value Opalescent: Spring Green (000126-0030), Sunflower Yellow (000220-0030), Tangerine Orange (000025-0030)

Dark Value Transparent: Red (001122-0030), Olive Green (001141-0030), Deep Royal Blue (001114-0030). These two photos show the same tiles. The image on the right is shown in transmitted light. The base color shows through.

◎ Quick Tip: Put a Ring on It

Explore the possibilities of a palette of green rings capped with Opaline! As an overlay, Opaline scatters light for a dramatic impact on base colors. Note the blue hue it adds to the dark-valued green here and the subtle changes with lighter-valued greens. But when held up to the light, it's as if the Opaline layer disappears.

Simple Secrets of Ring Cutting

For a good fit, inner pieces must be slightly smaller in diameter. A central circle cut to the same dimension as the inner ring will not fit, in the same way a ring and circle cut from the same sheet won't fit back together. Larger, narrower rings are easier to cut because they're more flexible than smaller, wider rings.

For a plate with a central circle and a ring

1. Cut a cap, or the top layer, of Opaline (000403-0030).

2. Cut a circle for the ring the same diameter as the cap. Before scoring the sheet, mark the placement of the circle cutter's suction cup on the sheet glass with an ultra fine point Sharpie. You'll use these to re-align the circle cutter in a later step.

3. Adjust the cutting head to the dimension that will be the inner diameter of the ring. Tip: Keep this ring relatively narrow, less than an inch wide.

4. Re-align the suction cup with the marks from Step 2. Score and run gently to avoid breaking the ring. Make a single score perpendicular to the inner circle and run it gently, then wiggle the ends of the ring up and down to ease it off of the central circle. This will leave a seam in the ring, but this usually fuses together with little visibility, particularly under a cap of Opaline.

5. Adjust the cutting head to a slightly a smaller dimension for the center of the design. A millimeter or two should do the trick. Score, run, and break out the circle as usual.

6. Once you're sure the pieces fit, clean and fire to a full fuse. We then slumped our plate into a Large Cone Bowl mold (8975).

Follow the same steps to add more rings, making sure the circles are slightly smaller at each color transition.

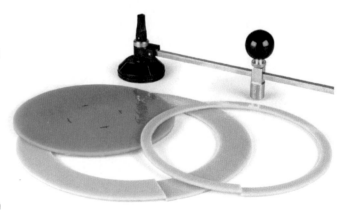

Glass styles: Opaline (000403-0030), Pine Green (001241-0030), Mineral Green (000117-0030), Celadon Green (000207-0030), Spruce Green Tint (001841-0030); **Tools and supplies**: Bohle Silberschnitt Studio Circle Cutter (7161), Large Cone Bowl Mold (8975), Cone Bowl Mold (8943)

Quick Tip: Working with Petrified Wood

Detail

Detail

Petrified Wood is Bullseye's magical unicorn streaky. Its unique combination of glasses results in dramatic internal reactions at full-fuse temperatures. Here are two ideas for making this glass sing.

Copper Reactions

The Clear areas of Petrified Wood contain Red Reactive Clear, a style that reacts with select copper-bearing glasses, developing deep red hues where they meet. Neighboring sepia-hued areas develop a variety of rich, earthy effects.

Tips:
- The red reactions may continue to deepen with additional heatwork. Maintain color with lower temp slump firings and other cautious heatwork. The piece pictured below became darker with a 1225°F (663°C) slump firing.
- Some favorite copper-bearing styles for creating a range of deep reds include 3mm Turquoise Blue in Opalescent and Transparent (000116 and 001116), Light Cyan (000216), and Robin's Egg Blue (000161).

Base: Robin's Egg Blue (000161-0030); Cap: Petrified Wood (002971-0030). Mold: Square Nesting Plate, medium (8758).

Displacement with Frit

Sepia-hued areas of Petrified Wood strike with varying opacity and colors. Play up this organic effect with various grain sizes of Clear Frit. We used Coarse and Extra Large. The frit rounds out and sinks in, creating shallow pools.

Tips:
- Leave space between the grains and give them room to melt and displace the underlying glass.
- Expect variation to occur within a single sheet and throughout production runs of Petrified Wood.

Base: Tekta Clear (001101-0030); Cap: Petrified Wood (002971-0030) with Clear Frit (001101-0003 and -0005) on top. Mold: Round Slumper (8630.)

◎ Quick Tip: Powder Power for Bubble Control

A thin layer of powder has power! Light Turquoise and Clear Powder (001101-0008-F), unfired.

Same, capped with Tekta Clear & fired with schedule provided. Very small bubbles.

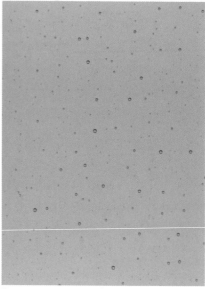

For comparison, same sheet glass lay-up fired without powder to a basic full fuse. Typical champagne bubbles.

Want to minimize the look of bubbles in fused pieces? Here's a technique—used in kilnforming circles for many years—that's also worked well for us.

Add a light application of Clear powder between the layers with a full-fuse firing schedule. That's right: *between* the layers! You'll actually trap more bubbles, but they'll be smaller than the usual "champagne" bubbles—and to that we say, "Cheers!"

Tip: To get an even distribution of powder, keep your sifter at least 18 inches (45 cm) above the surface and apply with multiple light taps to the handle.

Firing Schedule

Rate	Temperature	Hold
300°F (167°C)	1225°F (663°C)	1:00
600°F (333°C)	1490°F (810°C)	:10

Anneal and cool based on thickness.

This firing schedule has a built-in "bubble squeeze" when the glass is in the 1200-1225°F range. The glass softens in this range and, as the layers settle, much of the air is squeezed out. We've tested this extensively on 6" x 8" tiles. For larger works, you may want to extend the hold time at 1225°F.

Note that the smaller bubbles created by this technique can also result in a flatter piece, whether it's fired with transparent, opalescent, or iridized glasses.

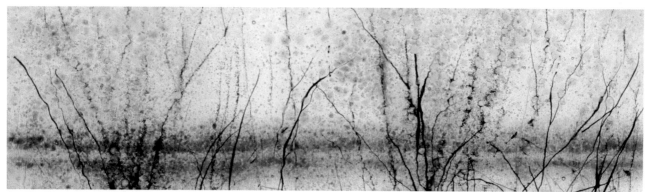

Angelita Surmon, *Oak Island Reflections* (detail), 8 x 12 x .25 inches, 2012. Surmon uses a variation of this bubble control technique to draw attention to imagery and quiet the negative spaces in her kilnformed landscape works.

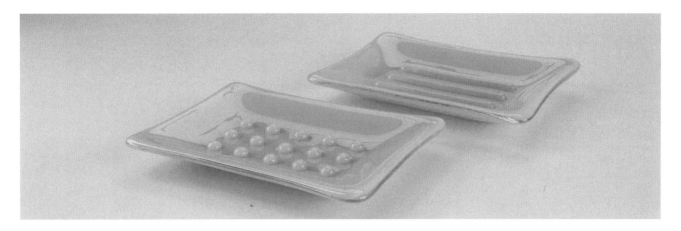

Add an accent color—and functionality—to your new soap dish with a little help from Bullseye fusible rods! We paired Robin's Egg Blue Opalescent with Driftwood Gray rod, but you could use any combination.

Step 1. Fuse a 10.5 x 15.5 cm piece of Robin's Egg Blue on a base of 3mm Clear.

Step 2. Tack fuse texture with Driftwood Gray rods—choose from two ways:

Rods for dots
- Make dots by snipping rod into 8-10mm lengths, standing the pieces on end on either a primed shelf or ThinFire (which we especially like for opals). Fire as fast as possible to 1500°F (816°C) for 20 minutes and crash cool.
- Clean and arrange dots in the center of the fused blank.
- We tack fused this piece at 1375°F. Remember to anneal for twice the thickness of the thickest area, following the Annealing Thick Slabs chart.

Rods for ridges
- Cut lengths of rod and arrange them on the blank. Use Glastac Gel sparingly.
- We tack fused this piece at 1400°F, again with an annealing cycle for twice the thickness of the thickest area. This higher temperature softens the cut ends of the rod and tacks them securely to the base.

Step 3. Slump into Soap Dish Mold (8981). The heatwork of this slump firing maintains the tack-fused texture. Again, we anneal for twice the thickness of the thickest area.

Suggested Firing Schedules

FULL FUSE

	Rate (Degrees/Hour)	Temperature	Hold
1	400°F (222°C)	1225°F (663°C)	:45
2	600°F (333°C)	1490°F (810°C)	:10
3	AFAP*	900°F (482°C)	1:00
4	100°F (55°C)	700°F (371°C)	:00
5	AFAP	70°F (21°C)	:00

*As fast as possible

TACK FUSE TEXTURE

	Rate (Degrees/Hour)	Temperature	Hold
1	300°F (167°C)	**	:10
2	AFAP	900°F (482°C)	3:00
3	45°F (25°C)	800°F (427°C)	:00
4	81°F (45°C)	700°F (371°C)	:00
5	270°F (150°C)	70°F (21°C)	:00

**1375°F or 1400°F (746° or 760°C)

SLUMP (SOAP DISH MOLD)

	Rate (Degrees/Hour)	Temperature	Hold
1	300°F (167°C)	1215°F (657°C)	1:00
2	AFAP	900°F (482°C)	3:00
3	45°F (25°C)	800°F (427°C)	:00
4	81°F (45°C)	700°F (371°C)	:00
5	270°F (150°C)	70°F (21°C)	:00

Supplies
- Robin's Egg Blue, Double-rolled (000161-0030-F)
- Clear, Double-rolled (001101-0030-F)
- Driftwood Gray Rod (000132-0576-F)
- Soap Dish Mold (8981)

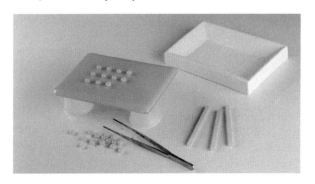

Quick Tip: Reaction Action

When certain Bullseye glasses are fired in contact with one another, their chemistries interact at the interface to create varied effects and colors. Here are close-up examples of some of our favorite reactions, including copper+sulfur, copper+reactive, and lead+sulfur.

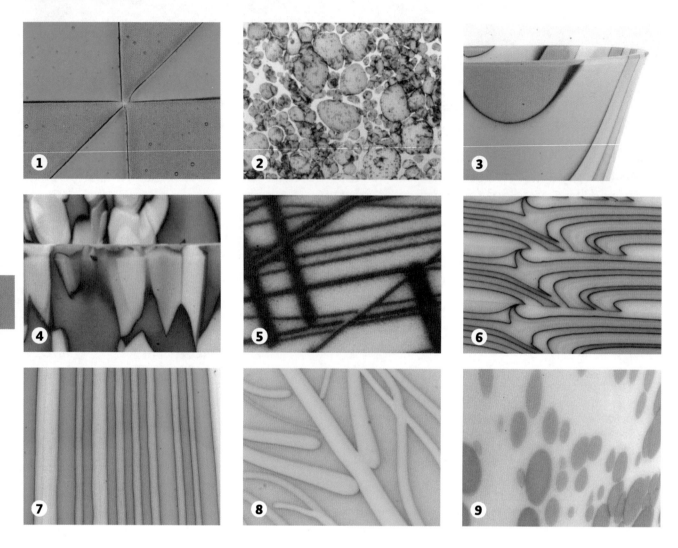

1. Copper: Light Turquoise Blue (001416) sheet
   Sulfur: Medium Amber (001137) sheet
2. Lead: Sunset Coral (001305) powder
   Sulfur: French Vanilla (000137), medium and coarse frit. For instructions, see *Quick Tip: River Rock Reaction.*
3. Copper: Light Cyan (000216) rod
   Sulfur: Golden Green (000227) rod
4. Sulfur: French Vanilla (000137) coarse frit
   Copper: Turquoise (000116) coarse frit
5. Sulfur: French Vanilla (000137) sheet
   Copper: Steel Blue (000146) powder
6. Copper: Robin's Egg Blue (000161) sheet
   Reactive: Reactive Cloud Opal (000009) sheet

7. Copper: Light Cyan (000216) sheet
   Reactive: Reactive Cloud Opal (000009)
8. Copper: Robin's Egg Blue (000161) sheet
   Sulfur: Spring Green (000126) Vitrigraph stringer
9. Sulfur: French Vanilla (000137) sheet
   Copper: Light Aquamarine Blue (001408), medium and coarse frit

Resources
Reactive Potential of Bullseye Glass (chart)
Get a Reaction: Bullseye Reactive Glasses (article)
TechNotes 2: The Vitrigraph Kiln (article)
Color Reactions and Special Effects (video)

Quick Tip: River Rock Reaction

Make a part sheet with stony effects—then cut it up to create projects!

Reactivity is key to achieving the pebbly look of the part sheet featured here. Under kiln heat, sulfur-bearing frits react with lead-bearing powder to create a rocks-in-a-streambed effect.

To make this part sheet, start with a base of 3 mm Clear (001101-0030-F) or Tekta Clear (001100-0380-F) sheet glass. Mix together French Vanilla frits (000137-0001, -0002, -0003) in equal portions by volume—enough to cover your base sheet with a layer that's one frit thick. Weigh the frits and pour them into a clean container with a lid. Using a spray bottle, spritz the frit grains with enough water to dampen them, then put the lid on the container and shake to distribute the moisture. Next, weigh out Sunset Coral powder (001305-0008) equaling 5% of the weight of your frits. Sprinkle the powder over the wet frits, replace the container lid, and shake. As the powder is distributed, it will stick to the wet frits. When the mix is relatively uniform, pour all of it onto your base glass and spread it out evenly. For firing we recommend the following schedule, which facilitates melting the stiff opalescent frits into the thin base, as well as proper annealing.

Once the part sheet has cooled, flip it over so the Clear is on top. Then you're ready to cut the sheet and use it in projects like the French Vanilla platter shown below.

When designing your part sheet, consider making it larger than needed by about an inch all the way around. Firing the unknown volume of frit onto the 3 mm base will likely distort the sheet's edges, and you may need to trim them if you want straight sides.

Rate	Temperature	Hold
400°F (222°C)	1000°F (538°C)	:30
600 °F (333 °C)	1500 ° (816 °C)	:10
AFAP*	900 °F (482 °C)	2:00
100 °F (56 °C)	700 °F (371 °C)	:00
AFAP*	70 °F (21 °C)	:00

*As fast as possible

◎ Quick Tip: Silver Stripe Jewelry

Wearable glass with flash! It's all in the details — torn silver paired with candy apple red, and drilled holes for stringing.

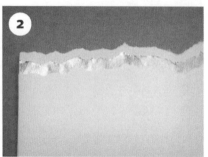
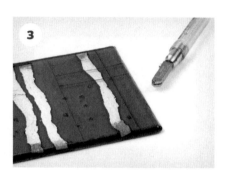
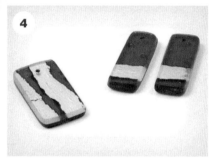

1. Materials: Clear, Thin (001101-50); Red, Thin (001122-50); silver foil (7217)

2. Place silver between layers of paper and tear into strips. Layer the silver between Red and Clear sheet glass. Keep the silver away from the perimeter to minimize potential shelf contamination. Fuse the layers together.

3. Cut the fired sheet into jewelry components.

4. Coldwork the edges to smooth them. We used a small flat lap grinder.

5. Drill small holes with a rotary tool and a diamond-coated drill bit. Then countersink or open up the hole by using a conical-shaped diamond-coated bit. This can help with stringing the finished piece. (See *Drilling Small Holes in Jewelry and Ornaments* for more information.)

6. Clean the drilled components, and then re-fire to firepolish according to the provided schedule. Note that cooler temperatures will maintain crisp edges, while hotter temperatures will achieve more softening. Fired effects will vary depending on the characteristics of the ground edges as well as how your kiln fires.

Suggested Fusing Schedule

Rate	Temperature	Hold
300°F (167°C)	1225°F (663°C)	:45
600°F (333°C)	1425°F (774°C)	:10
AFAP	900°F (482°C)	1:00
100°F (56°C)	700°F (371°C)	:00
AFAP	70°F (21°C)	:00

Suggested Firepolishing Schedule

Rate	Temperature	Hold
300°F (167°C)	1000°F (538°C)	:30
600°F (333°C)	1275-1325°F (691-718°C)	:10
AFAP	900°F (482°C)	1:00
100°F (56°C)	700°F (371°C)	:00
AFAP	70°F (21°C)	:00

Quick Tip: Smooth It Out

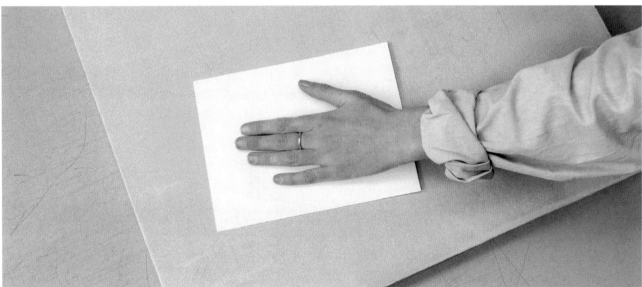

Create a smooth, uniform surface on the shelf side of your fired work—not a brush stroke in sight!

First, prepare a kilnshelf with Bullseye Shelf Primer. Follow the instructions in our free video *Preparing Kiln Shelves* to prime and dry the shelf.

Once the shelf has cooled, *gently* buff the surface with a sheet of standard copy paper.

Tip the shelf upright with the primer side away from you and tap it lightly against a hard surface to knock off the loosened primer (to ease cleanup, tap the shelf onto a piece of butcher paper). Ideally, this will be done with local ventilation, wearing a NIOSH approved respirator.

Note: The buffed surface is delicate. Avoid sliding pieces of sheet glass across it, as primer can collect in the seams.

This technique is ideal for works with a single base sheet or minimal seams. We're especially fond of the effect on iridized glass, though it's equally effective on non-iridized opals & transparents.

Create Hues with Sparkle and Depth

Did you ever wonder why Bullseye doesn't make an Aventurine version of other colors, like red, for example? We would if we could! The chemistry of those sparkles (a.k.a., flake) is deeply tied to green glass. In the kiln, however, you can layer to create new hues. When we were tipped off to this combination by Meryl Raiffe at *The Glass Underground*, we just had to try it and share the results!

001215-0030*
001412-0030

Light Pink (001215-0030)* fired over **Light Aventurine Green (001412-0030)** results in a dark, red-hued glitter effect. Remember to do a "gold hold" for two hours at 1225°F (663°C) in this full fuse firing.

*We fired Light Pink to illustrate its struck color.

At right, we've fired **Light Aventurine Green (001412-0030)**, from left to right, with caps of **Light Turquoise Blue (001416-0030)**, **Light Silver Gray (001429-0030)**, and **Light Orange (001025-0030)**. Each of these medium saturation transparent glasses is strong enough to affect Aventurine's color while transparent enough to let its sparkle shine through, creating deep hues that emanate an enchanting glitter effect.

◎ Quick Tip: Tint Overlay Palette

Create this soft, dreamy palette by layering Tint styles over neutral Opalescent styles. We're in love!

Tints: Pale Yellow Tint (001820-0030), Purple Blue Tint (001948-0030)

Opalescents: Light Peach Cream (000034-0030), White (000113-0030), Driftwood Gray (000132-0030)

And this is just the start — there are so many palette possibilities to explore!

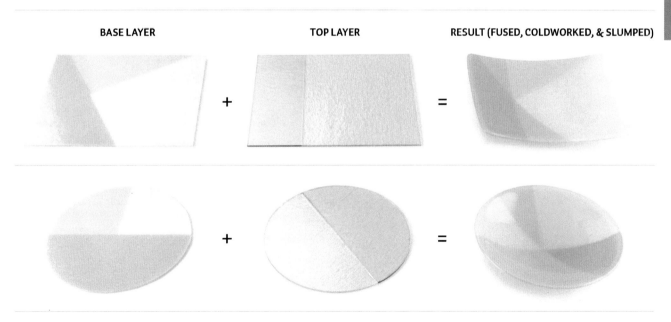

| BASE LAYER | TOP LAYER | RESULT (FUSED, COLDWORKED, & SLUMPED) |

For a semi-matte finish and crisp seams, design with a base layer of Tint glasses and cap with Opalescent styles. To keep the finish, slump with the shelf-side facing up and work with molds that require relatively little heatwork.

Product Use

◎ Alchemy Glasses

Alchemy Clear, Silver to Gold
001015

Reacts With: Silver
Cold Characteristics: Unfired sheet has a faint blue tint.

Working Notes

Upon firing, silver foil turns a golden color wherever it is in contact with 1015 (Alchemy Clear). On the sample tile above, the left side illustrates silver foil after being fired uncapped on top of 1015. The sample's right side illustrates silver foil after being fired between a layer of Clear (any style) and 1015, with 1015 as the cap. (Faint blue color may be evident in any fired work containing 1015.)

Expect variations in effects to result from different sources and thicknesses of silver, glass production runs, and heatwork (including firing times, temperatures, and number of times fired).

For color development, we recommend a 1 hour soak at 1225°F in the pre-rapid heat section of a firing cycle.

Note: When firing silver foil in the kiln, be aware that the silver can deposit onto the kiln shelf, potentially affecting silver-sensitive glasses in one or more subsequent firings. This can happen even when new shelf release (paper or primer) is applied to the kiln shelf. When fired between layers, silver is generally more contained and less likely to affect the firing surface.

1015 Alchemy Clear, Silver to Gold, with rainbow iridescent coating

Because iridescent coating acts as a barrier, don't expect much reaction when using silver directly against this coated glass. That said, the silver might still make contact with the glass through thinner sections of the iridescent coating. This may result in pale gold effects caused by 1015's silver reactivity, detailed above. Results vary widely, both in terms of the effect's strength and color.

Alchemy Clear, Silver to Bronze
001016

Reacts With: Silver
Cold Characteristics: Unfired sheet has a faint coral tint.

Working Notes

Upon firing, silver foil turns a bronze color wherever it is in contact with 1016 (Alchemy Clear). On the sample tile above, the left side illustrates silver foil after being fired uncapped on top of 1016. The sample's right side illustrates silver foil after being fired between a layer of Clear (any style) and 1016, with 1016 as the cap. (Faint coral color may be evident in any fired work containing 1016.)

Expect variations in effects to result from different sources and thicknesses of silver, glass production runs, and heatwork (including firing times, temperatures, and number of times fired).

For warm-hued bronze color development, we recommend a 1 hour soak at 1225°F in the pre-rapid heat section of a firing cycle. If fired rapidly through this temperature range, the resulting hue will be a lighter metallic.

Note: When firing silver foil in the kiln, be aware that the silver can deposit onto the kiln shelf, potentially affecting silver-sensitive glasses in one or more subsequent firings. This can happen even when new shelf release (paper or primer) is applied to the kiln shelf. When fired between layers, silver is generally more contained and less likely to affect the firing surface.

1016 Alchemy Clear, Silver to Bronze, with rainbow iridescent coating

Because iridescent coating acts as a barrier, don't expect much reaction when using silver directly against this coated glass. That said, the silver might still make contact with the glass through thinner sections of the iridescent coating. This may result in bronze effects caused by 1016's silver reactivity, detailed above. Results vary widely, both in terms of the effect's strength and color.

Amaco Black Underglaze Pencil

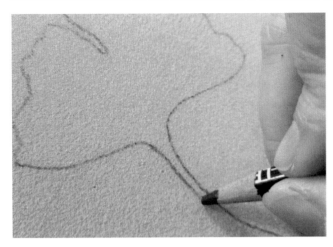 

You can make permanent marks on your glass projects with these underglaze pencils.

- Draw on one or more layers
- Create shading effects
- Sign your name or add other handwritten text

Using the Pencil

The pencil requires the friction of a rough surface to make a mark. Think of this as equivalent to "tooth" in paper. You can achieve this surface several ways:

1. Apply powder to sheet glass, tack fuse to around 1275°F–1300°F (691°C–704°C), then cool. This will create enough tooth for successful application of the pencil.
2. Coldwork the surface with loose grit, diamond hand laps, a diamond angle grinder, or anything that will leave a rough surface.
3. Sandblast prior to using the pencil. The coarser the grit used in the sandblaster, the rougher the resulting tooth.

If extremely precise lines are important, work on the flattest glass surface possible. This may mean you need to flatten sheet glass prior to creating a toothy surface, especially if roughening the glass by tack fusing powder or sandblasting. The flatter surface will make it possible to draw crisper lines.

Marks need to be fired to a full fuse or they may rub off. The lines will appear to be a dark gray, like marks made by a soft graphite pencil. Examined closely, they are in fact black but the color and transparency of the base glass dilutes the overall line. The pencil will look darker fired on white glass than it will on clear or light transparent glass. Repeated application will darken the hue, but it will never appear truly black.

Before firing, pencil marks on a sandblasted surface can be blended or erased, as with normal pencil work. Erasing marks from a highly textured surface, however, may be difficult and require scrubbing with water.

If you plan to stack multiple layers with marks, fire each layer individually to at least 1425°F (774°C) before fusing them together in a subsequent firing. Without this step you are likely to trap large bubbles between the layers. Likewise, be aware that unless the markings have already been fused to the glass, firing them against a primed kilnshelf or ThinFire can also cause bubbles.

Do you plan to roughen the surface again and add more markings? Protect your initial line work by sifting a layer of clear/transparent powder over it before firing. This buffer will preserve it during the next round of roughening and marking.

We recommend sharpening the pencil with a craft knife or blade because a pencil sharpener or an electric sharpener will likely snap off the pencil's tip.

BULLSEYE BRAINSTORM | TEXTURES & IRIDS

Jumpstart your ideas for using Bullseye textured and iridescent glasses by studying these examples. Each tile is made from two 4-inch squares of glass, each 3mm thick. The bottom piece of glass used for each tile is described here as the "base" glass. The top one is called the "cap."

1. BUBBLE TRAPPING

Create an even grid of trapped bubbles by using a base of reeded or prismatic textured glass face up and a cap of the same texture face down, crisscrossed at a 90-degree angle. These tiles are shown with the fire-polished side up.

1. Base: Clear Reed (001101-0043-F); Cap: Clear Reed (001101-0043-F) 2. Base: Black Prismatic (000100-0047-F); Cap: Clear Prismatic (001101-0047-F) 3. Base: Clear Prismatic (001101-0047-F); Cap: Clear Prismatic (001101-0047-F).

2. POWDER PATTERN

Simply sift a layer of glass powder in a contrasting color over a textured piece of glass. After a full fuse firing, the texture will disappear but the pattern will remain. These tiles are shown with the fire-polished side up.

1. Base: Clear Tekta (001100-0380-F); Cap: Black Prismatic (000100-0047-F) 2. Base: Clear Tekta (001100-0380-F); Cap: Clear Reed (001101-0043-F) 3. Base: Clear Tekta (001100-0380-F);
Cap: Black Herringbone Ripple (000100-0022-F)

3. CLEAR-ON-CLEAR COLLAGE WITH IRID

Place one of our iridized clear-on-clear collage glasses irid face down on the kiln shelf. Cap it with a dark 3mm piece of glass. After a full firing, the texture will be flat, but the irid pattern will remain. These tiles are shown with the fire-polished side down, kiln shelf side up. Note: Designs like these can be made subtler by choosing a light 3mm glass for the cap.

1. Base: Clear Irid with Clear Frit (004202-0031-F), irid down; Cap: Deep Cobalt Blue (000147-0030-F) 2. Base: Clear Chopstix Irid (004402-0031-F), irid down; Cap: Red (000124-0030-F) 3. Base: Clear Irid with Clear Fractures (004102-0031-F), irid down; Cap: Black (000100-0030-F)

4. CLEAR-CAPPED IRIDS

Iridescent patterns and textures gain intensity and shine when capped with 3mm clear glass. Tiles are shown here with the fire-polished side up. Tile #3 in the row shows a variation: the base glass is a 3mm opal capped with an irid texture, with the irid facing down.

1. Base: Black Accordion Irid (000100-0046-F), irid up; Cap: Clear Tekta (001100-0380-F) 2. Base: Black Patterned Irid (000100-0032-F), irid up; Cap: Clear Tekta (001100-0380-F) 3. Base: Deep Cobalt Blue (000147-0030-F); Cap: Clear Prismatic Irid (001101-0048-F), irid down

5. IRID TEXTURES FACE DOWN

The base is an iridized texture, placed face down on the kiln shelf. The cap can be any 3mm compatible glass. These tiles are shown with the fire-polished side down, kiln shelf side up.

1. Base: Black Prismatic Irid (000100-0048-F), irid down; Cap: Clear Tekta (001100-0380-F) 2. Base: Black Herringbone Ripple Irid (000100-0025-F), irid down; Cap: Clear Tekta (001100-0380-F) 3. Base: Clear Reed Irid (001101-0044-F), irid down; Cap: Red (000124-0030-F)

IRIDS AND SHELF SEPARATORS

If you plan to fire the irid side of a glass against the kiln shelf, coat the shelf with primer instead of using ThinFire paper, which can cause pitting on some irid coatings. For example, if you were making the tiles in sets 3, 4, and 5 on this chart, you would coat the shelf with primer. If making sets 1 and 2, you could use either shelf primer or ThinFire.

1.   2.   3.

Using Bullseye Shelf Primer

Hot glass will stick to most ceramic or metal surfaces and crack as it cools, unless prevented by a separator like Bullseye shelf primer. Careful application of our primer to shelves and molds will result in smooth, effective firing surfaces.

MIXING

Mix one part shelf primer powder to five parts (by volume) water. Stir the mix frequently during application.

Assuming a 20 x 20"(51 x 51cm) shelf, one pound (454 grams) of dry shelf primer will make enough mix to prepare about 32 shelves with the required five coats per shelf.

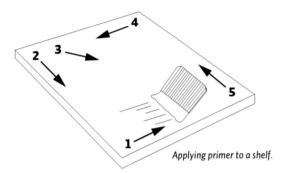

Applying primer to a shelf.

APPLICATION

Use five coats of primer on a new shelf or mold and also on subsequent applications.

For shelves and ceramic molds, apply shelf primer with a wide, natural-bristle brush. (A Chinese hake brush works well.) Brush in one direction, then at a 90° angle, and then diagonally, applying as uniformly as possible.

After applying five coats (see illustration), dry the shelf or mold in your kiln at 500°F (260°C) for 20 minutes. Mullite shelves may be fired up to temperature as quickly as your kiln permits. Take at least 30 minutes to bring ceramic molds up to temperature.

For steel, steep-sided, or non-porous molds, the liquid shelf primer can be sprayed onto the mold surface. A hand-held squirt bottle or garden sprayer will work, but an airbrush will give a smoother application. Heat the mold to 400°F (204°C) in the kiln, then remove and spray the warm mold surface with primer until it no longer dries quickly. Reheat the mold and re-spray. Repeat this process until the mold surface is thoroughly covered with primer. Metal molds with steep sides may require up to ten applications.

Allow shelves and molds to cool before use, to prevent thermal-shocking the glass.

REUSE

A newly prepared shelf that has not been fired (except at a very low temperature to dry it) will retain the fresh shelf-primer tint. On firing, this dye will burn out. Depending on the temperature at which you fire a shelf or mold, you may or may not need to clean and re-prepare it before your next firing.

If you are not firing over 1300°F (704°C), you can reuse shelves and slumping molds many times without reapplying primer, provided that the primer has not been scratched through.

When firing to 1300°F (704°C) and above, shelves and molds will need to be cleaned and recoated before each use. Scrape off the old primer with a wide window/tile scraper (razor type). Scraping, rather than sanding, minimizes dust. To remove primer from a contoured surface, use a Scotch-Brite pad.

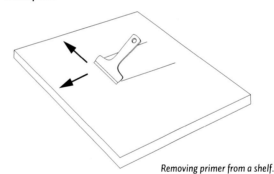

Removing primer from a shelf.

STORAGE

Keep the primer-powder container tightly closed and in a cool, dry place. Shelf primer that has been mixed with water will last for many weeks, if kept covered.

PRECAUTIONS

Unless your porous shelves and molds have been kiln dried after preparation, you cannot be completely confident that they are thoroughly dry. Surfaces that feel dry to the touch can still hold moisture and, therefore, cause bubbles, glass sticking, and breakage.

Shelf primer is extremely drying to the skin. Wear thin rubber gloves to prevent chapping.

Avoid breathing shelf-primer dust. Wear a respirator approved by NIOSH for dusts and/or clean your shelves outdoors or with a good, local ventilation system.

◎ Clean Shield Gel

When properly applied, Clean Shield Gel (8224) brings out luster and gives dry, matte surfaces the sealed appearance of a low-temperature firepolish. (Unfired, unsealed sandblasted surfaces have a "dry" appearance that can show fingerprints and other oils.) Ideal for glass that has been sandblasted or coldworked with loose grit, or in cases where firepolishing isn't practical. Reduces the appearance of fingerprints and heightens color and transparency.

How to use it
Make sure glass surface is thoroughly clean and dry. Squeeze a pea-sized amount of Clean Shield Gel onto the included nano-fiber application cloth, blot or rub the gel into the cloth until it is absorbed, then use the cloth to apply gel and burnish the surface. You'll notice the firepolished effect immediately. Keep in mind that a little goes a long way and that the gel is challenging to remove if too much is applied.

When not to use it
Clean Shield Gel brings about subtle changes in matte surfaces and will not create a glossy effect. It will not heal deep or linear scratches nor does it fix devitrification. Note: Once applied, the surface will resist most adhesives.

Safety guidelines
Clean Shield Gel is a concentrated, polymer-coating protectant designed for use on household fixtures. Non-toxic and solvent/VOC-free, but not recommended for food bearing surfaces.

Other applications
· Seals kilncast work that has been sandblasted
· Brightens matte, powder, and *pâte de verre* surfaces

Drilling Small Holes in Jewelry and Ornaments

These directions apply to using our 2.1 mm Drill Bits (7239) to produce high-quality hole with minimal blow-outs (chipping out the back side) in small-scale pieces of fired or unfired sheet glass.

These drill bits feature a diamond-abrasive coating applied to a fluted core. As the edges wear away, fresh diamonds are exposed, extending the effective lifespan of the bit.

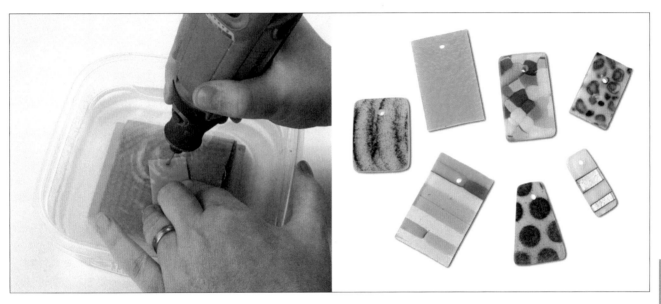

Directions

1. Insert the drill bit in the rotary tool. Adjust the abrasive area to accommodate the thickness of the glass with 0.5" to spare. Before drilling, turn the tool on to check that the bit is in straight. Adjust if necessary.

2. In a shallow waterproof container, place a support for the glass. Use a material that is softer than the glass and that will not clog up the diamonds. We recommend a piece of wood or mullite*. Place the glass on top of the support and add enough water to cover the glass. Too much water will make it difficult to see once the drill bit touches the water.

3. Steady the glass with one hand, start the bit rotating and bring the tool to the glass. (If not using a drill press, stabilize the hand with the tool against the edge of the container.) Apply enough pressure to break through the surface of the glass without skidding. If using a hand-held tool, start with the bit at an angle, and then tilt upright. Ground glass should start to cloud the area around the bit. With glass thicker than 2 mm, lift the tool periodically to allow water to flush the hole. You'll feel a change in resistance once the hole is complete. Lift the tool and bit straight out before letting go of the glass.

With thicker pieces or pieces you intend to refire, you may want to follow up with a countersink bit to flare out the hole slightly.

How long does a drill bit last?
In our studios, we generally make at least 8 holes in 4-6 mm thick fused glass or 20-plus holes in 2-3 mm unfired sheet glass before changing to a new bit. With use, you'll notice that a drill bit doesn't work as effectively. If a piece breaks while drilling, this may indicate that it's time to replace a bit.

Tip: If using a Sharpie to mark the spot for the hole, apply a thin layer of lip balm or petroleum jelly over the mark. This will prevent the ink from floating free of the smooth surface of the glass. (Yes, this can happen!)

Safety note: Wear safety glasses when drilling and take appropriate precautions using electric tool around water.

* Mullite is what many kiln shelves and dams are made of. If using mullite to support glass, wrap it in a few layers of thick paper to act as a cushion.

◎ Frit Tinting

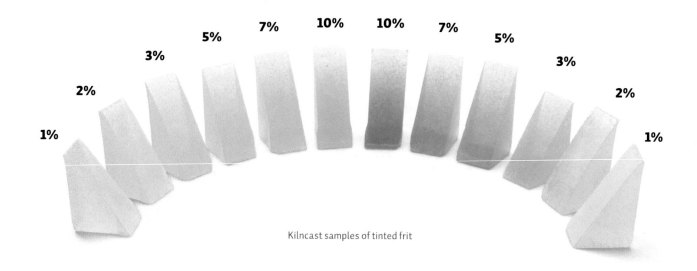

1% 2% 3% 5% 7% 10% 10% 7% 5% 3% 2% 1%

Kilncast samples of tinted frit

Frit tinting is a method that allows one to create specific color blends for kilncasting and pâte de verre. The process involves "tinting" or coloring clear glass by adhering colored powder (-0008) to larger-grained Clear frit (001101-0001, -0002, -0003) and then firing the mixture in a mold. By conducting careful tests with this method, you can learn to manipulate color saturation and translucence in frit-cast pieces with predictable results.

Both opalescent and transparent colored powders can be used for this process, and colored powders can be mixed to further extend one's palette. A surprisingly small amount of Bullseye powder will add substantial color to clear frit.

The image above shows the saturation resulting from various ratios of powder to frit. Note that the samples were cast as wedges, which allow the color to be viewed at different thicknesses. All of the samples were made with Clear medium frit (001101-0002). One series was mixed with Spring Green powder (001426-0008) and the other with Turquoise Blue (001116-0008). The percentage of colored powder to clear frit is indicated.

CHOOSING THE FRIT

Choose the percentage of colored powder (-0008) you want. It may be useful to make your own set of sample wedges to help accurately predict results. Next, select the grain size of Clear base frit to accomplish the look you desire. Note: the grain size will have a significant visual impact on the finished casting.

-0001 (fine) will tend to trap many small bubbles during the firing process. This will give the finished casting an opalescent appearance, even when Crystal Clear (001401-0001) is used.

-0002 (medium) will trap larger and slightly fewer bubbles than are trapped when using -0001. The result will be a homogenous blend with good light transmission.

-0003 (coarse) will create fewer but larger bubbles than the mixes made with -0001 and -0002, and the final casting will appear to be less blended. Each grain of -0003 will seem to retain its shape and be "coated" in color.

WEIGHING THE FRIT

Once the weight of the glass needed to fill the mold has been determined* the proportionate weights of frit and powder must be calculated, based on the percentage of color desired. For example, if the mold requires a total of 500 grams of glass, and the color is to be a 3% tint of Spring Green powder (001426-0008) with Clear frit (001101-0002):

Calculate that 3% of 500 grams is 15 grams (500 x 0.03).

Therefore, filling the mold will take:

15 grams of Spring Green (001426-0008) powder, plus 485 grams of Clear frit (001101-0002), for a total of 500 grams.

Weigh out the amounts of powder and frit needed in separate containers. The Clear container should have a lid and be large enough to allow for thorough mixing.

MIXING THE FRIT

Using a spray bottle filled with water, lightly mist the Clear frit. Close the lid and shake vigorously to coat every piece of glass with water. Next, sprinkle the colored powder evenly over the top of the wet frit. Shake vigorously until each piece of frit is covered with powder. Even a small percentage of powder should be mixed with the base frit evenly.

Load the mold with the damp frit mixture and fire promptly. If the mixture is left to sit for an extended period of time, the powder can separate from the base frit. For this reason, it is best not to make more of the mixture than is needed for any one firing.

SURFACES

You can achieve a wide array of surfaces when using frit as the casting medium. Fired to a low temperature, frits can be simply sintered together (made coherent, not melted) to produce a crusty/grainy surface. When fired hotter, the cast surface will become more glossy and smooth. After firing, surfaces can be altered further by employing the same coldworking methods applied to other types of kilnformed glass.

*To calculate how much glass will fill a mold, see page 5 of *TipSheet 5: Bullseye Box Casting* at bullseyeglass.com.

*To calculate how much glass will fill a mold, see page 5 of *TipSheet 5: Bullseye Box Casting* at bullseyeglass.com.

Tools and supplies you will need:
- Frit
- Powder
- A spray bottle filled with water
- A mold (appropriate for kilncasting)
- A gram scale
- Containers for weighing and mixing the powder and frit.

Susan Longini, *Pieced Quilt Triptych*, 2005. Pâte de verre, 36 x 11 x 2 in (91 x 28 x 5 cm) installed. Photo: Keay Edwards.

Longini fired her tinted components to a low temperature, retaining a delicate, granular appearance.

Steven Easton, *Snow Queen's Realm II* (detail), 2005. Pâte de verre, 5 x 36 x 84 in (13 x 91 x 213 cm) installed. Photo: Mark Johnston.

Easton fired his tinted components to a higher temperature, then coldworked them, giving them translucency and a lustrous surface.

Get a Reaction

Try fusing samples of Reactive Cloud Opal and Reactive Ice Clear with our copper-bearing glasses or copper leaf or silver foil. Their chemistries may react at the interface, resulting in special colors and effects. Reactions range from subtle to dramatic and can prove quite versatile in art and design.

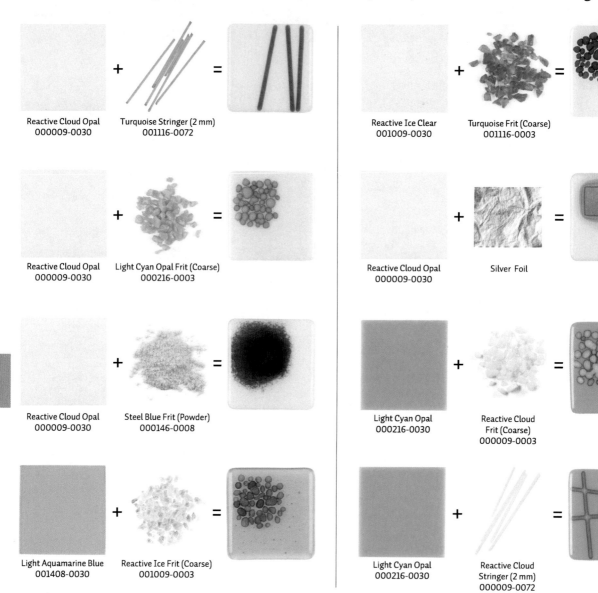

Reactive Cloud Opal
000009-0030
+
Turquoise Stringer (2 mm)
001116-0072
=

Reactive Ice Clear
001009-0030
+
Turquoise Frit (Coarse)
001116-0003
=

Reactive Cloud Opal
000009-0030
+
Light Cyan Opal Frit (Coarse)
000216-0003
=

Reactive Cloud Opal
000009-0030
+
Silver Foil
=

Reactive Cloud Opal
000009-0030
+
Steel Blue Frit (Powder)
000146-0008
=

Light Cyan Opal
000216-0030
+
Reactive Cloud Frit (Coarse)
000009-0003
=

Light Aquamarine Blue
001408-0030
+
Reactive Ice Frit (Coarse)
001009-0003
=

Light Cyan Opal
000216-0030
+
Reactive Cloud Stringer (2 mm)
000009-0072
=

155

Layups: 6 mm stacks (3 mm clear base + 3 mm reactive sheet), -0003 frit, 2 mm stringer, -0008 powder, Silver Foil Process temp: 1490°F (810°C)

Want a quick way to identify Bullseye's copper-bearing and other reactive glass styles? Download a free copy of our *Reactive Potential of Bullseye Glass* chart at bullseyeglass.com.

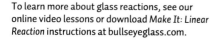

To learn more about glass reactions, see our online video lessons or download *Make It: Linear Reaction* instructions at bullseyeglass.com.

◎ Reactions with Sulfur

Fusing our sulfur- or copper-bearing sheet glass, powder, and frit with other reactive elements results in a range of colors and effects that can prove quite versatile in art and design.

Layups: 6 mm stacks (3mm clear base* + 3 mm sulfur or copper-bearing sheet glass), frit, 1 mm stringer, silver foil.

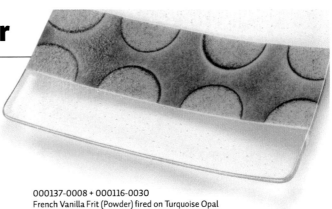

000137-0008 + 000116-0030
French Vanilla Frit (Powder) fired on Turquoise Opal

Sulfur + Copper

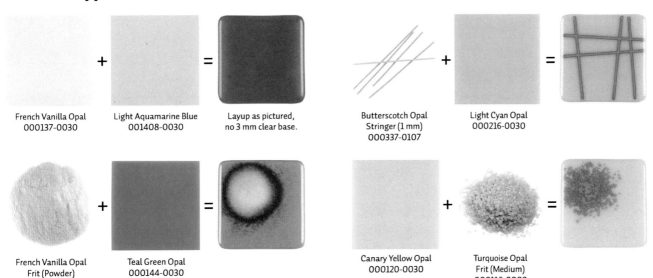

French Vanilla Opal
000137-0030

Light Aquamarine Blue
001408-0030

Layup as pictured,
no 3 mm clear base.

Butterscotch Opal
Stringer (1 mm)
000337-0107

Light Cyan Opal
000216-0030

French Vanilla Opal
Frit (Powder)
000137-0008

Teal Green Opal
000144-0030

Canary Yellow Opal
000120-0030

Turquoise Opal
Frit (Medium)
000116-0002

156

Sulfur + Lead

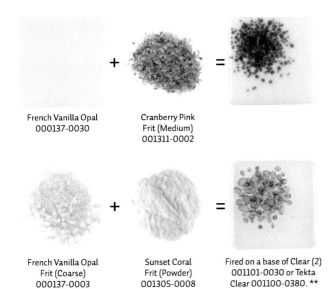

French Vanilla Opal
000137-0030

Cranberry Pink
Frit (Medium)
001311-0002

French Vanilla Opal
Frit (Coarse)
000137-0003

Sunset Coral
Frit (Powder)
001305-0008

Fired on a base of Clear (2)
001101-0030 or Tekta
Clear 001100-0380. **

Sulfur + Silver

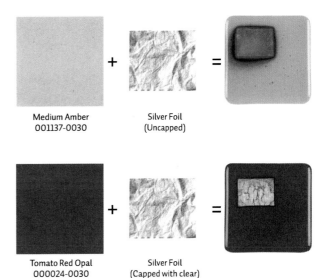

Medium Amber
001137-0030

Silver Foil
(Uncapped)

Tomato Red Opal
000024-0030

Silver Foil
(Capped with clear)

* Except where noted.   **See also instructions for *River Rock Reaction* part sheets at bullseyeglass.com.

◎ Reactive Potential of Bullseye Glass

Combinations with Reactive Potential

Glasses in the top row may react with glasses in the bottom row. Note: Many glasses can be stained or even react when fired with silver.

COPPER + SULFUR/SELENIUM	COPPER + REACTIVE

LEAD + SULFUR/SELENIUM	REACTIVE + COPPER

SULFUR/SELENIUM + COPPER	SULFUR/SELENIUM + LEAD

LEAD-BEARING

	000301	PINK OPAL
	000303	DUSTY LILAC OPAL
	000305	SALMON PINK OPAL
	000313	DENSE WHITE OPAL
	000334	GOLD PURPLE OPAL
	001205	LIGHT CORAL
	001215	LIGHT PINK
	001234	VIOLET
	001305	SUNSET CORAL
	001311	CRANBERRY PINK
	001332	FUCHSIA
	001334	GOLD PURPLE
	001823	BURNT SCARLET TINT
	001824	RUBY RED TINT
	001831	RUBY PINK TINT

REACTIVE

These glasses do not contain sulfur, copper or lead, but may react with copper-bearing glasses, copper leaf, and silver (foil, wire).

	000009	REACTIVE CLOUD OPAL
	001009	REACTIVE ICE CLEAR
	001019	RED REACTIVE CLEAR

ALCHEMY SERIES

Reacts with silver (foil, wire).

	001015	CLEAR, SILVER TO GOLD
	001016	CLEAR, SILVER TO BRONZE

COPPER-BEARING

	000104	GLACIER BLUE OPAL
	000116	TURQUOISE BLUE OPAL
	000144	TEAL GREEN OPAL
	000145	JADE GREEN OPAL
	000146	STEEL BLUE OPAL
	000161	ROBIN'S EGG BLUE OPAL
	000164	EGYPTIAN BLUE OPAL
	000216	LIGHT CYAN OPAL
	000345	STEEL JADE OPAL
	001116	TURQUOISE BLUE
	001145	KELLY GREEN
	001164	CARIBBEAN BLUE
	001176	PEACOCK BLUE
	001217	LEAF GREEN
	001226	LILY PAD GREEN
	001246	COPPER BLUE
	001408	LIGHT AQUAMARINE
	001416	LIGHT TURQUOISE BLUE
	001417	EMERALD GREEN
	001464	TRUE BLUE
	001808	AQUA BLUE TINT
	001816	TURQUOISE BLUE TINT
	001845	MING GREEN TINT
	001917	CILANTRO GREEN TINT

SULFUR/SELENIUM-BEARING

This category of glasses will also react with silver (foil, wire).

	000024	TOMATO RED OPAL
	000025	TANGERINE ORANGE OPAL
	000120	CANARY YELLOW OPAL
	000124	RED OPAL
	000125	ORANGE OPAL
	000126	SPRING GREEN OPAL
	000137	FRENCH VANILLA OPAL
	000203	WOODLAND BROWN OPAL
	000220	SUNFLOWER YELLOW OPAL
	000221	CITRONELLE OPAL
	000222	AVOCADO GREEN OPAL
	000224	DEEP RED OPAL
	000225	PIMENTO RED OPAL
	000227	GOLDEN GREEN OPAL
	000309	CINNABAR OPAL
	000310	UMBER OPAL
	000320	MARIGOLD YELLOW OPAL
	000321	PUMPKIN ORANGE OPAL
	000329	BURNT ORANGE OPAL
	000337	BUTTERSCOTCH OPAL
	001025	LIGHT ORANGE
	001119	SIENNA
	001120	YELLOW
	001122	RED
	001125	ORANGE
	001126	CHARTREUSE
	001137	MEDIUM AMBER
	001138	DARK AMBER
	001207	FERN GREEN
	001241	PINE GREEN
	001320	MARIGOLD YELLOW
	001321	CARNELIAN
	001322	GARNET RED
	001422	LEMON LIME GREEN
	001437	LIGHT AMBER
	001857	RED AMBER TINT

Visit the About Our Glass section at bullseyeglass.com for more information.

DO NOT CONTAIN LEAD, COPPER, OR SULFUR

000013	OPAQUE WHITE OPAL
000034	LIGHT PEACH CREAM OPAL
000100	BLACK OPAL
000101	STIFF BLACK OPAL
000102	BLUE BLACK OPAL
000108	POWDER BLUE OPAL
000112	MINT GREEN OPAL
000113	WHITE OPAL
000114	COBALT BLUE OPAL
000117	MINERAL GREEN OPAL
000118	PERIWINKLE OPAL
000119	MINK OPAL
000131	ARTICHOKE OPAL
000132	DRIFTWOOD GRAY OPAL
000136	DECO GRAY OPAL
000138	MARZIPAN OPAL
000139	ALMOND OPAL
000141	DARK FOREST GREEN OPAL
000142	NEO-LAVENDER OPAL
000143	LACY WHITE OPAL
000147	DEEP COBALT BLUE OPAL
000148	INDIGO BLUE OPAL
000206	ELEPHANT GRAY OPAL
000207	CELADON GREEN OPAL
000208	DUSTY BLUE OPAL
000212	OLIVE GREEN OPAL
000236	SLATE GRAY OPAL
000241	MOSS GREEN OPAL
000243	TRANSLUCENT WHITE OPAL*
000312	PEA POD GREEN OPAL
000332	PLUM OPAL
000336	DEEP GRAY OPAL
000349	GRAY GREEN OPAL

000403	OPALINE OPAL
000420	CREAM OPAL
000421	PETAL PINK OPAL
000920	WARM WHITE OPAL
001101	CLEAR
001105	DEEP PLUM
001107	LIGHT GREEN
001108	AQUAMARINE BLUE
001109	DARK ROSE BROWN
001112	AVENTURINE GREEN
001114	DEEP ROYAL BLUE
001118	MIDNIGHT BLUE
001128	DEEP ROYAL PURPLE
001129	CHARCOAL GRAY
001140	AVENTURINE BLUE
001141	OLIVE GREEN
001228	AMETHYST
001229	PEWTER
001401	CRYSTAL CLEAR
001405	LIGHT PLUM
001406	STEEL BLUE
001409	LIGHT BRONZE
001412	LIGHT AVENTURINE GREEN
001414	LIGHT SKY BLUE
001419	TAN
001426	SPRING GREEN
001428	LIGHT VIOLET
001429	LIGHT SILVER GRAY
001439	KHAKI
001442	NEO-LAVENDER
001444	SEA BLUE
001449	OREGON GRAY
001806	JUNIPER BLUE TINT

001807	GRASS GREEN TINT
001814	SAPPHIRE BLUE TINT
001818	INDIGO TINT
001819	BROWN TOPAZ TINT
001820	PALE YELLOW TINT
001821	ERBIUM PINK TINT
001826	GREEN TEA TINT*
001827	LIGHT AMBER TINT*
001829	GRAY TINT
001834	CORAL ORANGE TINT
001837	MEDIUM AMBER TINT*
001838	DARK AMBER TINT*
001841	SPRUCE GREEN TINT
001842	LIGHT NEO-LAVENDER SHIFT TINT
001844	LAVENDER GREEN SHIFT TINT
001845	MING GREEN TINT
001858	LT RHUBARB SHIFT TINT
001859	RHUBARB SHIFT TINT
001864	GRAY BLUE TINT
001867	OLIVE SMOKE TINT
001877	OLIVINE TINT
001917	CILANTRO GREEN TINT
001920	LEMON TINT
001932	FUCHSIA TINT
001934	COPPER TINT
001948	PURPLE BLUE TINT
001964	LAVENDER GRAY TINT
001977	PINE GREEN TINT

*Current production does not contain lead or sulfur. Visit the About our Glass section at bullseyeglass.com for more information.

Reactive Potential of Bullseye Rods & Stringers

Combinations with Reactive Potential

Glasses in the top row may react with glasses in the bottom row. Note: Many glasses can be stained or even react when fired with silver.

COPPER + SULFUR/SELENIUM	COPPER + REACTIVE

LEAD + SULFUR/SELENIUM	REACTIVE + COPPER

SULFUR/SELENIUM + COPPER	SULFUR/SELENIUM + LEAD

LEAD-BEARING

	Number	Name	ROD	STRINGER
	000113	WHITE OPAL		▪
	000243	TRANSLUCENT WHITE OPAL	▪	
	000301	PINK OPAL*	▪	▪
	000303	DUSTY LILAC OPAL	▪	
	000313	DENSE WHITE OPAL *	▪	▪
	000334	GOLD PURPLE OPAL *	▪	▪
	001215	LIGHT PINK	▪	
	001232	LIGHT FUCHSIA	▪	
	001234	VIOLET		▪
	001305	SUNSET CORAL	▪	▪
	001311	CRANBERRY PINK	▪	▪
	001342	CRANBERRY SAPPHIRINE	▪	
	001701	AMBER LUSTRE *	▪	
	001707	GREEN LUSTRE *	▪	
	001714	BLUE LUSTRE *	▪	
	001717	COPPER GREEN LUSTRE *	▪	

COPPER-BEARING

	Number	Name	ROD	STRINGER
	000016	TURQUOISE OPAQUE *	▪	
	000046	BLUESTONE OPAQUE *	▪	
	000116	TURQUOISE BLUE OPAL	▪	▪
	000144	TEAL GREEN OPAL	▪	▪
	000145	JADE GREEN OPAL	▪	▪
	000146	STEEL BLUE OPAL	▪	▪
	000164	EGYPTIAN BLUE OPAL	▪	▪
	000216	LIGHT CYAN OPAL	▪	▪
	001116	TURQUOISE BLUE	▪	▪
	001145	KELLY GREEN	▪	▪
	001164	CARIBBEAN BLUE	▪	▪
	001408	LIGHT AQUAMARINE BLUE	▪	▪
	001417	EMERALD GREEN	▪	▪
	001517	PALE EMERALD	▪	
	001717	COPPER GREEN LUSTRE *	▪	
	001808	AQUA BLUE TINT	▪	▪

SULFUR/SELENIUM-BEARING

This category of glasses will also react with silver.

	Number	Name	ROD	STRINGER
	000024	TOMATO RED OPAL	▪	▪
	000120	CANARY YELLOW OPAL	▪	▪
	000124	RED OPAL	▪	▪
	000125	ORANGE OPAL	▪	▪
	000126	SPRING GREEN OPAL	▪	▪
	000127	NOUGAT OPAL	▪	
	000137	FRENCH VANILLA OPAL	▪	▪
	000203	WOODLAND BROWN OPAL	▪	▪
	000217	GREEN GOLD OPAL	▪	▪
	000220	SUNFLOWER YELLOW OPAL		▪
	000224	DEEP RED OPAL	▪	▪
	000227	GOLDEN GREEN OPAL	▪	
	000309	CINNABAR OPAL	▪	
	000321	PUMPKIN ORANGE OPAL	▪	▪
	000329	BURNT ORANGE OPAL	▪	▪
	000337	BUTTERSCOTCH OPAL	▪	
	001022	RED ORANGE	▪	
	001119	SIENNA	▪	▪
	001120	YELLOW	▪	▪
	001122	RED	▪	▪
	001125	ORANGE	▪	▪
	001126	CHARTREUSE	▪	▪
	001137	MEDIUM AMBER	▪	▪
	001321	CARNELIAN		▪
	001322	GARNET RED	▪	
	001437	LIGHT AMBER	▪	

REACTIVE

These glasses do not contain sulfur, copper or lead, but may react with copper-bearing glasses, copper leaf, and silver.

	Number	Name	ROD	STRINGER
	000009	REACTIVE CLOUD OPAL		▪
	001009	REACTIVE ICE CLEAR		▪

* Indicates T grade rod.
Bullseye rods are graded as either F (recommended for both kilnwork and torchwork) or T (recommended for torchwork only). Unmarked styles are F grade.

DO NOT CONTAIN LEAD, COPPER, OR SULFUR

			ROD	STRINGER
	000013	OPAQUE WHITE OPAL *	▪	▪
	000017	MINERAL GREEN OPAQUE *	▪	
	000018	PERIWINKLE OPAQUE *	▪	
	000034	LIGHT PEACH CREAM OPAL	▪	
	000100	BLACK OPAL	▪	▪
	000101	STIFF BLACK OPAL	▪	▪
	000108	POWDER BLUE OPAL	▪	▪
	000112	MINT GREEN OPAL	▪	▪
	000114	COBALT BLUE OPAL	▪	▪
	000117	MINERAL GREEN OPAL	▪	
	000132	DRIFTWOOD GRAY OPAL	▪	
	000136	DECO GRAY OPAL	▪	▪
	000141	DARK FOREST GREEN OPAL	▪	▪
	000142	NEO-LAVENDER OPAL	▪	▪
	000147	DEEP COBALT BLUE OPAL	▪	▪
	000148	INDIGO OPAL	▪	
	000207	CELADON GREEN OPAL	▪	
	000212	OLIVE GREEN OPAL	▪	▪
	000236	SLATE GRAY OPAL		▪
	000241	MOSS GREEN OPAL	▪	▪
	000312	PEA POD GREEN OPAL	▪	▪
	000420	CREAM OPAL	▪	▪
	000421	PETAL PINK OPAL	▪	▪

			ROD	STRINGER
	000429	RHUBARB PASTEL OPAL	▪	
	000920	WARM WHITE OPAL	▪	
	001101	CLEAR	▪	▪
	001105	DEEP PLUM	▪	▪
	001107	LIGHT GREEN	▪	▪
	001108	AQUAMARINE BLUE	▪	▪
	001109	DARK ROSE BROWN	▪	▪
	001112	AVENTURINE GREEN	▪	▪
	001114	DEEP ROYAL BLUE	▪	▪
	001118	MIDNIGHT BLUE	▪	▪
	001128	DEEP ROYAL PURPLE	▪	▪
	001129	CHARCOAL GRAY	▪	▪
	001140	AVENTURINE BLUE		▪
	001141	OLIVE GREEN	▪	▪
	001401	CRYSTAL CLEAR	▪	
	001405	LIGHT PLUM	▪	
	001406	STEEL BLUE	▪	▪
	001409	LIGHT BRONZE	▪	▪
	001412	LIGHT AVENTURINE GREEN	▪	▪
	001414	LIGHT SKY BLUE	▪	▪
	001426	SPRING GREEN	▪	▪
	001428	LIGHT VIOLET	▪	
	001429	LIGHT SILVER GRAY	▪	▪

			ROD	STRINGER
	001439	KHAKI	▪	
	001442	NEO-LAVENDER	▪	▪
	001444	SEA BLUE		▪
	001506	PALE STEEL BLUE	▪	
	001514	PALE SKY BLUE	▪	
	001528	PALE AMETHYST	▪	
	001806	JUNIPER BLUE TINT	▪	
	001807	GRASS GREEN TINT	▪	▪
	001812	SEAWEED AVENTURINE	▪	
	001820	PALE YELLOW TINT	▪	▪
	001821	ERBIUM PINK TINT	▪	▪
	001834	CORAL ORANGE TINT	▪	▪
	001841	SPRUCE GREEN TINT	▪	▪
	001842	LIGHT NEO-LAVENDER SHIFT TINT	▪	▪
	001859	RHUBARB SHIFT TINT	▪	▪

Special Effects: Steel Blue Opalescent

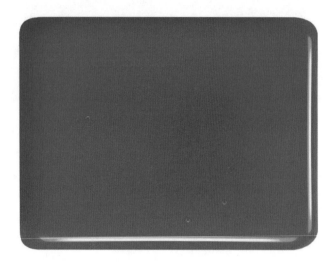

Kilnformed tiles, 4 x 4 x 1/4 in.

"When I put it in the kiln, the glass was blue. When I took it out, it was the color of mild steel. When I fired it again, it was blue. What's going on?"

On the surface, Bullseye's Steel Blue Opalescent glass (000146) is a deep teal blue. In transmission, it shows a slight shift to a deep aquamarine. But on firing, this glass seems to have a mind of its own.

When we were developing Steel Blue Opalescent, our quality inspectors tested it—as we test all our glass—by firing it to 1500°F (815°C) and it came out of the kiln looking as blue as when we put it in. But kilnformers soon called us to report the appearance a mysterious shiny silver-gray coating.

Through interviews and further testing, we discovered that between 1250°F–1425°F (677°C–773°C), the surface of the sheet exposed to the atmosphere did indeed take on a shiny silver-gray coating. This effect often disappeared once the glass reached full-fuse temperatures.

We considered discontinuing Steel Blue Opalescent at that point, but kilnworkers persuaded us to keep it, having discovered exciting ways to use this special effect glass. The areas of the sheet that are not exposed to air do not develop the metallic film. Artists worked up patterning schemes that allowed them to fire Steel Blue Opalescent to two colors simultaneously—covering portions of the glass with Clear Thin sheet glass, frit, or powder,

and firing or re-firing to lower temperatures to keep the metallic effect.

Steel Blue Opalescent is available in 3 mm sheets, Thin sheets, frit, powder, and rod.

Although the metallic effect coating is not entirely predictable, we have observed it on pieces fired to a full fuse (1490°F/810°C) as well as within the previously mentioned tack fuse range. If a piece was designed and constructed to achieve the metallic coating, but it did not develop, try a second firing within the range where this effect is more predictable (for example, 1375°F/746°C with a 10-minute hold).

Most forms of Steel Blue Opalescent share this metallic characteristic, though we've noticed that powder tends to exhibit this effect (as a dark gray hue) more reliably in the sinter or tack fuse range of 1250–1375°F (677–746°C). With greater heat work, Steel Blue Opalescent Powder often fires with a blue hue, even where exposed.

Learn more about Steel Blue Opalescent, including its reactive potential, in the About Our Glass section of bullseyeglass.com.

ThinFire Shelf Paper

ThinFire is a ceramic-impregnated shelf paper that provides excellent separation between glass and kiln shelf. Compared to other ceramic fiber materials, ThinFire is lightweight, creates less binder burnout odor, and produces a glossier finish on the shelf side of your project. As an alternative to shelf primer, ThinFire reduces shelf preparation time and improves surface release.

USE, CLEANUP & SAFETY

ThinFire Shelf Paper is intended for single use at temperatures up to 1500°F (815°C).

For Best Results

- Store ThinFire in a dry place. Moisture from a basement or garage can affect performance even if the paper later dries.

- Place the rougher, printed side of ThinFire against the shelf and the smoother, plain side against the glass. Firing glass against the rougher side may result in residue clinging to the glass.

- Weight the outer corners of the paper with small pieces of glass or bits of kiln shelf. This is helpful because at maximum temperature, the edges of ThinFire can otherwise pull into or curl over the top surface of the glass, leaving an undesirable haze.

Not for Every Application

ThinFire has been used with excellent results in Bullseye's Research and Education studios for many types of fusing applications. It does not work, however, in the following applications:

- Used in direct contact with iridized glass, ThinFire may cause a reaction resulting in surface pitting.

- When fitting a bunch of cut pieces together in a design down arrangement, unless those pieces fit together perfectly, using ThinFire can actually prevent the glass from fusing at the contact surface. If one proceeds with a slump firing, the areas where the glasses are not fused together will be prone to open up as the glass stretches.

- Under very large or heavy pieces ThinFire can rip, leaving a faint outline on the bottom of the piece.

Cleanup and Safety

After firing, ThinFire will be reduced to a fine layer of ash. As with all ceramic fiber material, avoid breathing its residual dust. Use a HEPA-filtered vacuum to remove ThinFire from the shelf. An alternative method of disposal is to remove the shelf from your kiln, spray the ThinFire with water, and collect the resulting paste in a garbage bag. If possible clean your shelves outdoors or near a good, local ventilation system, regardless of method. If you are not able to reduce dust exposure with these work practices or engineering controls, wear a NIOSH-approved respirator while cleaning. For more cleanup and safety tips, see "Safety in the Kiln-Glass Studio" at www.bullseyeglass.com.

PACKAGING

5-Sheet Pack	7090	20.5 x 20.5 in (52 x 52 cm)
100 Sheets	8210	20.5 x 20.5 in (52 x 52 cm)
Roll	8211	41 in x 250 ft (1.04 x 76.2 m)
Roll, Narrow	8710	20.5 in x 65 ft (52 cm x 19.8 m)
Roll, Short, Wide	8711	41 in x 32.75 ft (104 cm x 9.9 m)

Tips for Using Vermiculite Board

Bullseye Vermiculite Board is stronger and more durable than most fiberboard used for making casting molds. Here are some tips for handling it successfully:

1. **Work it like wood.**
   Vermiculite board can be cut or tooled like wood or particle board.

2. **Control dust and wear a respirator.**
   Our vermiculite is certified asbestos free. Regardless, whenever generating dust, work in a well-ventilated area and wear a NIOSH-approved respirator.

3. **Pre-fire vermiculite boards at 55°F (30°C) above process temperature.**
   After cutting to size, determine the process temperature for your intended project. Then fire at a rate of 500°F (278°C) per hour to a temperature approximately 55°F (30°C) higher than your planned process temperature. For example, if the process temperature for your intended project is 1525°F (829°C), you will add 55°F (30°C) to that temperature and pre-fire the vermiculite to 1580°F (860°C). Hold at that temperature for 30 minutes, then crash cool the kiln.

4. **Line with fiber paper after pre-firing.**

5. **Handle the vermiculite carefully.**
   The boards can become brittle after multiple firings, so always treat it carefully.

6. **Avoid using vermiculite boards as kiln shelves.**
   The boards are not designed to function as kiln shelves. Using them as such can put your project (and possibly your kiln) at risk.

7. **Use it for projects!**
   See Bullseye Vermiculite Box Assembly on the reverse side of this page for assembly instructions.

Bullseye Vermiculite Boards
008240
1″ × 24″ × 36″
(2.5 × 61 × 91.4 cm)

008743
1″ × 17″ × 20″
(2.5 × 43 × 50.8 cm)

Bullseye Circle Dams
008848
10″ (25.4 cm) square
8″ (20 cm) round opening

008768
7″ (17.7cm) square
5.25″ (13.3 cm) round opening

⊚ Vermiculite Box Assembly

Bullseye's vermiculite boxes come pre-cut and with a number of pilot holes already drilled. You will need to assemble, disassemble, and pre-fire the vermiculite components before using them in a glass project.

Phase 1: Build the sides of the box

1. Align a side that has a pre-drilled pilot hole with one that does not. (For Box 008427, this will mean aligning a long side with a short one.) Do this on top of the base, using the base as a guide to ensure the pieces are aligned correctly.

2. Using the existing pilot hole in one of the side pieces, drill through that hole and into the end of your second piece to create a new pilot hole. (Pilot holes help ensure that the screws do not overstress the material.) Use the pre-drilled pilot holes as handy guides for drilling the remaining pilot holes. Simply pass your drill through the pre-drilled hole to create a new pilot hole that will be aligned with the first. (Never push the drill so hard that you bend the material; this can cause the vermiculite to break.)

3. Using the aligned pilot holes, screw the two pieces together with stainless steel screws. (Non-stainless steel screws often come with metallic coatings that can contaminate your project and kiln during firing.)

4. Repeat this process with the third and fourth side pieces, arranging them on top of the base to ensure all side pieces are aligned correctly.

Phase 2: Attach the base to the assembled sides

5. Now place the base ON TOP of the assembled sides. Line it up squarely with the sides.

6. Drill through each of the four pre-drilled holes in the base to create pilot holes in the bottoms of each side piece.

7. Now that these pilot holes are drilled and aligned, use them to screw the base onto the sides.

Phase 3: Pre-fire the box and prepare it for a project

8. Disassemble the box, removing all stainless steel screws and setting them aside.

9. Fire the vermiculite pieces at a rate of 500°F (278°C) per hour to a temperature that is approximately 55°F (30°C) higher than the process temperature required by your specific project, hold for 30 minutes, then crash cool to room temperature.

10. Add a fiber paper liner and reassemble the vermiculite box. It is ready for a casting project!

Bullseye Vermiculite Boxes
008427
14″ × 10″ × 2.5″
(35.5 × 25.4 × 6.4 cm)

008249
10″ × 10″ × 4″
(25.4 × 25.4 × 10.2 cm)

Bullseye Ramp
008847
7.75″ (19.7 cm) wide.

Can be used with either of Bullseye's Vermiculite Boxes. Item sold separately.

◎ Using Color Line Screen Paste

Color line screen paste offers the ability to add high-pigmentation design elements and imagery onto sheet glass with no powdered enamels to mix. Pastes come ready to print, and are available in a wide range of mixable colors.

Preparation

The working consistency of color line screen paste should be close to that of honey. New pastes are ready to print, but will thicken with air exposure or prolonged storage. If your paste is too thick, gently stir in a few drops of Color Line Screen Printing Medium to thin to the desired consistency. Avoid creating bubbles in the paste, and pop any large bubbles before printing.

Application

Prefire your glass to 1425–1450°F to achieve a smooth printing surface, then cut your glass to the desired size, and bevel edges to avoid puncturing your screen. Follow standard printmaking procedures (first flood, then print).

Apply the paste to your screen (use 230 mesh silk screen for best results) by pouring it out of the tub or scooping it with a palette knife. You should use more paste than your print will require—this allows you to pull multiple prints if necessary, prevents the paste from drying too quickly in the screen, and excess paste can always be returned to the container.

Cleanup

Be sure to clean the screen, squeegee and tools using a wet sponge immediately after printing (see safety guidelines below for special instructions). Excess paste can be saved for future use. Do not store pastes in #6 plastic (polystyrene). The container will dissolve. Instead use glass, #5 plastic (polypropylene), or #2 (HDPE).

Safety

When using Color Line Screen Paste, always wear disposable gloves. No respirator is required. Contain waste water to a settling bucket (do not rinse down the drain) and check your local regulations for proper disposal instructions.

Firing/Layering

Once you've applied paste to the glass, it must be sintered by firing uncapped to 1350°F. This makes the enamel less susceptible to scratching/smearing. After sintering, the glass can be layered and full fused or capped. Printed imagery will distort a bit on the top layer of a full fuse firing, but you can prevent this by using a sheet of clear glass as your top layer.

Note: Red paste is sensitive to airborne carbon and requires special firing considerations.
- This color will not develop fully if the kiln is fired with no ventilation.
- Fire the kiln with peeps removed and door slightly ajar up to 1000°F.
- Hold at 1000°F for 15 minutes before closing the door for the remainder of your firing cycle.
- Other colors may be fired simultaneously. This will not affect their final hue.
- For more detailed instructions, refer to the Color Line Product Information packet.

Using Milestone Decals

Milestone decals are printed on water-release backing paper coated with an adhesive made from cornstarch. A layer of wax paper protects the decal. For best results, apply decals to pre-fired glass. We also recommend firing these decals on the surface, not between layers. (For supplemental video instructions, please visit bit.ly/fusedecals.)

Materials, Tools, and Supplies

To apply the decals, you'll need the following:

1. Glass with a smooth surface

2. A lint-free towel

3. A small rubber spatula or squeegee (our Polymer Rib Squeegee 7082 works well)

4. Scissors

Applying

Clean your glass before you begin with glass cleaner and a lint-free towel.

1. Remove the layer of wax paper.

2. Thoroughly wet the decal on its backing paper in a bowl of room-temperature water until it uncurls. This takes about 30 seconds, depending on the temperature of the water and the size of the decal. Do not let the decal sit in the water for more than a minute or two.

3. Remove the decal (still on its backing paper) from the water, and set it on top of the glass with the decal facing up. Let it sit for 1–2 minutes, at which point the decal should release from the backing paper with no resistance. If the decal is not releasing easily, re-wet the decal and allow it to rest a while longer on your glass while the glue softens. Larger decals may need more time in the water.

4. When properly wetted, the decal will slide straight from the backing paper and should not be flipped over. Gently position the decals as desired on the clean glass. Using a small squeegee or rubber/silicone spatula, gently press the water and any air bubbles from the center of the decal toward the edge. Starting with the gentle pressure, use a clockwise motion on the piece, increasing the pressure by increments at the end of each rotation until you squeeze all the water and air bubbles from underneath the decal.

5. Wick away any surface moisture with the lint-free cloth.

6. Once applied, you shouldn't be able to move the decal. If possible, let the applied decal sit in a dry environment overnight (or at least a couple hours) before firing.

Safety

The decals should be fired in a well-ventilated room, preferably one that vents to the outside.

Firing

- Make sure the kiln is ventilated up to 1000°F (535°C)

- The decal should be fired very slowly below 500°F (260°C)

- For best results, apply decals to pre-fired glass (see FAQ for more information)

- Slumping is an option in a subsequent firing

Below are suggested schedules for digital decals (four-color), metallic decals (platinum, gold, copper), and solid colors (black, blue, white) on Bullseye Glass. Your results may vary, depending on your kiln. You may want to do a few tests.

Solid Color & Metallic Decals

Rate	Temperature	Hold
80°F (44°C)	185°F (85°C)	:20
200°F (111°C)	600°F (316°C)	:15
600°F (333°C)	1370°F–1450°F (743°C–788°C)*	:10

Anneal according to the needs of the piece.

*Solid colors such as black, blue, and white mature towards the low end of the range, while metallic decals mature at the high end. Solid colors become slightly less opaque if fired at the high end. For decals that combine solid colors with metallic, we suggest firing to 1425° (774°C).

Digital Decals

Rate	Temperature	Hold
80°F (44°C)	185°F (85°C)	:20
200°F (111°C)	600°F (316°C)	:15
600°F (333°C)	1275°F–1380°F (691°C–749°C)	:10

Anneal according to the needs of the piece.

Notes on Digital Decals: These decals are not very opaque and will appear translucent on clear glass. They work best on white or other light colors and will not show up well on medium to darker shades of glass. They will adhere to glass from 600°F to 1420°F, but are best kept in a 1275°F to 1380°F range as opacity decreases at higher temperatures.

Goals for each segment:

1. Drying segment
2. Slow burning of the organics in the decal
3. Fusing with rapid heat to process soak

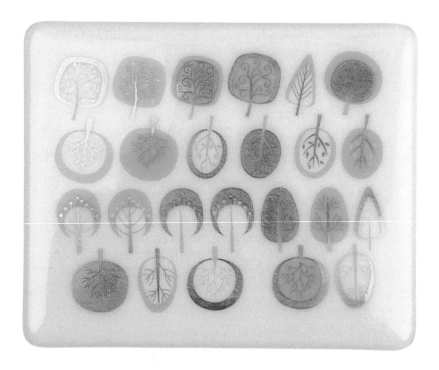

Frequently Asked Questions

1. Do I have to fire the glass before applying a decal?
   At Bullseye Glass studios, we have had success with applying decals directly to the smooth areas of unfired, double-rolled sheet glass. Take care to squeeze out any water and air as directed. This approach works well when working on a single layer object, such as a 3mm slumped dish (two firings; the first to fuse the decal to the sheet, the 2nd firing to slump). When using decals on a 6mm thick piece, composed of two layers of glass, it makes sense to pre-fuse the blank, apply and fire the decal, then lastly slump the piece (3 firings).

2. Why are the decals tinted orange/green?
   A tint is used to improve visibility while working with the decals and will not be visible after firing.

3. After firing, decals have pinholes and blowouts. What happened?
   These holes come from water or air bubbles that have remained underneath the decal. Review your decal application methods. Be patient and thorough. Pre-firing your glass to make it smooth can be helpful, as it allows air and water to escape more easily.

4. The decal wiped right off after firing. What happened?
   This can sometimes happen if you neglect to remove the white paper backing or wax paper on top before applying and firing. This can also happen if you accidentally apply the decal upside down, or under fire it.

5. My glass is hazy around the fired decal. What can I do?
   Sift a layer of clear powder over the decal and the hazed area. Fire to 1425°F (774°C) for a glossy finish to mask the devitrification. This technique is most effective with solid color decals. Metallic and digital decals may become slightly dappled if covered with powder.

6. Do decals fire the same on various styles (colors) of glass?
   We've noticed that Metallic decals fire shiny on transparent styles as well as Black and Opaline. Metallic decals fire to a semi-matte, antiqued finish on most Opalescent styles. The cornstarch layer tends to fire more cleanly on transparent styles as well as Black and Opaline.

These working notes are adapted from Milestone Decals for use with Bullseye Glass. For full instructions on using Milestone Decals with ceramic or other base materials, please see their instructions at their website: milestonedecalart.com/firinginstructions

You can also see our free video lesson at bit.ly/fusedecals

What Size French Cleat Do I Need?

Once you know the total weight of your piece, use this chart to select the right cleat(s).

8616 - Cleat, Small, 3" (76 mm)

Weight Limit	1.1 lbs. (0.5 kg) per cleat with 50% glue
Glue Surface Area	3" x 0.75" (76 x 19 mm)
Thickness	0.1875" (5 mm)
Lift off Clearance	0.5" (13 mm)
Mounting Channel	0.5" (13 mm)
Material	6005A high strength aluminum
Assembled Footprint	3" x 1.9375"

8615 - Cleat, Small, 6" (152 mm)

Weight Limit	2.25 lbs. (1 kg) per cleat with 50% glue
Glue Surface Area	6" x 0.75" (152 x 19 mm)
Thickness	0.1875" (5 mm)
Lift off Clearance	0.5" (13 mm)
Mounting Channel	0.5" (13 mm)
Material	6005A high strength aluminum
Assembled Footprint	6" x 1.9375"

8614 - Cleat, Small, 12" (304 mm)

Weight Limit	4.5 lbs. (2.04 kg) per cleat with 50% glue
Glue Surface Area	12" x 0.75" (304 x 19 mm)
Thickness	0.1875" (5 mm)
Lift off Clearance	0.5" (13 mm)
Mounting Channel	0.5" (13 mm)
Material	6005A high strength aluminum
Assembled Footprint	12" x 1.9375"

8613 - Cleat, Medium, 6" (152 mm)

Weight Limit	3 lbs. (1.36 kg) per cleat with 50% glue
Glue Surface Area	6" x 1" (152 x 25 mm)
Thickness	0.25" (6 mm)
Lift off Clearance	0.4375" (11 mm)
Mounting Channel	0.5625" (14 mm)
Material	6063 high strength aluminum
Assembled Footprint	6" x 2.625"

8612 - Cleat, Medium, 12" (304 mm)

Weight Limit	6 lbs. (2.72 kg) per cleat with 50% glue
Glue Surface Area	12" x 1" (304 x 25 mm)
Thickness	0.25" (6 mm)
Lift off Clearance	0.4375" (11 mm)
Mounting Channel	0.5625" (14 mm)
Material	6063 high strength aluminum
Assembled Footprint	12" x 2.625"

8611 - Cleat, Large, 12" (304 mm)

Weight Limit	9.75 lbs. (4.42 kg) per cleat with 50% glue
Glue Surface Area	12" x 1.625" (304 x 41 mm)
Thickness	0.40625" (10.3 mm)
Lift off Clearance	0.75" (19.05 mm)
Mounting Channel	1" wide x 0.25" (25 x 6 mm) deep
Material	6063 high strength aluminum
Assembled Footprint	12" x 4"

8657 - Cleat, Extra Large, 12" (304 mm)

Weight Limit	16.8 lbs. (7.62 kg) per cleat with 50% glue
Glue Surface Area	12" x 3" (304 x 76 mm)
Thickness	0.40625" (10.3 mm)
Lift off Clearance	0.75" (19.05 mm)
Mounting Channel	2.375" (60.325 mm)
Material	6063 high strength aluminium
Assembled Footprint	12" x 6.75"

◎ What to Expect from Opaline Striker Frit

Opaline Striker medium frit (000403-0002)

Frit balls made with Opaline Striker coarse frit (000403-0003). (Top and middle) Tack fused together, then slumped. (Bottom) Tack fused to a fully fused plate, then slumped.

BENEFIT

Like Opaline sheet glass, Opaline frit is a unique translucent style that transmits cool tones or warm fiery effects depending on how the light hits it.

CHALLENGE

Opaline frit tends to strike/go opaque with extensive heatwork.

SOLUTION

Kilnforming tests show that Opaline frit begins to develop color at 1400°F (760°C) and remains relatively stable through three full fuse firings to 1480°F (804°C). It can retain its unique characteristics in castings fired to 1480° F (804° C) and held for 10–60 minutes.

RECOMMENDED USES
- Full fuse "Painting with Glass" techniques.
- Open-faced kilncasting, where cold glass is packed inside the mold and minimal heatwork is required. Size may be restricted by length of time required at process temperatures for glass to completely flow to fill mold details.
- Making frit balls.
- Creating fading color fields.

SITUATIONS TO AVOID

Where Opaline frit will become opaque and lose its fiery quality
- Any method that requires extensive heatwork, such as kilncasting into a closed mold, where glass is heated to high temperatures to flow from a flowerpot or crucible.
- Firing in underpowered or over-insulated kilns, which may result in glass undergoing too much heatwork.

◎ **Working with Accucast 880 Blue**

Accu-Cast 880 Blue is an easily mixed alginate that sets in 5–10 minutes. If kept in a sealed container and treated carefully it can last a few weeks. If not, it will dry out and shrink over a couple of days.

Mixing Accucast 880 Blue
The manufacturer recommends mixing it 4 parts water to 1 part Accu-Cast 880 by weight. We have had success mixing it 7 parts water to 1 part Accu-Cast 880 by weight. We prefer mixing this alginate with a kitchen whisk in a bowl, starting at 1 beat per second until the dry powder incorporates into the water. When it does, we increase mixing speed to approximately 3 beats per second for 1–2 minutes (until the mixture is smooth but before it begins to set up). Work in a well-ventilated area and wear a NIOSH-approved respirator whenever working with powdered materials.

Pouring the Alginate
To begin, be certain that you are working on a flat and level surface. Also, be aware that poured molds typically involve a model that is attached to a work surface surrounded by walls or coddles to contain the mold material during pouring (often referred to as a "flask"). Pour a steady, uniform stream of alginate into the flask to one side of the model (not directly on it) so that the alginate rises up and around the model before covering its top. By enveloping the model in this manner, you help prevent air from getting trapped on its surface. Vibrating the worktable by drumming on it with the bottom of your fists will also help eliminate air bubbles.

Cleanup
Allow the remaining alginate to dry completely in the container; then immerse the container in a bucket of water. This will make it possible to remove the alginate in one large piece rather than peeling it out in chunks. Check local regulations for proper disposal.

And remember: never pour alginate down a drain as it will clog your pipes.

Bullseye Molds

Tips for Using Bullseye Slumping Molds

TIPS FOR USING BULLSEYE SLUMPING MOLDS

Bullseye slumping molds are slipcast from a specially formulated clay body. They have an exceptionally smooth surface and accept kilnwash uniformly. If prepared with Bullseye Shelf Primer and handled properly, they will not crack under repeated use. Some artists report using their molds for months and even years without re-priming.

Note: Mold measurements listed in our catalog and online store represent the outermost possible dimensions of the mold (the base). This is to help you determine whether a given mold will fit in your kiln. Since the molds are handmade, individual molds will vary in size. That is why you should *never cut glass to fit until you have measured your actual mold.*

PREPARING A BULLSEYE MOLD

A slumping mold must be prepared with a separator to prevent the glass from sticking to it during the firing process. When preparing a ceramic mold with Bullseye Shelf Primer, mix five parts water to one part dry powder. Wear a respirator to avoid inhaling dust.

Apply five layers of primer, each from different directions (ex: down, right, up, left, across), coating surfaces that will come in contact with glass. Use a natural-hair, fine-bristled brush, such as a hake brush.

To prevent breakage, kiln-dry the freshly prepared mold more slowly than you would a kilnshelf. Fire at 500°F (278°C) per hour to 500°F (260°C), with a 20-minute hold.

Clear the vent holes of primer and carefully remove any loose brush hairs prior to slumping. Store and handle primed molds with care to keep their prepared surfaces in good condition.

A prepared ceramic mold will serve for many firings, provided the primer remains free of chips and scratches, which could cause the glass to stick. Mold profiles with gentle curves fired to low process temperatures may not need to be re-prepared for 30 firings or more.

Note: steep-sided molds and molds with recessed details need more frequent re-priming. As glass slumps into a steep-sided form, it pulls small amounts of primer away from the surface. If the primer wears thin, glass can catch and slump unevenly. Re-prime after every two to three firings. To re-prime, gently remove the old primer with a dry scrub pad and reapply as directed.

SLUMP FIRING

The temperature and time it will take to successfully slump a piece depends on the profile and diameter of the mold, the depth of the slump, and the weight of the glass.

See *Mold Tips: Suggested Slumping Schedules*, which covers our recommendations for all the slumping molds we carry.

With any new mold, we suggest that you first fire a simple, inexpensive glass blank to confirm the correct cycle.

The ideal position for the mold is in the center of the kiln and 2" or more away from the elements. (In a front-loading kiln, you may want to center the piece on the mold outside of the kiln in order to get a better view.)

To promote better air and heat circulation, elevate molds from the floor of your kiln or kiln shelf. This also promotes more uniform heating and cooling for the glass.

Before firing, verify that the mold and glass are level.

Additional tip: For easy identification, use a ceramic underglaze pencil to mark the style number on the side of the mold.

ADDITIONAL RESOURCES

Bullseye Shelf Primer Instructions
Mold Tips: Big Bowl
Mold Tips: Cone Bowls
Mold Tips: Deep Form
Mold Tips: Pyramid Casting Mold
Mold Tips: Suggested Slumping Schedules
Tip Sheet 7: Platemaking Tips

Mold Tips: Big Bowl

Notes generated in the Bullseye Research & Education studios, firing in Paragon GL24 kilns.

Note: The following tips do not guarantee a uniform result. Because of the steep-sided nature of this mold, pieces may slump unevenly.

SLUMPING OPTIONS

We have achieved the most consistent results creating relatively even forms with the Big Bowl slumping mold (8973) by using it as the second part of a two-stage slump, combined with frequent re-application of shelf primer to the mold.

The first stage uses the center area of the 16.5" Ball Surface / Deep Form Step One mold (8738). Be sure to measure and cut the piece based on the diameter of the Big Bowl mold. After firing according to the Stage 1 schedule, the result should be a slumped piece with a symmetrical, rounded profile. Transfer it to the Big Bowl mold and fire according to the suggested Stage 2 schedule.

UNIFORM HEATING

The same characteristics that make this form unique—depth combined with a narrow lip and flat base—make it unforgiving of uneven heat. Elevating the mold on 2" (5 cm) posts will promote even heating, slumping, and cooling. Also, make sure the mold is in the center of the kiln, as this form may slump unevenly if one side is closer to the elements.

A Big Bowl mold may also be used to slump a flat blank, however results may vary.

MORE FREQUENT RE-PRIMING

Steep-sided molds like these need more frequent re-priming than forms with gentle curves, which are often fired to lower process temperatures with shorter hold times. As glass slumps into a steep-sided form, it pulls small amounts of primer away from the surface. If the primer wears thin, glass can catch and slump unevenly. Re-prime after every two to three firings, or as needed. To re-prime, gently remove the old primer with a dry scrub pad and reapply as directed.

SUGGESTED FIRING SCHEDULES

STAGE 1: CENTER OF 16.5" BALL SURFACE / DEEP FORM STEP ONE MOLD (8738)

	RATE (DEGREES / HOUR)	TEMPERATURE	HOLD
1	300°F (167°C)	1200°F (649°C)	:05
2	AFAP*	900°F (482°C)	1:00
3	100°F (56°C)	700°F (371°C)	:00
4	AFAP	70°F (21°C)	:00

STAGE 2: BIG BOWL MOLD (8973)

	RATE (DEGREES / HOUR)	TEMPERATURE	HOLD
1	300°F (167°C)	1200°F (649°C)	:15**
2	AFAP*	900°F (482°C)	1:00
3	100°F (56°C)	700°F (371°C)	:00
4	AFAP	70°F (21°C)	:00

* As Fast As Possible. Allow the kiln to cool at its natural rate with the door closed.
** Visually confirm slump progress.

Mold Tips: Cone Bowl Molds

The following tips do not guarantee a uniform result. Because of the steep-sided nature of this mold, pieces may slump unevenly.

Prepare either the Cone Bowl (8943) or Large Cone Bowl mold (8975) as directed in *Tips for Using Bullseye Slumping Molds* at www.bullseyeglass.com.

Measure the top edge of your mold to determine the diameter. Cut your glass to the same diameter as the mold or up to 1/16" (1.5 mm) larger all around. This slightly larger size allows the mold's narrow lip to support the glass and hold it in place as it slumps into this steep form.

UNIFORM HEATING

The same characteristics that make these forms unique— depth combined with a narrow lip and flat base—make it unforgiving of uneven heat. Elevating the mold on 2" (5 cm) posts will promote even heating, slumping, and cooling. Also, make sure the mold is in the center of the kiln as these forms may slump unevenly if one side is closer to the elements.

MORE FREQUENT RE-PRIMING

Steep-sided molds like these need more frequent re-priming than forms with gentle curves. (Forms with gentle curves are often fired to lower process temperatures paired with shorter hold times.) As glass slumps into a steep-sided form, it pulls small amounts of primer away from the surface. If the primer wears thin, glass can catch and slump unevenly. Re-prime after every two to three firings. To re-prime, gently remove the old primer with a dry scrub pad and reapply as directed.

SUGGESTED FIRING SCHEDULES

CONE BOWL (8943)

	RATE (DEGREES / HOUR)	TEMPERATURE	HOLD
1	300°F (167°C)	1200°F (649°C)	:30
2	300°F (167°C)	1225°F (663°C)	1:30*
3	AFAP**	900°F (482°C)	1:00
4	100°F (56°C)	700°F (371°C)	:00
5	AFAP	70°F (21°C)	:00

LARGE CONE BOWL (8975)

	RATE (DEGREES / HOUR)	TEMPERATURE	HOLD
1	300°F (167°C)	1200°F (649°C)	:30
2	300°F (167°C)	1225°F (663°C)	1:00*
3	AFAP**	900°F (482°C)	1:00
4	100°F (56°C)	700°F (371°C)	:00
5	AFAP	70°F (21°C)	:00

* If possible, visually confirm the slump. If you are not able to observe a slump in progress, remember that it is often easier to re-fire and increase the heatwork than to fix something that has slumped too much.

** As Fast As Possible. Allow the kiln to cool at its natural rate with the door closed.

Note on Segment 1: The purpose of this lower temperature hold is to begin the slumping process and facilitate a uniform slump before moving on to greater heatwork to resolve the form.

Note on Segment 2: We commonly hold at slumping process temperatures for over an hour, especially for molds with steep sides. This lower-for-longer approach reduces the amount of mold texture picked up by the glass and helps maintain a uniform thickness.

175

Mold Tips: Deep Form Three-Step Process

Notes generated in the Bullseye Research & Education studios, firing in Paragon GL24 kilns.

Note: The following tips do not guarantee a uniform result. Because of the steep-sided nature of these molds, pieces may slump unevenly.

MOLDS NEEDED FOR THIS PROCESS
- 16.5" Ball Surface / Deep Form Step One (8738)
- Deep Form Step Two (8990)
- Deep Form Step Three (8991)

OTHER HELPFUL ITEMS
- 10.8" Drop Out Ring mold (8631) or 5.8" Ball Surface mold (8746)
- A level and a flat straight edge that fits in the kiln to set across the top of the mold (we used a strip of sheet glass!)
- Suction Lifter, Large (7195) or Small (7196)
- Zetex Heat Protective Gloves (8265)
- Protective face shield (available at most hardware stores)
- Bullseye Shelf Primer (8220)

OVERVIEW

This process involves slumping a 15.5"-diameter circle over the course of three firings. (Note: always measure your mold before cutting your glass.) Each consecutive firing shapes the form, ultimately resulting in a relatively deep, tall, steep-sided vessel. For our testing, we worked with an assortment of uniform-color 6 mm pieces (two 3 mm layers of a single color or a single 3 mm color with a 3 mm Clear cap). Pieces were kept in the same orientation as the initial full fuse (i.e., not flipped) with the shelf side in contact with the mold.

16.5" BALL SURFACE / DEEP FORM STEP ONE MOLD (8738)

This is a relatively conventional slumping form. Elevate the mold from the floor of the kiln using 2" posts. As with other gently sloped molds, a standard five-coat application of Bullseye Shelf Primer will serve for many slump firings.

SUGGESTED FIRING SCHEDULE

	RATE (DEGREES / HOUR)	TEMPERATURE	HOLD
1	250°F (139°C)	1200°F (649°C)	:05
2	AFAP*	900°F (482°C)	1:00
3	100°F (56°C)	700°F (371°C)	:00
4	AFAP	70°F (21°C)	:00

Firing schedules are intended as a starting point. Results may vary.

DEEP FORM STEP TWO (8990)

A smooth, well-primed surface for this form contributes to a uniform slump. Apply five coats of Bullseye Shelf Primer and kiln dry as directed. If your mold has already been primed and slumped into, gently remove the remaining primer with a dry scrub pad before re-priming.

This mold does not have a flat base. To create a stable base, elevate either Drop Out Ring or 5.8" Ball Surface mold on 2" posts and set Deep Form Step Two on top. Once the base is ready, place the slumped bowl from Step 1 into Deep Form Step Two, making an effort to center and level the set-up.

SUGGESTED FIRING SCHEDULE

	RATE (DEGREES / HOUR)	TEMPERATURE	HOLD
1	200°F (111°C)	1200°F (649°C)	:45**
2	AFAP*	900°F (482°C)	1:30
3	100°F (56°C)	700°F (371°C)	:00
4	AFAP	70°F (21°C)	:00

Firing schedules are intended as a starting point. Results may vary.

* As Fast As Possible. Allow the kiln to cool at its natural rate with the door closed.
** Visually confirm slump progress.

Mold Tips: Deep Form Three-Step Process (continued)

ACTIVE PARTICIPATION

Artist Karl Harron has developed an approach that helps to control these slumped forms. When slumping Deep Forms Step Two and Three,

More information on Karl Harron is available at theglassstudioireland.com

observe the slump in action. When unevenness is detected, manipulate the mold to counteract it. Wearing heat-protective gear—gloves, face shield, etc.—reach into the kiln and tilt the mold so the highest point of the glass rim is even higher, encouraging it to slump further and even out the form. Keep the mold from touching exposed elements and thermocouples at all times.

It may be necessary to manipulate the piece many times during the course of the firing. These small adjustments over the course of the slumping process (as often as every few minutes, starting as early as 1100°F) can help achieve an even form. Note that if you are going to manipulate the pieces in this manner you will need to program a much longer process hold time to account for heat loss.

Note: Never insert other objects (metal tools, etc.) into the kiln to perform these adjustments.

DEEP FORM STEP THREE (8991)

As noted in Step Two, we recommend a fresh application of Bullseye Shelf Primer with each slump firing when using these deep vessel forms.

If you plan to adjust the mold during the firing, support it with either a Drop Out Ring or Ball Surface mold as described in Step 2. Otherwise, elevate on 2" posts.

SUGGESTED FIRING SCHEDULE

	RATE (DEGREES / HOUR)	TEMPERATURE	HOLD
1	100°F (56°C)	1200°F (649°C)	:20**
2	AFAP*	900°F (482°C)	1:30
3	75°F (42°C)	700°F (371°C)	:00
4	AFAP	70°F (21°C)	:00

Firing schedules are intended as a starting point. Results may vary.
* As Fast As Possible.
  Allow the kiln to cool at its natural rate with the door closed.

** Visually confirm slump progress.

OBSERVATIONS

- In GL24 kilns, it is not possible to see the bottom of the vessel, so reading the top rim becomes significant.
- The piece will adequately fit in Stage Three without having reached the bottom of Stage Two.
- Through the slump firings, the glass against the mold can change texture and develop a dry surface. As the walls of the vessel become more vertically oriented, they thicken slightly.

◎ Mold Tips: Heart Casting Mold (8976)

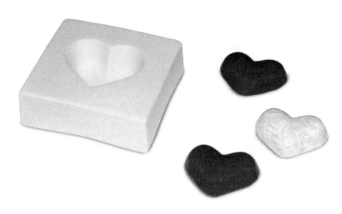

Mold preparation: Apply 5 coats of primer/separator with a soft bristle brush. Tilt the mold as you apply to prevent fluid primer from collecting in one spot. Kiln dry as you would any other small ceramic mold. Once dry, gently smooth the surface and tap out any excess primer. This mold should be re-primed before each casting.

Glass selection: It takes 50 grams of glass to make a heart casting that is approximately 0.7" (18 mm) thick. We've had success using various grain sizes of frit, as well as bits of 3mm sheet glass. Note that the form of glass used will impact the clarity of the casting. The form of glass may also be evident on the surface of the final casting as the shape of the material imprints against the mold. (To learn about selecting glass for casting, see TipSheet 8: Basic Lost Wax Kilncasting at bullseyeglass.com.)

For smoother edges around the fired base, heap material in the center. Some coldworking of the fired piece may be required.

SUGGESTED FIRING SCHEDULE

To promote even heating and cooling, place the Heart Casting Mold in the center of the kiln and elevate 1–2" (2.5–5 cm)

Suggested Firing Schedule following a 0.75" (19mm) annealing profile:

	Rate (Degrees/Hour)	Temperature	Hold
1	400°F (222°C)	1225°F (662°C)	1:30
2	600°F (333°C)	1500°F (816°C)	:10*
3	AFAP**	900°F (482°C)	3:00
4	45°F (25°C)	800°F (427°C)	:00
5	81°F (45°C)	700°F (371°C)	:00
6	270°F (150°C)	70°F (21°C)	

Fire gold-bearing styles with an appropriate hold of 2:00 at 1225°F.

*Plan to be present when the kiln is at process temperature, and visually inspect the piece. Skip to the next segment once cast is complete.

**As Fast As Possible. Allow kiln to cool at its natural rate with the door closed.

Fire gold-bearing styles with an appropriate hold of 2:00 at 1225°F.

Expect matte surfaces where the glass is fired in contact with the mold. Apply a small amount of Clean Shield Gel to impart a subtle sheen.

Re-preparation: Due to the heatwork involved, this mold must be re-prepared before each use. Primer is no longer effective once fired to this temperature. To re-prime, gently remove the old primer with a dry scrub pad and reapply as directed.

Helpful Resources
Clean Shield Gel product use
Frit Tinting (article)
Frit Tinting (video)
Mold Tips: Suggested Slumping Schedules
Tips for Using Bullseye Slumping Molds

Mold Tips: Pyramid Casting Mold (8948)

Notes generated in the Bullseye Research & Education studios, firing in Paragon GL24 kilns.

Prepare the Pyramid Casting Mold with primer/separator and kiln-dry as directed in *Tips for Using Bullseye Slumping Molds* at bullseyeglass.com. This mold should be re-prepared before each casting.

To promote even heating and cooling, place the Pyramid Casting Mold centrally in the kiln and elevate on 2" (5 cm) shelf posts.

It takes 2090 grams of glass to maximize the mold form. Billet or frit may be used. For smoother edges around the finished base, heap material in the center as shown. (We have not yet tested this mold using sheet glass, which will involve more complex preparation for successful casting.)

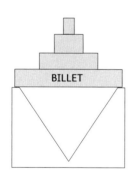
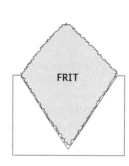

SUGGESTED FIRING SCHEDULE

Suggested firing schedule following a 2" (50 mm) anneal profile appropriate for thickness of glass and hollowed mold structure:

	RATE (DEGREES / HOUR)	TEMPERATURE	HOLD
1	200°F (111°C)	1225°F (663°C)	2:00 for billet 1:00 for frit
2	600°F (333°C)	1525°F (829°C)	2:00*
3	AFAP**	900°F (482°C)	8:00
4	6°F (3.8°C)	800°F (427°C)	:00
5	12°F (6.8°C)	700°F (371°C)	:00
6	41°F (22°C)	70°F (21°C)	:00

*   Visually inspect after :20. Skip segment once cast is complete. If bubbles have collected at the top surface, a continued hold will allow them to break open. Visually inspect bubble activity.

** As Fast As Possible. Allow kiln to cool at its natural rate with the door closed.

The topic of the firing cycle as it relates to the glass and kiln conditions is covered in depth in *TechNotes 4: Heat and Glass* at bullseyeglass.com.

Expect matte surfaces where the glass is fired in contact with the mold.

Re-preparation: Due to the high process temperatures and long hold times required, this mold must be re-prepared before each use. Primer is no longer effective once fired to these temperatures. Re-prime after every firing. To re-prime, gently remove the old primer with a dry scrub pad and reapply as directed.

Glass selection: The form of glass used (billet or frit) will have a direct impact on the clarity of the casting. Color is also a major consideration when choosing glass for thick works. To learn about selecting glass for casting, see *TipSheet 8: Basic Lost Wax Kilncasting* at bullseyeglass.com.

  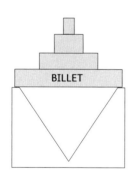 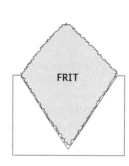

Mold Tips: Suggested Slumping Schedules (Fahrenheit)

The following slumping schedules have been collected over years of experience at Bullseye's Research & Education studios. Note that the schedules are intended as a starting point. Many variables factor in to developing an appropriate cycle. Every kiln fires differently, and different glass styles vary in viscosity.

Since no single slumping schedule will work for every project, we recommend that you visually confirm the slump during the firing. To do this, open the kiln door enough to take a quick look, then close it and think about what you've seen. Don't hold the door open for more than a few seconds.

Depending on the mold you're working with, this can happen either as you approach process temperature and/ or during the process soak until the slump is complete. Be sure to record your observations for future reference.

Suggested Video Lessons (subscription required)
Slumping Basics, Working with Drop-Out Molds

Using these schedules

Schedules are based on observations from slumping 6-mm-thick pieces in Paragon GL24 kilns. For each mold, the first segment of the firing is provided. Plug it into the provided template.

Segment	Rate (°F/hr)	Temperature	Hold
1			
2	AFAP*	900°F	1:00
3	100°F	700°F	:00
4	AFAP*	70°F	:00

* As Fast As Possible. Allow the kiln to cool at its natural rate with the door closed.

Soup Bowl
8665: 9.4" x 1.6"
(24 x 4 cm)
▶ 300°F | 1225°F | 1:15

Pasta Bowl
8909: 11.3" x 1.7" x 2"
(29 x 4 x 5 cm)
▶ 300°F | 1235°F | 1:00
8910: 13.1" x 1.9" x 2.4"
(33 x 5 x 6 cm)
▶ 300°F | 1225°F | :45

Plain Plate
8721: 14.6" x 1.2"
(37 x 3 cm)
▶ 300°F | 1200°F | :05
8722: 9.4" x 1.6"
(45 x 5 cm)
▶ 300°F | 1180°F | :05

Saturn Dessert Plate
8939: 11.3" x 0.7" x 5"
(29 x 2 x 13 cm)
▶ 300°F | 1225°F | 1:30

Round Plate
8928: 12.8" X 0.7"
(33 x 2 cm)
▶ 300°F | 1225°F | 1:30

Classic
8748: 5.9" x 1"
(15 x 3 cm)
▶ 300°F | 1225°F | 1:30
8749: 6.1" x 0.6"
(16 x 2 cm)
▶ 300°F | 1225°F | 1:30
8747: 8.5" x 0.9"
(22 x 2 cm)
▶ 300°F | 1225°F | :45

Classic
8723: 12.1" x 3"
(31 x 8 cm)
▶ 300°F | 1225°F | :45
8724: 15.7" x 3.3"
(40 x 8 cm)
▶ 300°F | 1225°F | :30

Cone Bowl
8943: 7.4" x 2.2"
(19 x 6 cm)
See Mold Tips: Cone Bowls

Large Cone Bowl
8975: 11.5" x 3.4"
(29 x 9 cm)
See Mold Tips: Cone Bowls

Big Bowl
8973: 12.5" x 3.7"
(32 x 9 cm)
See Mold Tips: Big Bowl

Note: The measurements given here are for the outer dimensions of the molds. This is to help you determine whether a given mold will fit in your kiln. Since they are handmade, individual molds will vary in size. Never cut glass to fit until you have measured your mold.

Seder Plate

8959: 12.3" x 1.4"
(31 x 4 cm)
▶ 300°F | 1250°F | 1:15

Swirl

8788: 11.9" x 2.1"
(30 x 5 cm)
▶ 300°F | 1225°F | 0:45

Round Slumper

8630: 7.5" x 1"
(19 x 3 cm)
▶ 300°F | 1200°F | :05

8629: 11.8" x 1.6"
(30 x 4 cm)
▶ 300°F | 1190°F | :05

Large Round Slumper

8628: 14.8" x 2.6"
(38 x 7 cm)
▶ 300°F | 1225°F | :20

Bowl

8651: 15.6" x 2.4"
(40 x 6 cm)
▶ 300°F | 1225°F | :45

8652: 16.1" x 3.4"
(41 x 9 cm)
▶ 300°F | 1215°F | :15

Oval

8744: 15.4" x 9.8" x 1.7"
(39 x 25 x 4 cm)
▶ 300°F | 1225°F | :40

Oval Dish

8536: 8.1" x 5.2" x 1.3"
(21 x 13 x 3 cm)
▶ 300°F | 1220°F | :20

8455: 11.3" x 7.4" x 1.5"
(29 x 19 x 4 cm)
▶ 300°F | 1225°F | :20

Short Oval

8919: 11" x 4.4" x 1.2"
(28 x 11 x 3 cm)
▶ 300°F | 1225°F | :10

8952: 14.8" x 6.3" x 1.7"
(38 x 16 x 4 cm)
▶ 300°F | 1215°F | :20

Long Oval

8920: 10.9" x 4.5" x 0.6"
(28 x 11 x 2 cm)
▶ 300°F | 1215°F | :20

8951: 18.1" x 6.7" x 1.3"
(46 x 17 x 3 cm)
▶ 300°F | 1225°F | :10

Snack Tray

8961: 9.8" x 6.7" x 1.2"
(25 x 17 x 3 cm)
▶ 300°F | 1250°F | 1:30

Ball Surface

8746: 5.8" x 1.7"
(15 x 4 cm)
▶ 200°F | 1220°F | :20

8736: 7.8" x 1.2"
(20 x 3 cm)
▶ 300°F | 1215°F | :05

8735: 9.4" x 2"
(24 x 5 cm)
▶ 300°F | 1200°F | :30

8734: 11.4" x 3"
(29 x 8 cm)
▶ 300°F | 1200°F | :20

Ball Surface

8733: 14.8" x 2.1"
(38 x 5 cm)
▶ 300°F | 1200°F | :05

8738: 16.5" x 3.3"
(42 x 9 cm)
▶ 200°F | 1200°F | :05

8737: 19.3" x 3.6"
(49 x 9 cm)
▶ 200°F | 1160°F | :20

8745: 21.7" x 4.2"
(55 x 11 cm)
▶ 200°F | 1170°F | :05

Deep Form Step Two

8990: 15" x 7.3"
(38 x 19 cm)
See Mold Tips: Deep Form

Deep Form Step Three

8991: 12.6" x 8.2"
(32 x 21 cm)
See Mold Tips: Deep Form

Pyramid Casting Mold

8948: 6.7" x 6.7" x 4.7"
(17 x 17 x 12 cm)
See Mold Tips: Pyramid Casting Mold

Heart Casting Mold

8948: 3.9" x 3.5"
(10 x 9 cm)
See Mold Tips: Heart Casting Mold

Note: The measurements given here are for the outer dimensions of the molds. This is to help you determine whether a given mold will fit in your kiln. Since they are handmade, individual molds will vary in size. Never cut glass to fit until you have measured your mold.

Mini Soft Edged Plate

8963: 6.1" x 6.1" x 0.8"
(16 x 16 x 2 cm)
▶ 300°F | 1250°F | 2:00

Small Dish

8926: 8.5" x 8.5" x 1.3"
(22 x 22 x 3 cm)
▶ 300°F | 1225°F | 2:15

Soft Edge Platter

8985: 9.1" x 9.1" x 0.9"
(23 x 23 x 2 cm)
▶ 300°F | 1225°F | 1:20

Retro Party Bowl

8936: 16.9" x 16.9" x 3.9"
(57 x 18 x 6 cm)
▶ 300°F | 1225°F | :35

Yin-Yang Plate

8341: 11.4" x 11.4" x 0.9"
(29 x 29 x 2 cm)
▶ 250°F | 1265°F | 1:30

One-Square Dish

8934: 3.5" x 3.5" x 0.9"
(9 x 9 x 2 cm)
▶ 300°F | 1250°F | 1:15

Square Bowl, Simple Curve

8647: 12" x 12" x 2.5"
(31 x 31 x 6 cm)
▶ 300°F | 1225°F | 1:00

Square Bowl, Double Curve

8648: 11.8" x 11.8" x 2.1"
(30 x 30 x 5 cm)
▶ 300°F | 1225°F | 1:00

Four-Square Dish

8935: 6.7" x 6.7" x 0.9"
(17 x 17 x 2 cm)
▶ 300°F | 1240°F | 1:00

Soft Edge Four Square Platter

8342: 14" x 14" x 1.2"
(36 x 36 x 3 cm)
▶ 300°F | 1225°F | 2:20

Very Gentle Curve

8982: 18" x 18" x 2.3"
(46 x 46 x 6 cm)
▶ 300°F | 1160°F | :05

Square Nesting Plate

8757: 5.5" x 5.5" x 0.9"
(14 x 14 x 2 cm)
▶ 300°F | 1225°F | 0:20

8758: 7" x 7" x 0.8"
(18 x 18 x 2 cm)
▶ 300°F | 1225°F | 0:25

8759: 8.6" x 8.6" x 1"
(22 x 22 x 3 cm)
▶ 300°F | 1225°F | 0:10

Square Slumper A

8636: 4.5" x 4.5" x 0.8"
(12 x 12 x 2 cm)
▶ 300°F | 1180°F | :05

8635: 8.5" x 8.5" x 1.5"
(22 x 22 x 4 cm)
▶ 300°F | 1180°F | :05

8634: 10.1" x 10.1" x 1.9"
(26 x 26 x 5 cm)
▶ 300°F | 1180°F | :05

8637: 12" x 12" x 2.2"
(30 x 30 x 6 cm)
▶ 300°F | 1180°F | :05

8739: 15.9" x 15.9" x 2.8"
(40 x 40 x 7 cm)
▶ 300°F | 1160°F | :05

8938: 20.9" x 20.9" x 3.7"
(53 x 53 x 9 cm)
▶ 150°F | 1160°F | :05

Square Slumper B

8998: 3.4" x 3.4" x 0.9"
(9 x 9 x 2 cm)
▶ 300°F | 1200°F | :05

8997: 5.2" x 5.2" x 1.3"
(13 x 13 x 3 cm)
▶ 300°F | 1200°F | :05

8996: 6.1" x 6.1" x 1.1"
(16 x 16 x 3 cm)
▶ 300°F | 1200°F | :05

8995: 6.8" x 6.8" x 1.6"
(17 x 17 x 4 cm)
▶ 300°F | 1200°F | :05

Square Plate

8901: 3.3" x 3.3" x 0.8"
(8 x 8 x 2 cm)
▶ 300°F | 1250°F | 1:30

8900: 5.3" x 5.3" x 1"
(13 x 13 x 3 cm)
▶ 300°F | 1240°F | 1:30

8899: 6.3" x 6.3" x 0.9"
(16 x 16 x 2 cm)
▶ 300°F | 1225°F | 1:30

Square Platter

8638: 9.6" x 9.6" x 0.8"
(25 x 25 x 2 cm)
▶ 300°F | 1250°F | 1:30

8641: 11.9" x 11.9" x 0.8"
(30 x 30 x 2 cm)
▶ 250°F | 1240°F | 1:15

8646: 14.8" x 14.8" x 0.8"
(38 x 38 x 2 cm)
▶ 250°F | 1225°F | 1:30

Soap Dish

8981: 6" x 4" x 0.8"
(15 x 10 x 2 cm)
▶ 300°F | 1215°F | 1:00

Circle in Square

8453: 5.9" x 5.9" x 1.6"
(15 x 15 x 4 cm)
▶ 300°F | 1250°F | 1:30

Flat Slumper

8972: 10.6" x 10.6" x 1.1"
(27 x 27 x 3 cm)
▶ 300°F | 1170°F | :05

182

Note: The measurements given here are for the outer dimensions of the molds. This is to help you determine whether a given mold will fit in your kiln. Since they are handmade, individual molds will vary in size. Never cut glass to fit until you have measured your mold.

Small Rectangle
8945: 9.5" x 5.4" x 1.5"
(24 x 14 x 4 cm)
▶ 300°F | 1250°F | 1:15

Medium Rectangle
8949: 11.4" x 9.1" x 1.3"
(29 x 23 x 3 cm)
▶ 300°F | 1225°F | :45

Party Platter
8539: 19.8" x 12.8" x 1.8"
(50 x 33 x 5 cm)
▶ 300°F | 1225°F | 1:45

One Candle Bridge
8903: 7.2" x 5.1" x 2"
(18 x 13 x 5 cm)
▶ 300°F | 1250°F | 1:30

Four Candle Bridge
8902: 12.4" x 5.7" x 1.6"
(32 x 15 x 4 cm)
▶ 250°F | 1250°F | 2:00

Simple Curve
8642: 15.6" x 13.1" x 2.8"
(40 x 33 x 7 cm)
▶ 300°F | 1170°F | :05

Serving Tray
8947: 14.8" x 9" x 0.9"
(38 x 23 x 2 cm)
▶ 250°F | 1225°F | 1:20

Concave Dish
8933: 13.9" x 9.5" x 1.7"
(35 x 24 x 4 cm)
▶ 300°F | 1225°F | :45

Convex Dish
8932: 13.5" x 9.7" x 1.4"
(34 x 25 x 4 cm)
▶ 300°F | 1225°F | :45

Soft Edge Platter Long
8962: 14" x 9.4" x 0.9"
(36 x 24 x 2 cm)
▶ 300°F | 1225°F | 1:00

Double Curve
8960: 9.4" x 8.7" x 1.7"
(24 x 22 x 4 cm)
▶ 300°F | 1220°F | :10
8643: 15.9" x 13.6" x 2.9"
(40 x 35 x 7 cm)
▶ 300°F | 1215°F | :10

Lamp Bender Conic
8740: 12.2" x 10.4" x 3.8"
(31 x 27 x 10 cm)
▶ 300°F | 1200°F | :15

Lamp Bender
8964: 6" x 4.9" x 2.1"
(15 x 12 x 5 cm)
▶ 300°F | 1200°F | :30
8725: 10.1" x 8.5" x 3.7"
(26 x 22 x 10 cm)
▶ 300°F | 1200°F | :20

Square Drop Out
8957: 9.5" x 9.5" x 0.7"
(24 x 24 x 2 cm); Inside
5.4" x 5.4" (14 x 14 cm)
▶ 300°F | 1250°F | 1:30 *

Rectangular Drop Out
8923: 15.4" x 8.7" x 0.9"
(39 x 22 x2 cm); Inside 10.2"
x 3.7" (26 x 9 cm)
▶ 300°F | 1250°F | 2:00 *

183

Channel Plate
8456: 12.6" x 4.1" x 1.4"
(32 x 10 x 4 cm)
▶ 200°F | 1200°F | :25
8944: 17.1" x 4.8" x 1.6"
(44 x 12 x 4 cm)
▶ 200°F | 1200°F | :15
8257: 22.6" x 6.9" x 2.4"
(57 x 18 x 6 cm)
▶ 200°F | 1200°F | :10

Rectangular Slumper
8924: 12.2" x 7.4" x 1.7"
(31 x 19 x 4 cm)
▶ 300°F | 1200°F | :05
8925: 14.8" x 7.4" x 1.7"
(38 x 19 x 4 cm)
▶ 300°F | 1200°F | :05
8929: 16.5" x 11.9" x 2"
(42 x 30 x 5 cm)
▶ 300°F | 1170°F | :05

Oval in Rectangle
8454: 9.1" x 6.1" x 1.5"
(23 x 16 x 4 cm)
▶ 300°F | 1250°F | 1:30

Ellipse Drop Out
8955: 17.7" x 10.8" x 0.9"
(45 x 28 x 2 cm); Inside 13.6"
x 6.9" (35 x 18 cm)
▶ 300°F | 1250°F | 1:30 *

* This schedule is for making
a shallow plate. The mold
is placed directly on the kiln
shelf—not elevated.

Drop Out Ring
8633: 7.1" x 0.4" (18 x 1 cm);
Inside 3" (8 cm)
▶ 300°F | 1250°F | 1:30 *
8632: 8.9" x 0.4" (23 x 1 cm);
Inside 4.9" (13 cm)
▶ 300°F | 1250°F | 1:30 *
8631: 10.8" x 0.5" (28 x 1 cm);
Inside 6.7" (17 cm)
▶ 300°F | 1250°F | 1:30 *
8756: 13.3" x 0.5" (34 x 1 cm);
Inside 7.5" (19 cm)
▶ 300°F | 1250°F | 1:30 *

Note: The measurements given here are for the outer dimensions of the molds. This is to help you determine whether a given mold will fit in your kiln. Since they are handmade, individual molds will vary in size. Never cut glass to fit until you have measured your mold.

Mold Tips: Suggested Slumping Schedules (Celsius)

The following slumping schedules have been collected over years of experience at Bullseye's Research & Education studios. Note that the schedules are intended as a starting point. Many variables factor in to developing an appropriate cycle. Every kiln fires differently, and different glass styles vary in viscosity.

Since no single slumping schedule will work for every project, we recommend that you visually confirm the slump during the firing. To do this, open the kiln door enough to take a quick look, then close it and think about what you've seen. Don't hold the door open for more than a few seconds.

Depending on the mold you're working with, this can happen either as you approach process temperature and/or during the process soak until the slump is complete. Be sure to record your observations for future reference.

Suggested Video Lessons (subscription required)
Slumping Basics, Working with Drop-Out Molds

Using these schedules
Schedules are based on observations from slumping 6-mm-thick pieces in Paragon GL24 kilns. For each mold, the first segment of the firing is provided. Plug it into the provided template.

Segment	Rate (°F/hr)	Temperature	Hold
1			
2	AFAP*	482°C	1:00
3	56°C	371°C	:00
4	AFAP*	21°C	:00

* As Fast As Possible. Allow the kiln to cool at its natural rate with the door closed.

Soup Bowl

8665: 9.4" x 1.6"
(24 x 4 cm)
▶ 167°C | 663°C | 1:15

Pasta Bowl

8909: 11.3" x 1.7" x 2"
(29 x 4 x 5 cm)
▶ 167°C | 668°C | 1:00

8910: 13.1" x 1.9" x 2.4"
(33 x 5 x 6 cm)
▶ 167°C | 663°C | :45

Plain Plate

8721: 14.6" x 1.2"
(37 x 3 cm)
▶ 167°C | 649°C | :05

8722: 9.4" x 1.6"
(45 x 5 cm)
▶ 167°C | 638°C | :05

Saturn Dessert Plate

8939: 11.3" x 0.7" x 5"
(29 x 2 x 13 cm)
▶ 167°C | 663°C | 1:30

Round Plate

8928: 12.8" X 0.7"
(33 x 2 cm)
▶ 167°C | 663°C | 1:30

Classic

8748: 5.9" x 1"
(15 x 3 cm)
▶ 167°C | 663°C | 1:30

8749: 6.1" x 0.6"
(16 x 2 cm)
▶ 167°C | 663°C | 1:30

8747: 8.5" x 0.9"
(22 x 2 cm)
▶ 167°C | 663°C | :45

Classic

8723: 12.1" x 3"
(31 x 8 cm)
▶ 167°C | 663°C | :45

8724: 15.7" x 3.3"
(40 x 8 cm)
▶ 167°C | 663°C | :30

Cone Bowl

8943: 7.4" x 2.2"
(19 x 6 cm)
See *Mold Tips: Cone Bowls*

Large Cone Bowl

8975: 11.5" x 3.4"
(29 x 9 cm)
See *Mold Tips: Cone Bowls*

Big Bowl

8973: 12.5" x 3.7"
(32 x 9 cm)
See *Mold Tips: Big Bowl*

Note: The measurements given here are for the outer dimensions of the molds. This is to help you determine whether a given mold will fit in your kiln. Since they are handmade, individual molds will vary in size. Never cut glass to fit until you have measured your mold.

Seder Plate

8959: 12.3" x 1.4"
(31 x 4 cm)
▶ 167°C | 677°C | 1:15

Swirl

8788: 11.9" x 2.1"
(30 x 5 cm)
▶ 167°C | 663°C | 0:45

Round Slumper

8630: 7.5" x 1"
(19 x 3 cm)
▶ 167°C | 649°C | :05

8629: 11.8" x 1.6"
(30 x 4 cm)
▶ 167°C | 643°C | :05

Large Round Slumper

8628: 14.8" x 2.6"
(38 x 7 cm)
▶ 167°C | 663°C | :20

Bowl

8651: 15.6" x 2.4"
(40 x 6 cm)
▶ 167°C | 663°C | :45

8652: 16.1" x 3.4"
(41 x 9 cm)
▶ 167°C | 657°C | :15

Oval

8744: 15.4" x 9.8" x 1.7"
(39 x 25 x 4 cm)
▶ 167°C | 663°C | :40

Oval Dish

8536: 8.1" x 5.2" x 1.3"
(21 x 13 x 3 cm)
▶167°C | 660°C | :20

8455: 11.3" x 7.4" x 1.5"
(29 x 19 x 4 cm)
▶ 167°C | 663°C | :20

Short Oval

8919: 11" x 4.4" x 1.2"
(28 x 11 x 3 cm)
▶ 167°C | 663°C | :10

8952: 14.8" x 6.3" x 1.7"
(38 x 16 x 4 cm)
▶ 167°C | 657°C | :20

Long Oval

8920: 10.9" x 4.5" x 0.6"
(28 x 11 x 2 cm)
▶ 167°C | 657°C | :20

8951: 18.1" x 6.7" x 1.3"
(46 x 17 x 3 cm)
▶ 167°C | 663°C | :10

Snack Tray

8961: 9.8" x 6.7" x 1.2"
(25 x 17 x 3 cm)
▶ 167°C | 677°C | 1:30

Ball Surface

8746: 5.8" x 1.7"
(15 x 4 cm)
▶ 111°C | 660°C | :20

8736: 7.8" x 1.2"
(20 x 3 cm)
▶ 167°C | 657°C | :05

8735: 9.4" x 2"
(24 x 5 cm)
▶ 167°C | 649°C | :30

8734: 11.4" x 3"
(29 x 8 cm)
▶ 167°C | 649°C | :20

Ball Surface

8733: 14.8" x 2.1"
(38 x 5 cm)
▶ 167°C | 649°C | :05

8738: 16.5" x 3.3"
(42 x 9 cm)
▶ 111°C | 649°C | :05

8737: 19.3" x 3.6"
(49 x 9 cm)
▶ 111°C | 627°C | :20

8745: 21.7" x 4.2"
(55 x 11 cm)
▶ 111°C | 632°C | :05

Deep Form Step Two

8990: 15" x 7.3"
(38 x 19 cm)
See Mold Tips: Deep Form

Deep Form Step Three

8991: 12.6" x 8.2"
(32 x 21 cm)
See Mold Tips: Deep Form

Pyramid Casting Mold

8948: 6.7" x 6.7" x 4.7"
(17 x 17 x 12 cm)
*See Mold Tips: Pyramid
Casting Mold*

185

Note: The measurements given here are for the outer dimensions of the molds. This is to help you determine whether a given mold will fit in your kiln. Since they are handmade, individual molds will vary in size. Never cut glass to fit until you have measured your mold.

Mini Soft Edged Plate

8963: 6.1" x 6.1" x 0.8"
(16 x 16 x 2 cm)
▶ 167°C | 677°C | 2:00

Small Dish

8926: 8.5" x 8.5" x 1.3"
(22 x 22 x 3 cm)
▶ 167°C | 663°C | 2:15

Soft Edge Platter

8985: 9.1" x 9.1" x 0.9"
(23 x 23 x 2 cm)
▶ 167°C | 663°C | 1:20

Retro Party Bowl

8936: 16.9" x 16.9" x 3.9"
(57 x 18 x 6 cm)
▶ 167°C | 663°C | :35

Yin-Yang Plate

8341: 11.4" x 11.4" x 0.9"
(29 x 29 x 2 cm)
▶ 139°C | 685°C | 1:30

One-Square Dish

8934: 3.5" x 3.5" x 0.9"
(9 x 9 x 2 cm)
▶ 167°C | 677°C | 1:15

**Square Bowl,
Simple Curve**

8647: 12" x 12" x 2.5"
(31 x 31 x 6 cm)
▶ 167°C | 663°C | 1:00

**Square Bowl,
Double Curve**

8648: 11.8" x 11.8" x 2.1"
(30 x 30 x 5 cm)
▶ 167°C | 663°C | 1:00

Four-Square Dish

8935: 6.7" x 6.7" x 0.9"
(17 x 17 x 2 cm)
▶ 167°C | 671°C | 1:00

**Soft Edge Four
Square Platter**

8342: 14" x 14" x 1.2"
(36 x 36 x 3 cm)
▶ 167°C | 663°C | 2:20

Very Gentle Curve

8982: 18" x 18" x 2.3"
(46 x 46 x 6 cm)
▶ 167°C | 627°C | :05

Square Nesting Plate

8757: 5.5" x 5.5" x 0.9"
(14 x 14 x 2 cm)
▶ 167°C | 663°C | :20

8758: 7" x 7" x 0.8"
(18 x 18 x 2 cm)
▶ 167°C | 663°C | :25

8759: 8.6" x 8.6" x 1"
(22 x 22 x 3 cm)
▶ 167°C | 663°C | :10

Square Slumper A

8636: 4.5" x 4.5" x 0.8"
(12 x 12 x 2 cm)
▶ 167°C | 638°C | :05

8635: 8.5" x 8.5" x 1.5"
(22 x 22 x 4 cm)
▶ 167°C | 638°C | :05

8634: 10.1" x 10.1" x 1.9"
(26 x 26 x 5 cm)
▶ 167°C | 638°C | :05

8637: 12" x 12" x 2.2"
(30 x 30 x 6 cm)
▶ 167°C | 638°C | :05

8739: 15.9" x 15.9" x 2.8"
(40 x 40 x 7 cm)
▶ 167°C | 627°C | :05

8938: 20.9" x 20.9" x 3.7"
(53 x 53 x 9 cm)
▶ 83°C | 627°C | :05

Square Slumper B

8998: 3.4" x 3.4" x 0.9"
(9 x 9 x 2 cm)
▶ 167°C | 649°C | :05

8997: 5.2" x 5.2" x 1.3"
(13 x 13 x 3 cm)
▶ 167°C | 649°C | :05

8996: 6.1" x 6.1" x 1.1"
(16 x 16 x 3 cm)
▶ 167°C | 649°C | :05

8995: 6.8" x 6.8" x 1.6"
(17 x 17 x 4 cm)
▶ 167°C | 649°C | :05

Square Plate

8901: 3.3" x 3.3" x 0.8"
(8 x 8 x 2 cm)
▶ 167°C | 677°C | 1:30

8900: 5.3" x 5.3" x 1"
(13 x 13 x 3 cm)
▶ 167°C | 671°C | 1:30

8899: 6.3" x 6.3" x 0.9"
(16 x 16 x 2 cm)
▶ 167°C | 663°C | 1:30

Circle in Square

8453: 5.9" x 5.9" x 1.6"
(15 x 15 x 4 cm)
▶ 167°C | 677°C | 1:30

Square Platter

8638: 9.6" x 9.6" x 0.8"
(25 x 25 x 2 cm)
▶ 167°C | 677°C | 1:30

8641: 11.9" x 11.9" x 0.8"
(30 x 30 x 2 cm)
▶ 139°C | 671°C | 1:15

8646: 14.8" x 14.8" x 0.8"
(38 x 38 x 2 cm)
▶ 139°C | 663°C | 1:30

Flat Slumper

8972: 10.6" x 10.6" x 1.1"
(27 x 27 x 3 cm)
▶ 167°C | 632°C | :05

Note: The measurements given here are for the outer dimensions of the molds. This is to help you determine whether a given mold will fit in your kiln. Since they are handmade, individual molds will vary in size. Never cut glass to fit until you have measured your mold.

Small Rectangle
8945: 9.5" x 5.4" x 1.5"
(24 x 14 x 4 cm)
▶ 167°C | 677°C | 1:15

Medium Rectangle
8949: 11.4" x 9.1" x 1.3"
(29 x 23 x 3 cm)
▶ 167°C | 663°C | 1:00

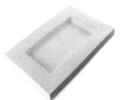

Party Platter
8539: 19.8" x 12.8" x 1.8"
(50 x 33 x 5 cm)
▶ 167°C | 663°C | 1:45

One Candle Bridge
8903: 7.2" x 5.1" x 2"
(18 x 13 x 5 cm)
▶ 167°C | 677°C | 1:30

Four Candle Bridge
8902: 12.4" x 5.7" x 1.6"
(32 x 15 x 4 cm)
▶ 139°C | 677°C | 2:00

Simple Curve
8642: 15.6" x 13.1" x 2.8"
(40 x 33 x 7 cm)
▶ 167°C | 632°C | :05

Serving Tray
8947: 14.8" x 9" x 0.9"
(38 x 23 x 2 cm)
▶ 139°C | 663°C | 1:20

Concave Dish
8933: 13.9" x 9.5" x 1.7"
(35 x 24 x 4 cm)
▶ 167°C | 663°C | :45

Convex Dish
8932: 13.5" x 9.7" x 1.4"
(34 x 25 x 4 cm)
▶ 167°C | 663°C | :45

Soft Edge Platter Long
8962: 14" x 9.4" x 0.9"
(36 x 24 x 2 cm)
▶ 167°C | 663°C | 1:00

Double Curve
8960: 9.4" x 8.7" x 1.7"
(24 x 22 x 4 cm)
▶ 167°C | 660°C | :10

8643: 15.9" x 13.6" x 2.9"
(40 x 35 x 7 cm)
▶ 167°C | 657°C | :10

Lamp Bender Conic
8740: 12.2" x 10.4" x 3.8"
(31 x 27 x 10 cm)
▶ 167°C | 649°C | :15

Lamp Bender
8964: 6" x 4.9" x 2.1"
(15 x 12 x 5 cm)
▶ 167°C | 649°C | :30

8725: 10.1" x 8.5" x 3.7"
(26 x 22 x 10 cm)
▶ 167°C | 649°C | :20

Square Drop Out
8957: 9.5" x 9.5" x 0.7"
(24 x 24 x 2 cm); Inside
5.4" x 5.4" (14 x 14 cm)
▶ 167°C | 677°C | 1:30 *

Rectangular Drop Out
8923: 15.4" x 8.7" x 0.9"
(39 x 22 x2 cm); Inside 10.2"
x 3.7" (26 x 9 cm)
▶ 167°C | 677°C | 2:00 *

Channel Plate
8456: 12.6" x 4.1" x 1.4"
(32 x 10 x 4 cm)
▶ 111°C | 649°C | :25

8944: 17.1" x 4.8" x 1.6"
(44 x 12 x 4 cm)
▶ 111°C | 649°C | :15

8257: 22.6" x 6.9" x 2.4"
(57 x 18 x 6 cm)
▶ 111°C | 649°C | :10

Rectangular Slumper
8924: 12.2" x 7.4" x 1.7"
(31 x 19 x 4 cm)
▶ 167°C | 649°C | :05

8925: 14.8" x 7.4" x 1.7"
(38 x 19 x 4 cm)
▶ 167°C | 649°C | :05

8929: 16.5" x 11.9" x 2"
(42 x 30 x 5 cm)
▶ 167°C | 632°C | :05

Oval in Rectangle
8454: 9.1" x 6.1" x 1.5"
(23 x 16 x 4 cm)
▶ 167°C | 677°C | 1:30

Ellipse Drop Out
8955: 17.7" x 10.8" x 0.9"
(45 x 28 x 2 cm); Inside 13.6"
x 6.9" (35 x 18 cm)
▶ 167°C | 677°C | 1:30 *

* This schedule is for making
a shallow plate. The mold
is placed directly on the kiln
shelf—not elevated.

Drop Out Ring
8633: 7.1" x 0.4" (18 x 1 cm);
Inside 3" (8 cm)
▶ 167°C | 677°C | 1:30 *

8632: 8.9" x 0.4" (23 x 1 cm);
Inside 4.9" (13 cm)
▶ 167°C | 677°C | 1:30 *

8631: 10.8" x 0.5" (28 x 1 cm);
Inside 6.7" (17 cm)
▶ 167°C | 677°C | 1:30 *

Note: The measurements given here are for the outer dimensions of the molds. This is to help you determine whether a given mold will fit in your kiln. Since they are handmade, individual molds will vary in size. Never cut glass to fit until you have measured your mold.

187

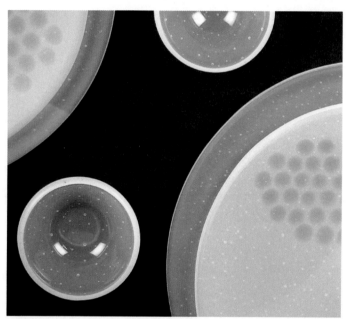

Learn. Grow. Make.

Visit one of our Resource Centers and explore the possibilities of kilnformed art glass. There are many introductory and advanced classes from which to choose.

Visit our website for more details.
www.bullseyeglass.com

Bullseye Resource Center Portland
3610 SE 21st Avenue
Portland, OR 97202
503.227.2797
portland@bullseyeglass.com
bullseyeglass.com/portland

Bullseye Resource Center Bay Area
4514 Hollis Street
Emeryville, CA 94608
510.595.1318
bayarea@bullseyeglass.com
bullseyeglass.com/bayarea

Bullseye Resource Center Los Angeles
143 Pasadena Avenue, Suite B
South Pasadena, CA 91030
323.679.4263
losangeles@bullseyeglass.com
bullseyeglass.com/losangeles

Bullseye Resource Center New York
115 Hoyt Avenue
Mamaroneck, NY 10543
914.835.3794
newyork@bullseyeglass.com
bullseyeglass.com/newyork

Bullseye Resource Center Santa Fe
805 Early Street, Building E
Santa Fe, NM 87505
505.467.8951
santafe@bullseyeglass.com
bullseyeglass.com/santafe

BULLSEYE GLASS
RESOURCE CENTER

Colours to buy

meduim Amber 1137 sky
glass - Sunsets.

Stands . Reading Stained glass.